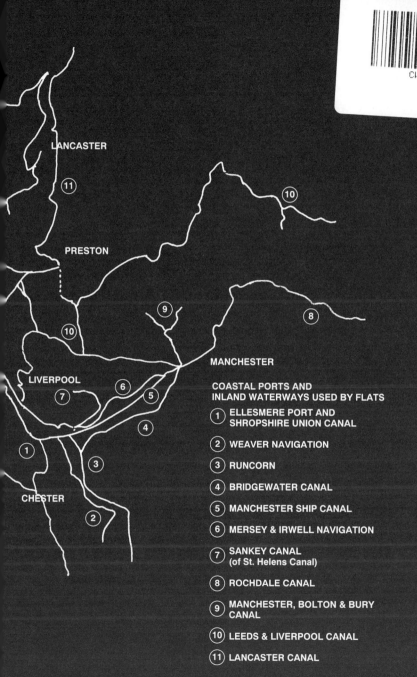

LANCASTER

11

10

PRESTON

9

10

8

Liverpool

MANCHESTER

6

5

7

COASTAL PORTS AND
INLAND WATERWAYS USED BY FLATS

4

1 ELLESMERE PORT AND
SHROPSHIRE UNION CANAL

1

2 WEAVER NAVIGATION

3

3 RUNCORN

CHESTER

4 BRIDGEWATER CANAL

2

5 MANCHESTER SHIP CANAL

6 MERSEY & IRWELL NAVIGATION

7 SANKEY CANAL
(of St. Helens Canal)

8 ROCHDALE CANAL

9 MANCHESTER, BOLTON & BURY
CANAL

10 LEEDS & LIVERPOOL CANAL

11 LANCASTER CANAL

MERSEY FLATS

AND FLATMEN

MERSEY FLATS AND FLATMEN

MICHAEL STAMMERS

TERENCE DALTON LIMITED
LAVENHAM, SUFFOLK
NATIONAL MUSEUMS AND GALLERIES
ON MERSEYSIDE, LIVERPOOL 1993

Published by

TERENCE DALTON LIMITED AND

NATIONAL MUSEUMS AND GALLERIES ON MERSEYSIDE

In memory of Dr Frank Howard

Text photoset in 10/11pt Baskerville

Printed in Great Britain at
The Lavenham Press Limited, Lavenham, Suffolk
© National Museums and Galleries on Merseyside, 1993

Contents

Foreword

by

Major James Forsythe, TD
Chairman of the World Ship Trust

In the middle of the nineteenth century, there were over two
hundred different types of small trading and fishing craft working
solely under sail around the coasts of the British Isles. As recently as
the early nineteen-thirties there were still over two thousand of the
famous Thames sailing barges still trading on the Thames estuary and
adjacent coasts. It is a sobering thought for a maritime nation, largely
dependent on its seaborne trade, that now these types are practically
all gone. Some three dozen Thames barges are still in use, no longer
in active trade but mainly as homes and for holiday charter. There are

*Loaded flat running before
the wind on the Mersey.*
Williams Collection,
Trustees of NMGM

a few other survivors, either in museums or kept afloat by charitable trusts and the like. There has also been a significant revival of interest in and actual rebuilding of some typical nineteenth-century types, purely for the pleasure of once again sailing such interesting reminders of the great days of sail.

The author of this book, Michael Stammers, is well known in wider fields, but especially in the North West as the Keeper of the Merseyside Maritime Museum in the Albert Dock, Liverpool. He is therefore well qualified and well placed to record the history of the once famous Mersey flats. At one time these were to be seen trading in their hundreds, not only on the Mersey but along the adjacent coastline – not forgetting the connecting canals and other inland waterways which linked Liverpool with Manchester and embraced the whole surrounding area, with links with the whole national waterways system.

The flats were the principal carriers, under sail alone for generations, until supplemented and eventually taken over by steam power and finally the diesel engine. Over the same period first the railway and finally the ubiquitous motor lorry took over most of their carrying trade, until now, alas, all these interesting and historic vessels are gone.

The author, by profession obviously an authority on the shipping of Merseyside and the north-west coast, and the adjoining canals and rivers, has carried out detailed research and is able to present in full detail the history and derivation of these fascinating local craft, explaining fully their development from earliest times, until their ultimate eclipse by modern forms of transport. In many ways the flat can be likened in local importance to the perhaps better-known Thames sprittie, of which some still survive. Sadly the last of the flats ceased trading soon after Second World War.

The flats had an ancient lineage, being descended from earlier medieval craft. Records exist to show the flats in active trade in considerable numbers at least as far back as the early eighteenth century. It is indeed sad that not one now remains in use, although it is good to note that two – the *Mossdale* and the *Oakdale* – have fortunately been preserved.

The author also presents numerous personal interviews which make up a fascinating record of historic local reminiscences, together with a fine collection of photographs and plans that adds considerably to the interest of the book for posterity.

To sum up, the author is to be congratulated for including so many interesting anecdotes of the flats and the families involved with them. Theirs was a separate and proud community with a distinctive history of its own.

Preface and Acknowledgements

Flats have been a continuing interest of mine ever since I first arrived on Merseyside in 1969. At that time I was fortunate to work at Liverpool Museum for Edward Paget-Tomlinson, who has a deep knowledge of not only flats but also canal craft in general. I must thank him for his considerable help, especially with the text on the steam packets and the canal flats and for producing some superb drawings for this book. I am also much indebted to Mike Clarke, the leading authority on the Leeds & Liverpool Canal and its boats, for all his help on locating early documents and advising me on the construction of flats.

The late Dr Frank Howard was a great inspiration; he gathered a wealth of information on flats and much of this was incorporated in the plans he drew up, including those of the *Bedale* in this book and in the two fine flat models he built. I know he intended to write a book on flats. His family very kindly donated his papers to the Merseyside Maritime Museum and their deposit spurred me to dig out my own notes and to write this book, which I have dedicated to Frank's memory.

From the mid-nineteen-seventies, I was able to spend time talking to and recording a few of the surviving flatmen. Many of them were in their eighties and are unfortunately no longer with us. In particular, I should mention the Warburton brothers of Sankey Bridges, Richard Hart and John Brown of Widnes, George Wharton of Hough Green, Albert Caldwell of Maghull and Lou Atkin of Fleetwood. Still with us are Reg Wood of Rochdale, Harry Connell of Kirkby, Bill Leathwood of Runcorn, Jack Abel, Dick Johnson, Mr Kilner of Liverpool, Mr K. H. Hockaday of Crosby and Ralph Ashton of Llay near Wrexham. Thanks also to flat experts Jim McDougall, David Knowles, Dave Keenan (owner of the *Oakdale*), Harry Hignett of Liverpool Nautical Research Society and the late Peter Norton of Sankey.

The staff of the local libraries, record offices and museums have all been helpful and in particular I would like to record thanks to Paul Sillitoe, formerly archivist at the Boat Museum, Ellesmere Port; and the staffs of Liverpool City Library and the Cheshire and Lancashire Record Offices. Alan Leigh, curator of Warrington Museum, Mike McCaughan of the Ulster Folk and Transport Museum and David McDougall of the National Waterways Museum, Gloucester, were all of great help. I received much help from many of our own staff, in particular Gordon Read and his staff; Tony Tibbles, curator of

Maritime History; Adrian Jarvis, curator of Port History; my secretary
Julie Stanley who typed the manuscript (several times!). May I also
thank my wife and my family for their patience while I wrote the book.

    All major sources are acknowledged in the bibliography. All
photographs, many of which have not been published before, are
credited in the captions. In this context, I must particularly thank the
Trustees of National Museums and Galleries on Merseyside who
permitted me to use many photographs from the Maritime Museum's
collection. It should be noted that their credit is abbreviated to
'Trustees of NMGM'.

*'Barrow flat' topsail
schooner running before the
wind on the Mersey about
1925.*
David Smith Collection,
Trustees of NMGM

X

Introducing Flats: 1
their Origins and the
Waterways of the
North West

Stand at the Pier Head, Liverpool, at tide time today and you will see a wide estuary with a fierce current, its south bank with the houses, factories and docks of Birkenhead and Wallasey. To the left there are the brick slabs of the Albert Dock warehouses and the widening upper estuary, to the right a glimpse of the New Brighton lighthouse and the cranes and sheds of the North Docks. On a good day, you will be passed by perhaps a coaster in ballast and inward for the upriver port of Garston, two or three coastal tankers from the Manchester Ship Canal, a hundred-thousand-ton tanker docking at the Tranmere oil terminal and a Mersey ferry. Down river, out of sight, a fifty-thousand-ton container ship might be undocking.

Go back a hundred years and the river is alive with ships: passenger liners for North America; cargo liners from every continent; full-rigged ships and barques inward bound with grain; cross-Channel steamers for Belfast, Dublin and the Isle of Man; fishing trawlers and shrimpers under sail; steam coasters and tugs; ferries bringing office workers from the Wirral dormitory towns; sprit-rigged gig boats and sailing barges with rust-red sails. Some of the latter are deep loaded and their decks are awash; but if light their bluff black bows send up a cloud of spray as they work close hauled. On the nearest barge the skipper can be seen at the helm in blue guernsey and peaked cap. His tiller is a ten-foot (3 m) beam, a monster that could sweep him overboard. He has the tiller tackle hauled taut and his feet braced hard against the foot grips nailed to the deck.

Up forward, his crew – a lad rising eighteen and a relative – tends the bowline of the foresail. Its set is critical. The wide hatches (good for loading but vulnerable on a coastal trip) are protected by heavy tarpaulins, lashed, battened and wedged. Towlines, mooring ropes, stowers, boat hooks and sounding poles are neatly arranged on top of them. A big windlass for handling two anchors and barrel lines takes up much of the foredeck, and aloft the tree trunk of a mast carries big red-painted blocks for the running gear and is supported by three cable-laid shrouds to port and starboard and a forestay fashioned from

Opposite page: *Flat under way off the Albert Dock, Liverpool about 1900. Note the length of the tiller and the derrick stowed along the main hatch.*
Liverpool City Engineer

an iron rod to the stem. Its topmost section is painted white and is
crowned by a brass wind vane with a couple of yards of red bunting.
Everything is well painted and varnished. Down below in the hold, the
cargo is salt in white linen bags for export to West Africa. Behind the
hold bulkhead aft there is a small cabin, panelled and grained, with
cupboard bunks, a cast-iron stove and a flapdown table. There is a
kettle on the hob. A stout carvel cock boat is being towed in the wake.
There are more Mersey flats – for this what these barges are – in the
river. A liner, one of the biggest ships in port, is anchored midstream
off the Landing Stage at the Pier Head. Half a dozen flats lie alongside
her black hull. Their curved hatchboards are off and teams of labourers shovel steam coal into big wicker tubs for hoisting into her
bunkers. This black fuel will raise the steam to power her huge hull at
twenty or more knots across the Atlantic to New York in five and a half
days. An empty jigger flat, ketch rigged with topsails set, is outward
bound for Flint to pick up an export cargo of chemicals. A tug
manoeuvres a train of wooden barges away from Morpeth Dock
entrance wall at Birkenhead.

The barges look familiar because they too are flats, as is obvious
from the set of the bow, the big windlass and so on. They have all the

sailing flat's fittings except that they have only a token mast to carry a navigation light and no sails. They are loaded with parcels from the goods depot of the Great Western Railway. The GWR has no direct rail access into Liverpool thanks to the dominance of the London & North Western Railway on the north bank. It therefore has to transship consignments into flats and take them over the Mersey to Manchester Dock at the Pier Head, Liverpool where they can be packed onto carts for delivery. The tug will tow them across the river and release them off the dock gates. They will have sufficient way on to carry them into the dock.

Out of view, elsewhere around the port of Liverpool, flats are to be found at other work. The maintenance flats of the Mersey Docks & Harbour Board engineer's department carry cargoes of stone to repair quay walls. Highly painted Leeds & Liverpool canal boats – a subspecies of flat – deliver coal to the Liverpool gasworks at Athol Street and the local sugar refineries of Fairrie & Company and Tate & Lyle. Steam-powered flats – the Weaver packets – lie alongside sailing ships in Salthouse Dock. With their steam winches and derricks they are unloading soda ash (alkali) for export. Once empty, they will return up the Mersey to their owner's works on the Weaver with per-

3

haps a dumb flat or two in tow. As the steam packets go upstream they pass the 'powder hoys' loading at the gunpowder hulk *Swallow* off Bromborough, and the 'sand hookers' heading back from Eastham to Widnes with a cargo of fine-grained river sand for Pilkington's, the glass makers. These are both specialized trades for flats. At low tide, when most waterborne activity on the river stops apart from the regular criss-crossing of the ferries, the sand hookers are sitting high and dry on a sandbank. Around them, men steadily shovel sand into their holds, anxious to pack in as much as possible before the arrival of the incoming tide.

Mersey flats were a distinctive type of barge which developed in and around the River Mersey. Their purpose was to deliver and collect cargo from the port of Liverpool. This might be to or from the inland hinterland or along the coasts of the Irish Sea. The flat was a vehicle of distribution, the equivalent of a modern road-going 'juggernaut', capable of delivering 30 to 150-ton parcels of cargo to and from the most important deep-sea west coast port. Indeed, some reporter of the eighteen-nineties unkindly called them 'floating wheelbarrows'. It is difficult to imagine how important lighterage was before roads and railways were improved, and even into the mid-twentieth century there was a large traffic in goods delivered 'over the side'. It was cheaper than landing on the quay. The flat was a small but vital cog in the Industrial Revolution, that complex mechanism that made Britain a world economic power in the nineteenth century.

Flats had to operate over a wide range of conditions – from inland waterways to the open sea, from lying alongside bigger ships at anchor or in dock to drying out on a tidal mud berth. They were always strongly built and combined good carrying capacity with seaworthiness and sailing capability. The Mersey itself was a testing place for any craft and all the inland waterways linked with Liverpool (except the Leeds & Liverpool Canal) used the Mersey estuary for the last part of their route. This versatile hull design was capable of being fitted with several different rigs and propulsion systems. It was fitted with square sails, sloop rig with or without bowsprit and topmast, schooner, ketch, galliot or jigger rigs; it could be towed by teams of men, horses or tugs, or it could be self-propelled by steam or diesel engines. The steam packets especially in their early days, were a standard flat hull with round stern or a conversion of a sailing flat. They could be built in wood, iron or steel or a composite of wood and metal. They have not attracted the interest that has made the Thames barges famous; but their masters and crews were adept at working the tides and moving around the crowded docks and small ports and wharves beside the river and along the coast.

The flatmen were drawn from small communities up and down the river. Theirs was a distinct calling that was handed down from father to son. That tradition was still seen until recently on the self-

Opposite page: *Jigger flats* Edward Blower *(1874) and* Shooting Star *(1877) and an unknown single-masted flat in Salthouse Dock, Liverpool, about 1900. Note the windlass with the barrel line over it and the large size of the blocks.*
Trustees of NMGM

4

propelled barges that succeeded the last wooden flats in the nineteen-sixties. The men were proud of their craft and went to great lengths to look after them. Although it was a hard life, it was well rewarded compared with land work. But prosperity was always dependent on good tides and fair winds. Flatmen valued their independence and the skippers considered themselves the equals of any other master.

The Mersey has a character all of its own. Its source is in the Pennines, and it is joined by the Irwell below Manchester. Its estuary starts at Warrington, which is the highest point to be affected by tides. The estuary below Warrington has three main parts: the upper, the Narrows and the lower. The upper estuary, which is like a large bottle accumulates the tidal water and outpourings of the tributary rivers. The Narrows, with Liverpool on the north bank, is the neck of the bottle. Here the mass of water from the upper estuary tries to force its way out to the sea. The result is a current flowing at up to seven knots. About seven miles below Liverpool, the estuary widens out into Liverpool Bay, the outer section. Here the current begins to slow down and all the sand and mud carried in suspension past the Narrows from the upper estuary starts to drop to the bottom to form a shifting system of sand bars and banks which can trap the careless ship. At low tide the upper estuary is also a mass of sandbanks, with the main channel little more than a stream. This is because the Mersey (to make the sailor's task still more dangerous) has the second highest rise and fall of tide in the United Kingdom. On the highest spring tides it could be as much as thirty feet (10 m). In such an estuary it was difficult for deep-sea ships to go beyond the neck of the bottle at Liverpool. A flat-bottomed barge was a very efficient vehicle by which to deliver cargoes to and fetch cargoes from inland upriver wharves, mines and industries.

There has been maritime activity on the Mersey for a long time. More than a dozen early dug-out canoes have been found in the upper reaches around Warrington. Close by at Norton's Marsh a Roman cargo of lead was dug up in the sixteenth century and at Wilderspool the Romans had iron smelting and other industrial works which were linked to water transport. There was also a considerable amount of seaborne Viking settlement in the ninth and tenth centuries. Local place names such as Bootle, Formby and West Kirby provide evidence of this. Liverpool was designated a town by royal charter in 1207 and was involved in military campaigns against the Irish as well as trade. But Chester was the major port of the North West in the Middle Ages. Frodsham at the mouth of the Weaver also attracted Irish traffic, and in 1280 the ship tolls of the town totalled ten pounds. In 1354 Richard Starkey of Runcorn claimed to have boats on the Mersey 'to fish and to carry to all manner of lands being in the place of the Lord the King'. Maritime traffic though small and elusive seems to have been continuous on the medieval river. Trade increased by the sixteenth century and in 1540 Leland wrote of Liverpool: 'Irish merchants come much thither as a good haven. Good merchandise at Liverpool and much Irish yarn which Manchester men do buy here.' The chances are that there were barges for the Manchester men who were moving their packs of yarn up river to Warrington or Runcorn before transfer to cart or pack horse. Beyond the estuary Liverpool had trading connections with the Dee and the vital anchorage of Hoyle Lake, with North Wales, Lancashire, Cumberland, the Isle of Man and Irish ports such as Carrickfergus, Belfast, Drogheda and Dublin. Flats traded regularly to such destinations as the coastal trade of Liverpool grew from the late seventeenth century onwards. They principally carried bulk cargoes. Salt and coal were the main outward commodities; timber, metal ores (iron and copper), stone, slate, linen yarn and agricultural produce were among the inward cargoes. Smaller ports such as Tarleton at the mouth of the Ribble and Bagillt on the Dee also used sailing flats to shift cargo. It is often forgotten just how important the coastal trade was for the well-being of Liverpool. It probably accounted for a third to a half of the port's traffic in the eighteenth and nineteenth centuries.

However, the growth of coastal and estuary traffic does not account for the growth in the number of flats. Liverpool without an expanding industrial hinterland would have been a place of little importance. It was strategically placed to handle the exports of Lancashire coal and of textiles and salt from the Cheshire salt region around Northwich and Winsford. The expansion of British overseas trade after the restoration of Charles II in 1660 benefited the west-coast ports such as Bristol, Liverpool, Lancaster and Glasgow. They were all well sited to receive cargoes from the new colonies, North America and the West Indies and to meet the growing demand for tobacco, sugar, rum and other tropical produce. Liverpool, the point of exchange, was linked by a growing network of navigable rivers and canals for the distribution of goods inland. By 1715 Liverpool had opened its first dock to accommodate deep-sea shipping, and in 1720–21, Liverpool merchants played a leading role in obtaining three Acts of Parliament to open up the Rivers Weaver, Mersey, Irwell and Douglas. Raising finance and tackling lock building and deepening took longer. The Weaver was opened from Frodsham to Winsford via Northwich in 1732. The Mersey & Irwell Navigation, twenty and a quarter miles long, ran from Bank Quay, Warrington, to Manchester and was opened in 1736. The Douglas, which linked the important coal fields of Wigan with the coast, was opened to Wigan by 1742. The very important Sankey Canal opened 'for the passage of flats to the Haydock and Parr collieries' was operating by the spring of 1757. The Sankey-Weaver-Liverpool triangular trade of coal and salt was the most important reason for the expanding number of flats.

The next phase of waterways extended the Mersey links beyond the immediate region. The Duke of Bridgewater's canal, opened to

Runcorn in 1776, not only provided a second link with Manchester via a massive ten-lock staircase at Runcorn but also connected with the Trent & Mersey Canal. This opened up links with the east coast and the Midlands and, most importantly, it meant that consignments of china clay could reach the Staffordshire potteries and that the fine wares of Wedgwood and his colleagues could be exported by water, involving transshipment from the narrow boats to the Bridgewater flats. The Leeds & Liverpool canal was started in 1770 and although the route through to Yorkshire was not finished until 1816, the Lancashire half improved links with Wigan and the north Lancashire towns by 1800. Another trans-Pennine link was achieved with the opening of the Rochdale Canal in 1804. The Ellesmere Canal's Wirral line to the Mersey at Ellesmere Port meant that flats could reach Chester and go on to the Dee. Flats could also navigate to the Lancashire textile towns of Bolton and Bury by the Manchester, Bolton & Bury Canal, opened in 1808. Existing waterways were also improved by extensions to avoid the shallow reaches of the upper Mersey. The Mersey & Irwell was extended by the Runcorn & Latchford Canal in 1804, the Weaver was extended to Weston Point in 1810 and the Sankey to Widnes in 1833.

Contemporaries estimated that there were eighty flats working on the river by 1750. Half a century on, this figure had shot up to over three hundred craft. By 1852 there were four hundred on the Weaver alone, and they continued to increase until about 1900 in spite of railway competition, such was the rapid growth of industry and trade. To give just one indication, Liverpool's total due-paying shipping traffic rose from 450,000 tons in 1800 to three and a half million in 1850 and to 12,380,000 in 1900. The Bridgewater Navigation Company owned 258 flats in 1888, and 1,040 boats worked on the Leeds & Liverpool in 1894. Steam power was applied to flats as well as to railways. The first tentative experiment with a steam tug was as long ago as 1801, but canal proprietors feared bank erosion would result from a steam paddle-boat's wash. But they were acceptable on the Mersey estuary and steam towing was well established by 1840. It did not come into general use on inland canals until after 1860. The first steam 'packet' on the Weaver was launched in 1863; essentially this was a flat with an engine capable of propelling itself and towing two more flats. Many sailing flats were stripped of their masts and rigging and converted into dumb flats; a few were converted into steamers. Further new dumb flats were built without sails and the sailing flats were increasingly limited to the Mersey and the coastal trade. The opening of the Manchester Ship Canal in 1894, which gave deep-sea ships access to the heart of the industrial North West, meant a slackening of flats' traffic from Liverpool to Manchester. The Mersey & Irwell, which had been in decline, was incorporated in the new canal and the Bridgewater's traffic was affected. At the same time foreign competition and the supply of brine to chemical works at Runcorn and Widnes by pipeline, replacing salt, meant less work on the Weaver. The late nineteenth century saw a rapid fall in the number of sailing flats. Very few flats were under sail after 1920. New dumb flats and Leeds & Liverpool boats were being built until 1955. River, dock, lighterage and coastal traffic all slackened, especially because of competition from road vehicles. The last flats finished trading in the nineteen-sixties. Steel barges, many of them of flat design with tugs and motor craft, continued carrying traffic such as grain to Manchester, palm oil to Bromborough and soda ash from Northwich. One by one, all this traffic was abandoned and today only one firm – Frodsham Lighterage – does any business on the Mersey.

That is a brief summary of the development of the flat and its waterways. It is not my intention to write a history of canals; some excellent works such as those by Hadfield & Biddle – *The Canals of North West England* – and Clarke on the Leeds & Liverpool Canal are to be found in the bibliography. The volume and character of the flat traffic will be examined in chapters six and seven.

Dumb flats Ellesmount, Joan, George, Alice *and others, and the motor tug* Marina *in Stanley Dock, Liverpool, in 1942. The boats without windlasses in the second tier are Leeds & Liverpool Canal long boats. There are two steel swim-headed lighters beyond the flats. Note the bow decoration and fender on the* George.
Stewart Bale Collection, Trustees of NMGM

So far, I have used 'flat' as an all-embracing term. As was the case with many other types of traditional boat there was no single standard flat but a range of variations and developments. There were differences in hull design, dimensions, fittings and decoration between the various inland flats. The Leeds & Liverpool 'boats' were distinct from the Bridgewater or 'Dukers' flats and the Rochdale Canal flats. It has often been stated that Weaver flats were different from Mersey flats. This is more difficult to prove because although there are a large number of flats recorded in the Liverpool Ship Registers from 1786, the inland flats are more sparsely documented. Flats would be registered if they were used for coastal work. On the other hand, a high proportion of the registered flats were built on the Weaver, particularly at North-wich. The alleged difference can probably be traced back to the fact that a number of eighteenth- or early nineteenth-century square-sterned flats – including the famous *Daresbury* of 1772 – survived into the nineteen-fifties. Their shorter length and a stern that was markedly different from the round sterns of most other surviving flats seem to have misled observers into believing that they had character-istics that were unique to the Weaver. In fact they were survivors of an era when virtually all flats had square sterns. Leeds & Liverpool 'boats' came in long and short varieties – seventy-two or sixty-one feet (21.9 m or 18.6 m) – according to whether they were required to work the whole length of the canal or only between Liverpool and Wigan. The steam barges or 'packets' were a development of the flat hull to take an engine and boiler with a round stern and generally had larger dimensions. The 'Barrow flat' topsail schooner which was built from Connah's Quay up to Barrow-in-Furness for coastal trading, was also a development of the flat's hull design. All these variations will be covered later to a greater or lesser extent according to their import-ance to the main subjects – the sailing and dumb flats of the Mersey. The essential point is that they all appear to have developed from a common flat hull design, and this leads to the question of the origins of the flat.

The word 'flat' as applied to barges on the Mersey and connect-ing rivers was in common usage by the seventeen-forties and fifties. To give two examples, there is a contract for a flat to be built at Wigan on the Douglas in 1742; and the Act of 1755 to make the Sankey navigable states that it was for 'Boats, *Flats* and other Vessels'. In other words, flats were recognized as a separate type of vessel. The difference between a 'flat' and a 'boat' may be one of beam. According to a Leeds & Liverpool boatbuilder, any craft below fourteen-foot (4.3 m) beam was a 'boat' and any over was a 'flat'. This distinction could well go back to the eighteenthth century. Earlier writers have tended to imply that the flat was introduced with the opening up of the river navi-gations between their Acts of 1720–21 and their completion within the decade 1732–1742. Indeed, it has been suggested that it was an alien

Opposite page: 'Barrow flat' top-sail schooner at low tide, probably at Tranmere on the Mersey, having her hull tarred. Note the similarity of her hull to that of the single-masted flats. She is also deeper and has more sheer.
Dr Dennis Chapman

import: a Dutch type of barge directly copied for use on the Mersey. The shape of the bow, the style of the rudder and the flat bottom can all be advanced as evidence. What is more, Thomas Steers, the engineer for the Mersey & Irwell and the Douglas, served in the army on campaigns in the Netherlands and could have designed the first flats. This theory is undermined by the underlying structural differences between the flats and the Dutch barge. It is altogether more plausible to suggest that the post-1732 flat was a continuation of an existing design of barge. The expansion of the inland waterways undoubtedly contributed to the growth in the numbers of flats and possibly to their design. But there is plenty of documentary and pictorial evidence from before 1742 for sailing barges working on the Mersey and along the coast. Before providing some examples, it must be pointed out that the word 'flat' has been discovered in use as early as 1702. The context was not the Mersey but it has a connection with the river and Liverpool.

Bryan Blundell was a Liverpool master mariner, shipowner and merchant. He is chiefly remembered for his generosity towards his town by his foundation of the Bluecoat School. His journal is one of the treasures of the Lancashire Record Office. Most of his voyages were to the British colonies of North America and on 17th January 1702 he was off the coast of Maryland: 'At six in the morning we were off Cheritons and having a *flat* there and a sloop at Pangiteaque, I sent our yawl and five hands ashore to fetch them to Rappahannock'. On 20th April he wrote, 'our sloops came with fifty hogsheads [of tobacco]. As we could not have the liberty of going, so I thought our longboat and *flat* would get it aboard her time enough'; and on 30th May, 'I went to the Eastern Shore to call upon our sloop and *flat* and came back the 6th June.' There is something to be deduced from these passages. Blundell, the Liverpudlian seafarer, was describing a distinctive type of craft that could be used up river and for lightering hogsheads of tobacco out to an anchored deep-sea sailing ship. It may be significant that in later life, sometime after 1736, he wrote of Liverpool's ships:

'We had more than a hundred: some of the ships of 300 tons. Between thirty or forty ships we had in the Guinea trade [slave trade] some of which had good success and made great voyages. The rest was in the West India trade, besides all the coasting vessels, river boats and flats of which there was great numbers.'

There is evidence of boats of about the same size as the first documented eighteenth-century flats in the coastal trade from the late sixteenth century. The Liverpool Customs records list twenty-eight ships belonging to Liverpool which sailed or arrived in the Mersey between 28th March and 22nd June 1586. Four do not have their tonnage listed and the other twenty-four had an average 'burden' of fifteen tons. Tonnage measurement was not a precise science, but if 'burden' meant cargo capacity then these craft were the same size as the flats plying the Douglas and Ribble in 1751–52. The Liverpool Port Book for 1660–61 gives an interesting glimpse. Among the vessels entering was the *Ann Gabbart* of Liverpool from Formby and Bristol. 'Gabbart' may be a surname or the full name may be a description (like the barque *Jane*), 'gabbart' being the name given to sailing barges on the west coast of Scotland. The Liverpool Port Books for 1681–82 have records of many more Liverpool ships of about the fifteen- to twenty-ton range and the same can be found in the Belfast Port Books for 1683-87. Among the vessels recorded, the *Margaret* of Liverpool delivered fourteen cargoes to Belfast between 29th January 1683 and 1st October 1687. These were mainly salt, with some earthenware and fine goods. Slightly later, in 1722–23, the port books have further evidence of an important trade in 'potters clay' from Carrickfergus in vessels such as the *Industry*, of twenty tons. Vessels of a similar tonnage were also present on the Dee. In 1704 the Chester merchant Peck was regularly exporting lead from Flint in the twenty-ton *Good Intent*, and out of the twenty vessels entering or sailing from the port of Chester between 1st April and 24th June 1740 eight were of the above-mentioned tonnage and another seven of thirty tons. The north Welsh coast had also witnessed a significant amount of maritime activity in past eras. In the late seventeenth century there is evidence of barge traffic between the River Conway and Liverpool in the accounts of the Gwydir estate. Seven shipments of oak felled on the banks of the Conway were made between 13th May 1665 and 1st June 1686. Two 'great boats' were being loaded for Liverpool, one owned by Mr Trygan and the other by Richard Thomas, and payment of three pounds was made to each for the voyage. They arrived at Liverpool on 20th May. On 1st June Richard Thomas's open boat of fourteen tons took planks to Liverpool. There were also accounts for building a boat of about seven tons in May 1686. The anchor and ropes were purchased in Liverpool:

> 'May 31st. Richard Lusting, Anchor Smith of Leverpoole for one anchor weighing 30 lb at $3\frac{1}{2}$d pro new boat as appears 8s 9d Pd. then to Henry Dobson ropemaker there pro new cable and ropes for ye new boate as appears being 3 grs + 21 lb at 3d. per lb. or 28s per cwt.
>
> £1 6s 3d'

The new boat was equipped with oars and a sail fashioned from twenty-four yards (22 m) of 'course linnen cloth' at sevenpence (3p) a yard cost fourteen shillings (70p). The Liverpool connection is clearly important, as is the account of the sail, which must have been a single square sail.

In the next decade Captain Grenville Collins, in his book *Great Britain's Coasting Pilot* of 1693, includes detailed descriptions of the Hoyle Lake, off the Wirral peninsula the main approach anchorage for the Mersey and the Sloyne in the river. The Hoyle Lake: '. . . here the great ships that belong to Liverpool put out of the part of their lading till they are light enough to sail over the flats to Liverpool. . .' and the Sloyne, '. . . the ships lie aground before the town of Liverpool . . . 'tis bad riding afloat because of the strong tides; therefore the ships that ride afloat ride up at the Sloyne where is less tide . . .'. In other words, there was a need for flats to lighter cargo from these two anchorages to the town. Another example of lighterage took place in 1706 when Liverpool merchant Thomas Johnson sent flats to Frodsham to deliver 1,250 tons of salt to six Danish ships anchored in the Mersey.

In 1696 Sir Thomas Patten of Warrington, the MP for Liverpool pointed out the benefits to trade if the river could be made navigable to Manchester. He reported that he made some improvements on the stretch below Warrington and claimed that two thousand tons of cargo (much of it tobacco) was being carried annually between Liverpool and Warrington. There was also cross-river traffic with ferry stations at Eastham with good access to Chester and the south; Rock Ferry, Tranmere, Birkenhead, and Seacombe the northern side of the big tidal creek of Wallasey pool. It must not be assumed that these services were run by mere rowing boats. The stormy estuary and cargoes such as horses, sheep and cattle called for a larger type of sailing vessel. Celia Fiennes who published an account of her travels all round England wrote about her crossing from Eastham to Liverpool in 1694 ". . . I ferry'd over and was an hour and a half in the passage; it's of great breadth and at low water is so deep and salt as the sea almost . . . it's in a sort of hoy that I ferried over and my horses.' She then goes to say that 'the hoy' could hold up to a hundred people. This was no rowing boat but a barge. Fiennes would no doubt have been familiar with the hoys which plied the Thames estuary with passengers, freight and naval stores at this period.

Pictorial evidence reinforces the idea that the flat existed before the opening up of the inland rivers between 1732 and 1742. However, this must be treated with caution. All the pictures that contain sailing craft are topographic views. The main subject is a building, a haven or a town viewed from the opposite bank of a river or from the sea. The ships are subsidiaries which are useful for filling in the foreground. They should not be taken at face value. The artist could distort the image of the ship to make it look more interesting, or could have a standard ship for every situation. There are few models, no plans and little archaeological evidence against which to check these pictures. But they can be checked against each other and against other work of the same artist. The British Museum's Cottonian Collection (*Augustus I* ii 42) contains a drawing of the castle and harbour at Carrickfergus in 1580. The haven contains several different types of vessel, from a three-masted ship to double-ended open boats. In the centre of the harbour lie two large double-ended boats, one bow on with no mast and one stern on with a square-sail and bowsprit. Both, in spite of the relative crudeness of the picture, look remarkably like flats, even down to the round stern and 'out-of-doors' rudder. The rigged vessel has a kind of canvas wagon tilt rigged aft and possibly an open hold. Carrickfergus was a military garrison which was supplied from Liverpool. The Liverpool Customs records mention on 22nd April 1586: 'the *Spedewell* of Wallazie cleared out for Carrigfargos with twenty barrels of malt and twelve barrles of wheat to be delivered to the Queen's Majesties Victualler in the said town (and fortress) of Carrigfargos for her Majesties use, for provision.'

The first authentic view of Liverpool, as opposed to some rather fanciful nineteenth-century reconstructions, is an oil painting on a wooden panel dated 1682 in the Merseyside Maritime Museum. It shows the main landmarks: St Nicholas's Church, the town hall and the castle; and the river in the foreground contains two- and three-masted square-rigged ships, gaff-rigged single-masted craft with a raised poop and flat-type barges with square sails. The images of the larger ships can all be cross-checked against other contemporary paintings and are reasonably accurate; even though they cannot be checked, there seems to be no good reason to assume that the smaller 'flats' are not accurate as well. Chadwick's plan of Liverpool of 1725 shows the new dock with ships and two square-rigged barges like flats complete with wind vanes at the masthead; and a painting of Chester from the River Dee by Tillemans dated about 1710 also shows square-rigged barges of a similar kind.

Samuel and Nathaniel Buck's *South West Prospect of Liverpool* of 1728 shows a complete panorama of the town with its new dock filled with ships, ships under construction and ships under way and at anchor in the river. Eight of these are gaff rigged, five with raised poops and with windows in their transom sterns. There are three gaff-rigged boats with round sterns and two square-rigged 'flats'. The latter listed in the key as the Rock House and the Eastham ferry boats, and this of course brings us back to Fiennes's remarks about the Eastham ferry. They are similar to the square-rigged barges in the 1682 picture and Chadwick's plan. They all look like flats but before becoming carried away, it should be borne in mind that the Bucks were prolific artists. What was to stop them reproducing the same ships, whatever the town or the river? The degree of detail in each view does suggest they were drawn from life. When the Liverpool view is compared with, for example, the Newcastle and Tyne prospect of about the same date the differences are striking. The Newcastle one (reproduced as the endpaper of Roger Finch's *Coals from Newcastle*, 1973) shows a recognizable fleet of Tyne keels rowing or sailing together with coasting hoys that are square rigged with a bowsprit and jibs and with a lateen mizzen on one. The Liverpool view, in my opinion, shows two kinds of flat: square-rigged ones for up river and gaff-rigged ones for the estuary and in particular for working round to the Hoyle Lake for lightering deep sea ships. Edward Paget-Tomlinson has redrawn all these 'flats' to what we think is a likely scale for comparison with some later eighteen- and nineteenth-century flats.

Taken in combination, the documentary and pictorial evidence provide enough to support the theory that flats existed on the Mersey before 1732. Neither of them reveals the origins of the flat. Continuity of hull shape and structure and the slow evolution of design over several centuries have been recognized features of traditional coastal and inshore boat types such as the flat. The late Eric McKee in his book *Working Boats of Britain* (1983) produced an overall classification for the hull forms of the major types of traditional wooden boats around the British Isles. His classification is based on hull proportions: length to beam ratios, beam to depth and so on together with the shape of ends and bottoms. What he wrote about the Mersey flat is intriguing: 'Starting with those [hulls] that are both narrow and deep (more than 3.75 beams long and more than half a beam deep) we find a group of vessels which include the old herring busses, the Mersey flats and the Humber keels and sloops.' He found there were distinct similarities between the flat, the Humber keel and the North Sea herring busses in their proportions and their bluff-ended, boxy shape. Both the keel and the buss are known to be descended from medieval ships. Perhaps the flat is descended from the medieval ships of the Irish Sea. What is needed is the discovery of a datable medieval wreck off the Mersey.

Opposite page: *Sailing flats. These drawings are based on contemporary pictorial evidence and are to the same scale:*
1. *Coasting vessel, 1580, from a drawing of Carrickfergus Castle in the British Museum's Cottonian Collection.*
2. *Square-rigged flat, based on an anonymous painting of Liverpool of 1682, Perry's map of Liverpool 1725, and S. and N. Buck's* South West Prospect of Liverpool, *1728.*
3. *Square-rigged flat, on Mersey & Irwell Navigation, based on John Harris's* South West Prospect of Manchester and Salford, *1736, and Casson and Berry's map of 1741.*
4. *Mersey flat based on S. and N. Buck's 1728 'Prospect'.*
5. *Flat based on J. Lightoller's plan of Liverpool docks, 1765. Note short gaff.*
6. *Daresbury, built c1772 at Northwich, afloat until 1958, and still surviving as an abandoned wreck; based on photographs by E. W. Paget-Tomlinson taken in 1957.*
7. *Avon, round-sterned flat built 1868, owned by Worsley Battersby and Company (and referred to in chapter eight); based on photographs of a contemporary model in the Liverpool Museum's shipping collection which was destroyed in the Second World War.*
8. *Eastham, built 1861 – at only sixteen tons gross, one of the smallest flats, built as a 'gunpowder hoy' (see chapter seven), based on photographs c1940-45.*
9. *Pilot, jigger flat, built 1894 by Pimblott's at Northwich; based on model in Merseyside Maritime Museum Collection (model based on the builder's plans).*

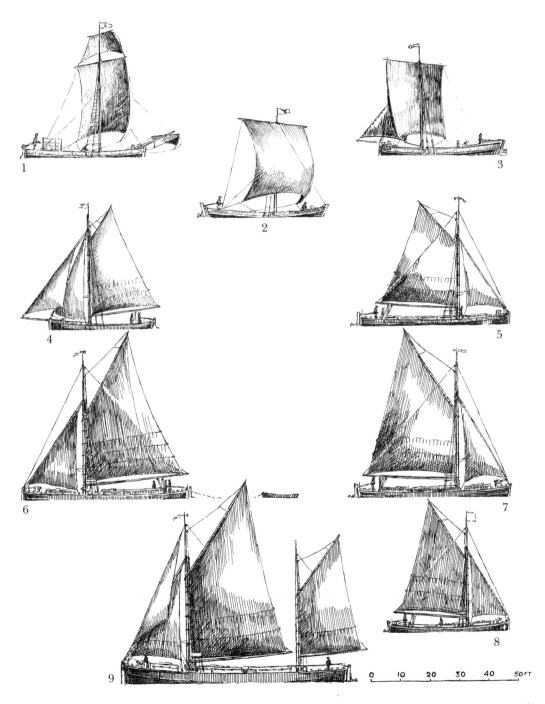

Hull design and construction   2

The majority of flats and their subspecies were built to the same overall pattern, although there was a lot of variation in size, shape and construction. This chapter will examine design, construction and deck fittings and equipment. Sails and other forms of propulsion will be dealt with in the following two chapters. The main design considerations for an eighteenth-century merchantman (which is what the sailing flat was) were laid down by the great naval architect F. H. Chapman as:

1. To be able to carry a great lading in proportion to its size (true of flats).
2. To sail well to wind, in order to beat easily off the coast where it may be embayed, and also to come about well in a hollow sea (for sea, read ability to tack in the confined reaches of the upper Mersey).
3. To work with a crew small in proportion to its cargo (two crew on a flat).
4. To be able to sail with a small quantity of ballast (none on a Mersey flat).

Seaworthiness to survive the gales that sweep the Mersey was vital as was strength to withstand grounding at low tide and heavy usage in crowded docks. The size of locks and depth of rivers or canals were major determinants of length, beam and draught. Appendix one gives the dimensions of the locks of the main north-west waterways. The overall length was generally about 68 feet (20.7 m) except for the River Douglas and the Leeds & Liverpool Canal. Nobody is quite sure what the precise dimensions of the Douglas locks were. Some idea can be gained from the dimensions of vessels built on the Douglas, such as the *Speedwell* built at Parbold in 1773: 47 ft (14.3 m) long, 13 ft 8 in. (4.2 m) beam and 4 ft 6 in. (1.4 m) depth of hold. The Leeds & Liverpool Canal's locks were 62 ft (18.9 m) in length on the Leeds–Wigan section and 72 ft (21.9 m) from Liverpool to Wigan. The river locks of the St Helens Canal, which extended the Sankey to Widnes, permitted large jigger flats to discharge stone and slate at Sankey Bridges. The Weaver's changes in the nineteenth-century reflected the huge volume of the salt traffic. With locks up to 230 feet (70 m) long, a hundred feet (30.5 m) wide and twelve feet (3.7 m) deep, the navigation was designed for trains of flats and steam coasters.

Opposite page: *A small flat, The* Gladys *was only seven tons gross, according to the 1914 Mercantile Navy List. She is about the size of the seventeenth century flats that served the Hoyle Lake anchorage where she is aground at low tide.*
Trustees of NMGM

The sailing flats of the first half of the eighteenth-century were in two main sizes. The smaller had a capacity of about twenty tons. The River Douglas flats *Success* and *Expedition* of 1751–52 were of this capacity and traded from Wigan to Tarleton and the Ribble estuary only. According to Sir Peter Warburton, who was objecting to further improvements to the Weaver Navigation in 1760, the first Weaver flat of 1832 carried twenty tons. The *Concorde*, which was built at Wigan in 1742, had a keelson 45 ft (13.7 m) long, which made her overall length over 50 ft (15 m). She also carried a compass, which proves that she was intended for coastal work (probably coal to Liverpool). The *Friend's Goodwill* built at Northwich in 1740 had a registered tonnage of 50 tons, was 50 ft (17.7 m) long and had 14 ft 6 in. (4.4 m) beam and 5 ft 4 in. (1.62 m) depth of hold. This remained more or less the standard size for a century. The collector of Customs wrote to London in 1785 about the Mersey traffic: 'The size of the vessels that ply there from 40 to 120 tons burthern. This chiefly employed in the coal trade from 40 to 60 tons and their construction very flatt and are decked . . .'.

The development of larger packets, dumb and jigger flats after 1850 led to an increase in size, as the following table shows.

Average tons of flats

1740–50	48.6
1750–75	57.4
1775–1800	57.3
1800–25	55.5
1825–50	65.2
1850–75	69.4
1875-1900	76.2

The sample is for twenty-five flats for 1750–1900 and three for 1740–50. Sources are the Liverpool Shipping Registers 1786–88, *Marwood's Liverpool Register* 1854 and the 1914 *Mercantile Navy List*. This can be only a rough indication because of the changes in measurements in 1773, 1836 and 1854. The average tonnages between 1775 and 1800 may be slightly high because the early ship registers do not have as many canal flats and are therefore biased towards the larger sea-going flats, which had to be registered. D. J. Pope in his article in *Mariner's Mirror*, volume 60, pages 84–91 (1974) has produced some interesting figures. He listed all the flats registered between Beaumaris and Carlisle from 1786 to 1823: 48.2 per cent were in the fifty-one to seventy-ton range, and another 27.1 per cent were between seventy-one and eighty tons. His figures again do not take into account the non-registered inland vessels. Wide variations in size were possible. The *Ant* and the *Luce* show the two extremes: the *Ant* was built in 1837 at Winsford and was twenty-three tons, forty feet (12.2 m) long; whereas the *Luce* built at Fiddler's Ferry in 1872 as a coal bunkering dumb flat, measured a hundred feet (30.5 m) long and 143 gross tons.

There were also small flats in the sand trade, such as the *Little Alice* out of Widnes, the *Flatfish* at Bangor and the *Gladys* of Liverpool. The upper Dee above Chester also had some very small square-rigged open-decked flats but nothing is known about them apart from a small late eighteenth-century view.

The problem of what the tonnage figures mean also applies to the other dimensions. Registry rules changed and do not equate to length overall, length between perpendiculars or length on the waterline. The same applies to the beam which could be overall including the rubbing strakes, to the outside or to the inside of the planking. Depth usually means depth of hold as against draught. The complexities of the changes are excellently explained in David MacGregor's book *Fast Sailing Ships 1715–1815* (1973) and for the purposes of this chapter it is enough to be aware of the problem. Flats tended to become deeper in the nineteenth-century; length and breadth increased if the locks used were extended. The range of dimensions over a span of dates and different types of flat can be found in appendix two. These dimensions can be regarded as typical of the date and the kind of craft. The dimensions of typical Thames barges, Humber keels and Severn trows are included for comparison.

Flats were not in fact completely flat bottomed; unlike the Thames barge with a hard chine or the Severn trow which was flat with a small radius curve at the bilge, the flat had a rising floor and larger radius curve at the bilge. A plan of a 1782 flat in a private collection, a half-model in Merseyside Maritime Museum and survivors such as the *Mossdale* of about 1860 and the Leeds & Liverpool short boat *George* all show this characteristic. Later dumb flats used on the Mersey and the Bridgewater Canal tended to be much flatter than the older sailing flat-hull form. Although the bottom might not be completely flat, flats working in the Mersey estuary and around the coast frequently took the ground at low tide. They were heavily built to cope both with this strain and with their weakness on deck because of their large hatches. Canal flats tended to be of lighter construction, smaller section timbers and wider frame spacings because they did not have the same stresses of grounding. John Sutton's account of the flat *Protection* in volume six of *Sea Breezes* (1948), pages 318–25 shows just how much hard usage a flat could take. She could carry 150 tons of stone from the Welsh coastal quarries to the Mersey:

> often she would run alongside the loading jetty and dry out on the ebb tide and be loaded while she lay dry. Sometimes the weight of cargo must have been miscalculated for it was a common experience for the decks to be awash, and frequently the cargo was manhandled and dumped overboard to get her to lift. . . . Sometimes when she was on the beach in bad weather, the heavy sea coming up the beach on the flood made her pound the bottom with her stern-post enough to make you think she was going to break up at any time.

Plan of a flat dated 12th November 1782.
M. Clarke

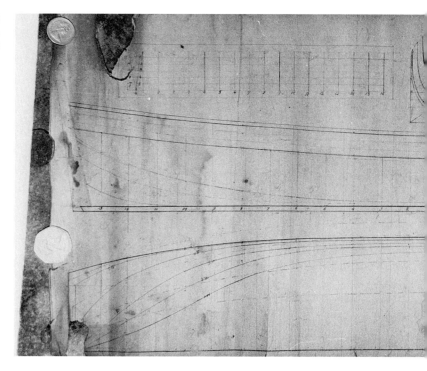

At this point, I should bring in the question of the 'Barrow flats'. The term was a nickname given to the flat-bottomed topsail schooners of the North West by the schoonermen of West Country ports such as Appledore. The 'Barrow flat' may have developed from the Mersey flat. There were two-masted galliots and galliot flats at the end of the eighteenth century and beginning of the nineteenth century. The Liverpool Ship Registers list six schooners with similar dimensions to flats built at flat-building yards at St Helens. The schooner *Margaret* was launched in 1834 and measured sixty-two feet (18.9 m) by fifteen feet (4.6 m) by seven feet four inches (2.3 m), sixty-seven tons with a lifting bowsprit, no figurehead and a square stern. Another, the *William Edwards* (65.3 gross tons), built in 1838, was altered from sloop to schooner in 1868. The design was refined, particularly by the builders of north Lancashire (especially the Ashburner family). Their ends were made sharper and their bilges were more rounded than those of a flat. They retained the massive strength of the flat hull. The 'out-of-doors' rudder and the stern formed by cant frames as in the round-sterned flat were retained as well.

Returning to the dumb and mast flats, they had a curved stem and raked stern post and their bows were rounded but not as a bluff and square as in a Humber keel. They could be described as 'apple

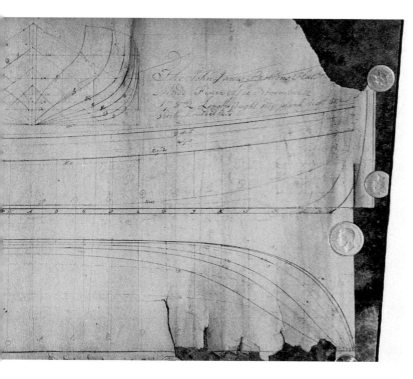

cheeked' and they had a distinct hollow at the base of the stem and a good run aft, particularly in the round-sterned flats. The shape hints at an older origin, possibly medieval, and within the overall pattern lies a range of subtle variations of fineness and bluffness. The survivors illustrate the variety of shape: the *Oakdale* of 1951 is very bluff and flatter in the floors than earlier flats such as the *Bedale*. The main body of the hull had parallel sides with a well-rounded bilge, which varied in radius. Bridgewater 'Dukers' had much less of a curve than Shropshire Union flats. The sheer could be absolutely flat in the case of later dumb flats, and 'Dukers' had less than the Shropshire Union boats. Sailing flats working on the Mersey and the coast had a very small rise forward and more aft and the coastal 'outside' flats had most of all. Early flats had more tumblehome than later ones. The round stern was probably the original form but it was overtaken in the early eighteenth century by the square stern. This owed its introduction to the huge increase in inland waterways traffic. The square stern allowed the maximum cargo capacity within a fixed set of dimensions. Like the bow, the square stern had various designs. It could be high and elegant, as in the Leeds & Liverpool Canal boats; or low and heavy, as in some of the flats built on the Weaver. It was also easier and cheaper to build than the round one. The square stern sacrificed steering and sailing capability because it restricted the flow of water to the rudder. But as the sailing flats spent a large proportion of the time being towed on the Weaver, the Irwell and the Sankey and only had to leave the towpath at Runcorn or Warrington for the final part of the passage down the estuary to Liverpool, it was satisfactory. One must also bear in mind the fact that flats invariably sailed with the strong tides of the river. Frank Ogle in volume forty-five of *Sea Breezes* (1971), pages 882–9 remarked, 'How the square sterned flats were persuaded to sail fully loaded is hard to understand; I imagine the progress was really a controlled tidal drift.'

It is clear that by 1786 square sterns were predominant, but the round stern continued to be built. Of the twenty-three flats listed in the Liverpool register for that year only two had round sterns. After 1850 the round stern became more common: for example all of Thomas Robinson's fleet of twelve flats (built between 1868 and 1892) had round sterns. A round stern was essential for the Weaver steam packets and the Leeds & Liverpool tugs which were introduced in 1864 and 1871 because they needed a good flow of water to the propeller to operate efficiently. Dumb flats towed by steam power moved faster through the water than their horse-drawn equivalents and therefore needed to be more responsive to their helm. The revival of the round stern helped to make the flats easier to steer while under tow in the Mersey and quicker to manoeuvre into locks.

Like other builders of traditional barges, flatbuilders probably used a half-model to develop the shape of the hull and, once agreed with the purchaser, this would be used to draw up a set of moulds for the frames in full size. There are half-models of a flat, a Leeds & Liverpool boat and a Weaver packet in the collection of Merseyside Maritime Museum. Half-models were also used for later metal boats to work out the layout of the plates. Where large quantities of boats were built to a standard size, for example on the Leeds & Liverpool Canal, the builders retained a set of standard frame patterns. The Leeds & Liverpool Canal Company also had a written specification which was issued to builders. The Brocklebank Collection at Merseyside Maritime Museum contains a set of offsets for the flat *Mite*, built at Whitehaven in 1830. But one must not assume that plans were not drawn at all for wooden flats. The 1782 plan has already been mentioned and there is another later, undated builder's plan from Taylor Brothers' yard at Chester. It is not clear whether this was built by Taylor's or by the Shropshire Union. Pimblott's, the Northwich builders, drew plans for the jigger flat *Pilot* of 1894. These were borrowed by the Liverpool Museum's model maker to build a model in 1933. They are referred to in some surviving letters but have themselves vanished. The Boat Museum, Ellesmere Port, holds plans for Bridgewater dumb flats and two plating half-models for the later steel barges that replaced them. The building process for many flats also put the stress on making the shape of the hull by hand and eye. Once the keel had been laid down, key frames would be sawn out and positioned and long flexible battens called ribbands stretched round them to provide the skeletal shape of the hull. The shape of the intermediate frames could be taken off the ribbands. The builders of the *Mite* used four and in 1950 Abel's at Runcorn used one to mark the line of the sheer.

Records of the flat's shape have also been made by outside researchers. In 1825 William Strickland, a canal engineer from Pennsylvania, was commissioned by that state's society for promoting improvements to go to England and draw up a report on the progress of dock, canal and road engineering. He was impressed by the Mersey & Irwell Canal flats and drew a plan of one for his report. Dr Frank Howard spend many hours in difficult conditions measuring the remains of the *Bedale* at Runcorn and the *Sir R. Peel* at Widnes West Bank Dock and then transforming the data into plans for both of them. Other archaeological excavations at Widnes and St Helens between 1977 and 1980 have contributed details of the variations in the methods of construction and scantlings of flats. While we know the main considerations behind the design of flats, there is no record of any of the flatbuilder's own thoughts of how lines for a particular flat were developed. Albert Andrews, the manager of Abels' yard at Runcorn gave the *Manchester Guardian* an interview in October 1950. He began designing flats with the *Fred Abel* in 1939 and in 1950 he designed the *Oakdale*: '. . . it has been designed as a canal and river barge, the aim of Mr. Andrews having been to secure the maximum amount of cargo with the minimum amount of displacement'. In the same context there is also an interesting caption to the 1782 plan: 'the John James Boltons flatt. Made Finer after November 12th 1782.' In other words, this plan had been altered after discussions between the builder and the customer on the shape of this new flat.

Flats were carvel built with one exception. The Leeds & Liverpool boats built on the Yorkshire side of the canal probably owed more to keel-building traditions than flats. This included the construction of some clinker-built boats. Mike Clarke's *The Leeds & Liverpol Canal, a History and Guide* (1990) has a photograph of one of these craft at Leeds. The scantlings of a wooden flat were always massive. The earliest surviving example is in the building accounts of the *Concorde*. She was built between 1742 and 1743 on the Douglas at Wigan for coasting:

> Paid Mr. John Walmsley (by Richard Roper) for a ffir bulk
> 45 ft long by 13½ inches, contents 56¼ for a kelson for
> ye flatt on ye stocks £3 10s 11d.

At the end of the eighteenth century, the Brockbank's contracts provide more detailed information. These are the dimensions and

Overleaf: *Mersey flat* Bedale *lines and construction profile, surveyed and drawn by the late Dr Frank Howard.*
Dr Frank Howard Collection, Trustees of NMGM

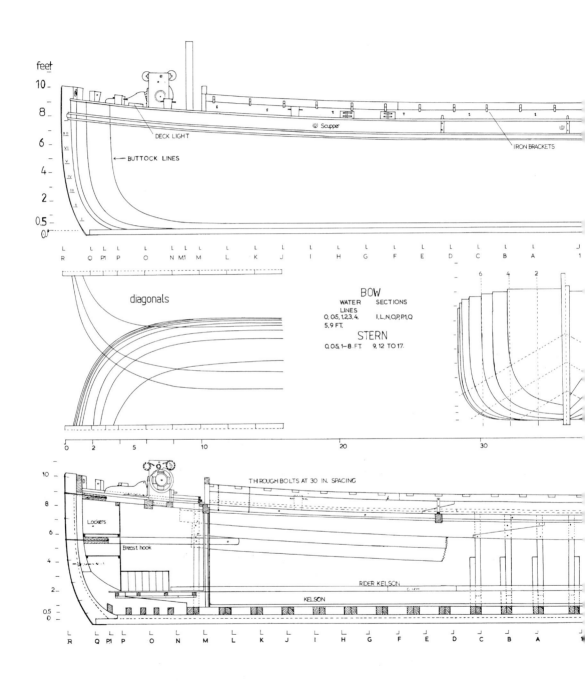

feet

10
8
6
4
2
0.5
0

DECK LIGHT

BUTTOCK LINES

Scupper

IRON BRACKETS

X II
V I
V
IV
III
II
I

L   L L L   L   L L L   L   L   L   L   L   L   L   L   L   L   L   L   J
R   Q P1 P   O   N M1 M   L   K   J   I   H   G   F   E   D   C   B   A   1

diagonals

BOW
WATER   SECTIONS
LINES
0, 0.5, 1,2,3, 4,   I, L,N,O,P, P1,Q
5, 9 FT.

STERN

0, 0.5, 1-8 FT.   9, 12 TO 17.

6   4   2

0   2   5   10   20   30

10
8
6
4
2
0.5
0

THROUGH BOLTS AT 30 IN. SPACING

Lockers

Breast hook

RIDER KELSON

KELSON

L   L L L   L   L   L   L   L   L   L   L   L   L   L   L   L   L
R   Q P1 P   O   N   M   L   K   J   I   H   G   F   E   D   C   B   A   1

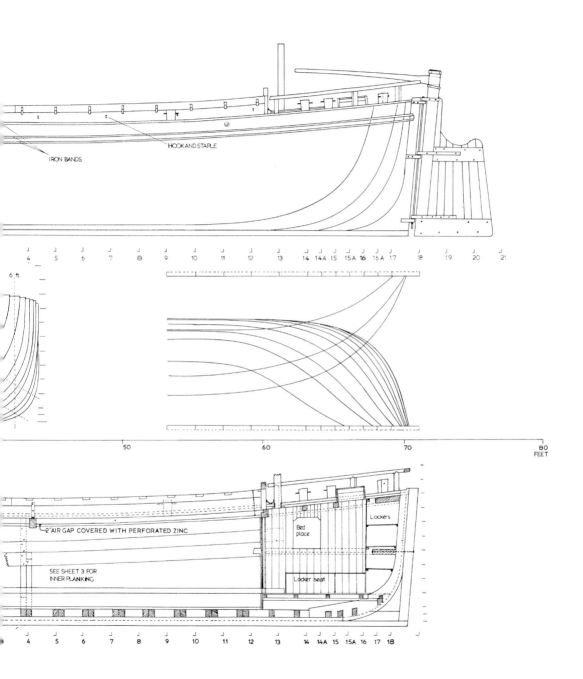

HOOK AND STAPLE

IRON BANDS

6 ft

4 5 6 7 8 9 10 11 12 13 14 14A 15 15A 16 16A 17 18 19 20 21

50 60 70 80 FEET

Lockers

Bed place

2" AIR GAP COVERED WITH PERFORATED ZINC

SEE SHEET 3 FOR INNER PLANKING

Locker seat

4 5 6 7 8 9 10 11 12 13 14 14A 15 15A 16 17 18

scantlings of the *Fox*, which was contracted to be built at Lancaster between 11th January and 15th March 1792:

DIMENSION & SCANTLINGS of a Flat Building by John Brockbank The FOX at Lancaster January 11th 1792

	Ft	in			
Length of Keel Square	52	0	Rake forward	9 ft	3 in
Ditto Extream aloft	63	6	Do, aft per foot	0	2
Breadth Molded	17	6			
Depth Hold	8	0			

TONS 83 81/95

KEEL	American Oak and Elm sided 12 inches depth $12\frac{1}{2}$ inches outboard $7\frac{1}{4}$ inches
KEELSON	of Fir $14\frac{1}{2}$ inches and Depth $18\frac{1}{2}$ inches
STEM	Sided 9 inches by 11 inches broad. STERN POST sided 9 inches
FLOOR TIMBERS	in midships sided 10 inches forward and aft 8 inches depth on keel
1st FOOTHOOKS	sided from 8 to 7 inches
2nd do. do	from 7 to 6 inches
TOPTIMBERS	from 7 to 6 inches and $4\frac{1}{2}$ inches in and out at gunwale
OUTSIDE PLANK	the flat bottom $2\frac{1}{2}$ inch oak or elm with 2 inch ends. Bilge 2 of 3 inches and 2 of 4 inches each side, from thence to the Bends $2\frac{1}{2}$ inches in midships and 2 inch ends – 2 BENDS of 4 inch thick, brightwork $2\frac{1}{2}$ topstrake $2\frac{1}{2}$ inches Foreign oak may be wrought below the light water mark.
INSIDE PLANK	Strings for the Beams $3\frac{1}{2}$ inch oak, Bilge 3 strake of 3 inch oak, foothook feet 3 inch oak, the rest of her ceiling in flat floor to be $2\frac{1}{2}$ inch. Deal in midships and 2 inch oak at each end, Foreign oak may be used in the inside bilge and Flat Floor to be caulked.
BEAMS	two for the mast $8\frac{1}{4}$ by $7\frac{3}{4}$ inches rest $7\frac{1}{2}$ by $6\frac{1}{2}$ inches
DECK PLANKS	3 inch Deal, WATERWAYS solid Deal.
WINDLASS	a patent one $14\frac{1}{2}$ inches diameter whelped on 4 sides with Elm.
WINCH	to be fixed to the mast
THE HULL MASTS	YARDS and other poles to be completely finished together with ironwork, Joiner Plumber and Painter's work a boat and 4 Deal Oars, 4 Handspikes, 2 Setting Poles, Anchor Stocks and Boat Chocks and to be launched on or before the 15th day of March 1792 for the sum of seven pounds a ton paying on delivery.

83 31/95 Tons at £7 is £537.

The different types of wood in the *Fox* are interesting, particularly the use of imported woods. Although it is not stated, it is almost certain that her frames were made from English oak. Indeed oak seems to have been the preferred wood for framing components and, according to the Liverpool Museum Shipping Guide (1935), flats built on the Weaver in the nineteenth century had all the frames and deck framing in oak. The bow planking was also of English oak; the four bilge planks were of rock elm, the bottom planking was of softwood, the midships planking was of oak or pitch pine and the deck planking was of pitch pine.

The backbone of the flat consisted of a keel and keelson with frames sandwiched between them except at the bow and the stern. The keel projected between 5 in. (127 mm) and 9 in. (229 mm) below the garboard strake. The stem and sternposts (about 11–12 in. (279–305 mm) deep by 8–9 in. (203 mm–229 mm) wide) were mortised into each end of the keel and the joint was sometimes reinforced by an iron staple known as a stopwater. The rake of the stem varied between five and ten degrees. The stern was less, between three and five. A keelson could be as much as 2 ft 6 in. (762 mm) deep (in the case of the *Eustace Carey*) by 16 in. (406 mm) wide. Its two ends were scarphed into the deadwoods. Sailing flats usually had a lighter rider keelson about 6 in. (152 mm) deep on top; this had strips of half-rounded iron to protect it from damage when cargo was being handled. Canal flats and later dumb flats had smaller keelsons sometimes with no rider and sometimes with side keelsons. H-section steel girders were a popular substitute in the times of timber scarcity and were found in many of the Leeds & Liverpool long boats – for example in the *Scorpio* (ex-*Helena*) of 1890 preserved by the Boat Museum, Ellesmere Port. Side keelsons were also found in dumb flats. At each end the keelson was scarphed with the inner stem, which consisted of a deadwood below and an apron on top. There were four or five cant frames to make up the shape of the bow and three to four for a round stern. The fan-shaped arrangement of these seems to have been a unique feature of flat construction.

The 'Barrow flat's characteristic stern was framed in the same fashion and it apparently proved seaworthy because it did not slam down onto the waves as much as the normal counter stern found in other kinds of coastal schooner. A square stern was framed by a pair of curved quarter timbers fastened together and clamped against the sternpost by the deadwood and jointed with a horizontal beam at the top. There were also two smaller beams below this to provide strength and more fastening points for the planking. All curved timbers were cut from oak crooks of more or less the correct curve. In this way the strength of timber was conserved because the builder did not have to weaken it by sawing across the grain to achieve the correct shape. The first cant frame next to the bow was a single timber and those following were made of two pieces overlapping approximately 2 ft 6 in. (762 mm). The heels were either fastened flush with the deadwood or

29

mortised in perhaps as much as an $1\frac{1}{2}$ in. (38 mm). There were about thirty double square frames in the main body of a sailing flat and twenty to thirty single ones in a canal flat. The 'floor' was curved up at its ends to form the rounding of the bilge and a vertical piece butted on to its top. The two were then joined together by a long doubling timber that extended 2 ft (610 mm) along the floor and 4 ft (1.2 m) up the side. This was fixed on the after side of the frame forward of amidships and forward side from midships to the stern. Dumb or canal flats had single frames up to about 2 ft (610 mm) apart. Floors could be 10–12 in. (254–305 mm) deep and top frames were about 5 in. (127 mm) by 6 in. (152 mm) inches in section.

The bow (and stern on a round-stern flat) were reinforced by up to four horizontal oak brackets (breasthooks), 5–7 in. (127-177mm) thick. The breasthook below the deck planking went aft to the forward deck beam and was made up of two pieces of wood scarphed together to obtain the necessary curve. At their apex at the stempost they were clamped together to the stempost by a triangular chock. The main deck beams were 7–8 in. (178–203 mm) deep and fitted – at the fore end of the forward hatch, the same hatch's aft end, the main hatch forward of the mast, at its centre and the aft end. At each side they were supported on horizontal timbers (clamps), 15–16 in. (381–406 mm) deep and 3 in. (76 mm) thick. These were fastened to the frames and ran the whole length of the parallel section of the hull. Beams and clamps were fastened together by horizontal wooden and wood or iron vertical brackets (knees). In some flats there were vertical posts (stanchions) to support them at their centres. The decks at each end were supported by smaller beams and those at the fore end were reinforced by shorter beams (carlins) to carry the windlass.

Like builders of other wooden vessels, nineteenth-century flat-builders used an increasing number of iron knees and flat straps to strengthen the flat's hull. The two cargo hatches of a sailing flat or the single hatch of a dumb flat were framed at each end by headledges fastened on top of deck beams and on the side by heavy side pieces (carlins) to which the vertical sides (coamings) of the hatch were fixed. The latter were about 15–17 in. high (381–432 mm). A series of short carlins was fastened between the shelf and the coamings to support the side decks. The outer edge of the deck was framed by a heavy waterway or covering board about 10 in. (254 mm) wide by 5 in. (127 mm) deep and the timber heads for mooring were mortised through this. There were two or three lead-lined scupper holes drilled through it in its straight sections to allow water to be cleared from the deck. Quite often there was inner covering board at the bow and stern. The flat's outer skin was made up of about twenty strakes. They were about $2\frac{1}{2}$ in. (64 mm) thick on the bottom, 3 in. (76 mm) on the bilge and had two planks 4 in. (102 mm) thick above the bilge itself. They tapered to about 3 in. (76 mm) at each end to fit the curve of the bow.

Top and bottom planks (sheerstrake and garboard) were 9 in. (229 mm) deep and the rest about 6 in. (152 mm). It must have taken a lot of steaming to make them fit the tight curves of the bow. The overall length was too great to use one plank and care had to be taken to make sure that the butt joints of one strake did not coincide with those below and above it. Planks were fastened to the frames with iron spikes though earlier ones used oak pins (treenails). The planking of a square stern was vertical, not horizontal. Some Bridgewater flats had bottom planks that were fastened across (athwartships) like in narrow boats. The inner skin or ceiling was fastened inside the frames and not only provided a smooth surface for the cargo hold but added to the strength of the hull. The ceiling was confined to the straight section of the hull and the hold was closed off from the ends by a double-skinned bulkhead with tarred canvas between each layer of boards. For Leeds & Liverpool coal boats the ceiling was no more than a series of vertical oak boards (shuts) nailed between the frames to protect the planking. There were normally two rubbing strakes at the bow of a sailing flat which went back to where the parallel body of the hull started. The stern was the same and there was a continuous strip of half-round iron to protect the gunwale. Bridgewater and Rochdale boats had four rubbing strakes or 'guards' at the bow. Finely made rope stem and sternpost fenders were a feature of canal flats. The Rochdale ones had three on the stem to protect it, especially in locks. Big coir fenders hung in loops were used to protect the bow and the stern. Many photographs show sailing flats with side fenders improvised from planks tied to the timber heads; and latterly rubber motor tyres were often used.

The design of the Rochdale Canal Company's flats had to combine seaworthy qualities for work on the Mersey with good cargo capacity and the shallow draught of the canal. Note the lutchet or towing mast just forward of amidships, the curved hatchboards (typical for all flats) and the three bow fenders (the sail, stem and feather board fenders). The bow is protected by sheet iron plates for working through ice on the canal.

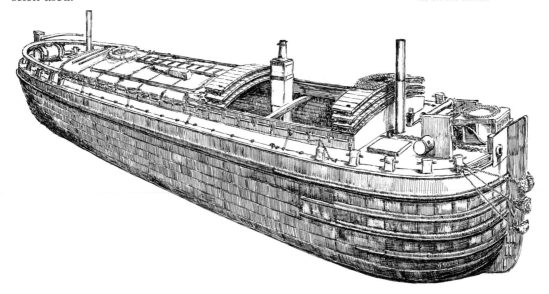

A relatively small number of flats were of composite build with iron frames and wood planking. The earliest I have found is the *Curlew*, built at Liverpool in 1863 and owned by the Chester Leadworks Company. Many of the steam packets were of similar construction. Some of the last flats built by Abels' at Runcorn had wooden cants and steel frames in the main body. Most surviving wooden flat hulks have iron knees and straps to reinforce beams, stems and the ends of the keel. Iron-hulled sailing flats were more rare. The earliest, built in 1834, was designed by the engineer to the Mersey & Irwell, Samuel Wylde, and could carry a third more than the company's existing flats, increasing the average cargo to thirty-nine tons. The new design was tried out in iron and wood and the metal version was considered successful enough to order another four. Wylde's lead was not followed, partly because of the cost and partly because wooden flats were easier to repair. Iron flats were built intermittently. The *Decempedes*, the *Opus* and several others were built in the late eighteen-seventies and then converted to steam. The *Decempedes*'s stout wrought iron was later motorized. The Shropshire Union's managers debated the merits of steel in 1887 and decided to order four steel dumb flats from Royden's, the Liverpool shipbuilders. They cost seven hundred pounds each, which was £125 more than a wooden one, and as a result wooden flats continued to be built. Similarly in 1875 the directors of the Leeds & Liverpool found an iron boat would cost a hundred pounds more than a wooden one – £360 as against £260.

Wood was the material for 'Barrow flats' but their design influenced that of later steel schooners. The Ashburners of Barrow were noted for their fine schooners, which were of the 'Barrow flat' type. Richard Ashburner was a trained naval architect who prepared a full set of drawings – sheer, body and half-breadth plans – for the vessels they built and in many cases owned. He worked continually to improve on the design. The *Result* built of steel in 1893 at Carrickfergus, was considered to be his masterpiece and was a long way from a 'Barrow flat', let alone a Mersey flat with a clipper bow and counter stern. But she retained a flat midship section.

The first steam packet, the *Experiment* was launched by Falk's, salt producers at Winsford, in December 1863; and apparently she was built out of tough Low Moor wrought iron recovered from old salt pans. The design of the iron and later steel packets was basically an enlarged version of the wooden flats. However, wood did not give way to metal, even among the packets. In 1914 there were 152 packets in the Mercantile Navy List. Seventy-six were iron or steel and only two were listed as composite with the balance recorded as wood built. The wooden ones did contain a substantial number of metal components and are generally regarded as composites. Some owners, such as the Salt Union, preferred wood to iron. The former was often cheaper to build and easier to repair. Wooden flats and packets were still being built in the twentieth century: the last flat, the *Ruth Bate*, was launched at Runcorn in 1953; the last Leeds & Liverpool boat in 1955; and the last wooden packet, the *Gwalia* built by Yarwood's, at Northwich in 1907. Their steel successors still continued to be built along the same lines, but gradually modifications were introduced. The Canal Transport Company, H. & R. Ainscough's and Appleby's, millers of Burscough and Blackburn, had steel motor and dumb barges built in the nineteen-thirties with a distinct chine at the turn of the bilge aft. Iron boats were also built for the Lancaster Canal by Allsup's, the Preston shipbuilders, and were of broadly similar design to those of the Leeds & Liverpool.

In an iron flat the keel and frames were fashioned from angle iron. These were not as closely spaced as wooden frames. The outer skin consisted of iron or steel plates rivetted together. They were much wider than the timber strakes of a wooden flat. There was no structural inner skin, but there were wooden floors in the holds to carry the cargo and bulkheads across the vessel at either end of the hold. Frames and plates were fastened by rivets. After the Second World War, British Waterways had some motor boats built for the Leeds & Liverpool which were welded and made out of high tensile steel.

The flat's deck layout was simple. In the bows on either side of the stem were two heavy timbers for the hawse holes. They had cast-iron liners to stop wear from the cables. A heavy knee back from the stem-post (the pawl chock) carried the pawls for the windlass. The windlass drum was supported on two heavy uprights (cheeks), and one heavy anchor and one lighter kedge anchor were normally carried. The main gear wheel was on the starboard side with the pawl race in the centre. There were warping drums at each side and these could be brought into use by hanging the three turns of chain from a row of hooks hanging from a bar above the windlass drum. There could be one or two smaller winch barrels on top of the main windlass. The one aft carried the barrel lines for warping the flat in dock. The lines (up to ninety fathoms) could be led over the bow via a block on the forestay. If a second were fitted it could be employed to wind up the four sheave purchase at the end of the forestay to raise the mast or for working cargo with a derrick. Beside the windlass was a small hatch or a companion (the scuttle) which provided access to the fo'c'sle. A heavy iron rod (the transom) was fitted abaft the forehatch for the foresail sheet. The two hatches had high coamings and curved wooden hatch covers. They could be wide – about 10–11 ft (3–3.4 m) on a 15–16 ft (4.6–4.9 m) beam – with side decks about 2 ft (610 mm) wide on later dumb flats. 'Barrow flats' had smaller hatches because they were sea-going. Dumb flats and packets had one hatch, as did Strickland's Mersey & Irwell flat. They were covered with canvas tarpaulins which were held tight along each side by battens wedged

Overleaf: Bedale, *deck and construction plans. Note the fan-shaped arrangement of the cant frames at the bow and the stern.*
Dr Frank Howard Collection, Trustees of NMGM

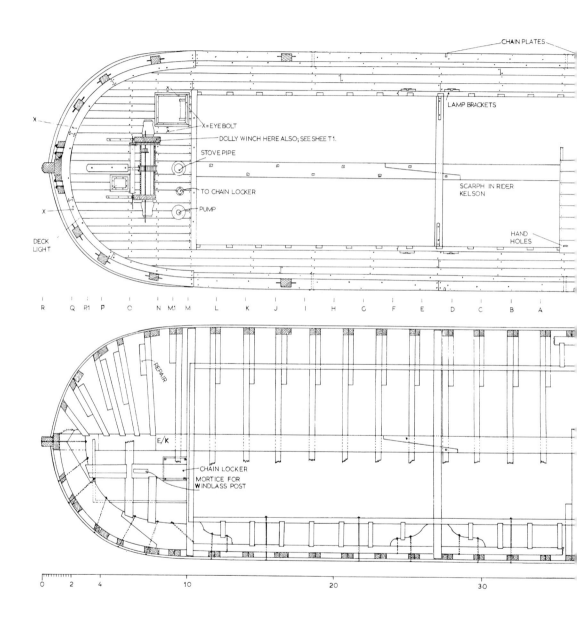

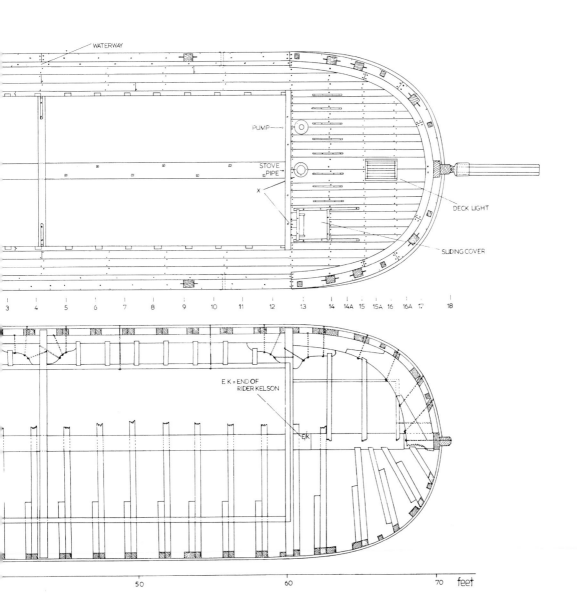

WATERWAY

PUMP

STOVE
PIPE

X

DECK LIGHT

SLIDING COVER

3   4   5   6   7   8   9   10   11   12   13   14   14A   15   15A   16   16A   17   18

E K = END OF
RIDER KELSON

E K

50   60   70   feet

tight in metal lugs. Some eighteenth-century flats such as the *Concorde* were 'open flats' without hatch covers. This tradition was perpetuated in coal carriers on the canals such as the long boats plying between the Wigan pits and Liverpool. The mast case was fixed to the forward side of the main hatches or inside the headledge. The packet's mast carried a light derrick worked from the barrel winch on the windlass. The following equipment was normally carried on the main hatch: tow lines, mooring warps, up to four boat hooks, sounding pole about eighteen feet (5.5 m) long for checking the depth of water and a mop. Rochdale flats had a stower with a forked end for poling the flat in the shallow waters of the canal. The packet's cock boat was carried on the hatches. They also had a trestle on which the mast and derrick could be lowered when passing under fixed bridges between Winsford and Northwich. Quite often there were a couple of bicycles as well. The mast case for the light mast of a dumb flat was about a quarter the length back from the stem, mounted on a beam across the hold.

The pump was traditionally fitted at the aft end of the main hatch and was made from an elm tree trunk. It had a valve at the bottom and a second valve or bucket hooked into a long iron spear rod which was worked by a wooden lever. The latter worked on an iron pin between two uprights fashioned from the trunk. It had to be primed with two buckets of water and pumping the bilges for any length of time was laborious. On the aft side of the pump there was a cleat for the main sheet on a sailing flat. Dumb flats and packets also had wooden pumps. Later flats had cast-iron pumps. The *Oakdale*, for example, has two 'Deluge' pumps, one forward and one aft. There was a chimney for the cabin stove and to port a water barrel on chocks and a companionway. The latter could be a flat sliding hatch or a half-round one with a sliding top. There were glass lights let into the deck to illuminate down below. Sometimes circular cast-iron ventilators with screw-down tops were fitted. Many flats had low side rails at the stern. Sailing flats also had an iron horse over the top of the rudder to stop ropes becoming entangled with it. Coasting flats might have detachable rails running forward to the mast; and some of the eighteenth- and early nineteenth-century ones had solid bulwarks. Twentieth-century dumb flats and steam packets rigged manropes along the side decks. Dumb flats might also have short rails amidships to carry brackets for the navigation lamps. The steam packets' boiler casing dominated its after deck. It carried the funnel (hinged for the Winsford ones), the safety valves and the whistle. There were iron lids on the deck for the coal bunkers and a filler cap for the water tank.

The tiller took virtually the whole length of the stern deck and was controlled by tiller lines attached to posts to port and starboard. There were foot grips fastened to the deck, again to ensure that the tiller did not take charge. It fitted into a square mortise in the top of the rudder post and might have a stay or bottle screw to keep it tight.

Some photographs show sailing flats carrying a second, shorter tiller on deck which would have been handier for working in the docks. A cranked iron tiller was used on Rochdale flats when carrying high loads. The rudder was large and made up of five or six vertical boards fastened between two horizontal sloats. It raked forward at the aft end and the end plank had a curved top (the saddle) which looked good and was functional, preventing ropes from fouling the rudder. The stern and the rudder post had three rudder braces each and the rudder was attached by a long rudder pin. This enabled the rudder to lift if the vessel took the ground. Some of the coastal jigger flats had steering wheels. Packets were fitted with a wheel and worm-type steering gear. A packet had a canvas dodger to protect the helmsman from the weather. Later packets had a wheelhouse forward of the funnel. Some 'Barrow flats' had open-fronted ones. The last steel packets were like coasters, with a raised superstructure and bridge. There were up to five timber heads at the bow and stern, with four amidships for belaying mooring ropes. Some had a horizontal iron bar fixed through them. Dumb flats had stout towing posts on either side of the stem and stern. A packet had towing posts at the stern. Sea-going vessels would carry a compass, sometimes in a binnacle. The eighteenth-century version was like a cupboard with sliding doors lashed to the deck. One is illustrated in the Brockbank specification of the *Juno* of 1789.

I shall leave the description of the accommodation to chapter nine. The hull was caulked, pitched and painted with 'black varnish' or gas tar. Although the decorative scheme of the sailing flat was not as extensive as the Thames barge, there was a tradition of brightly painted fittings – such as the rails, the tops of the stem and sternposts and the timber heads. Red was popular and nineteenth-century views of the port of Liverpool bear this out. Hatch combings, windlass and so on were brown. Lou Atkin, who worked with his father on the *Keskadale*, recalled: 'The coamings were grained, brush grained with a mixture of burnt sienna and raw sienna and cold tea!' Large organizations such as the canal companies had their own liveries. Green was considered an unlucky colour according to one flatowner. Painted or grained panels were an important decorative feature on the bows and the stern. Lou Atkin recalled: 'The flat's name was painted on the starboard. Below the name was a little grained or varnished panel. Every flatman had his own tiny scraper (made out of old files) for doing this work and there was usually a little feather (scrollwork) round it.' Older flats, such as the *Chester* of 1828 and the eighteenth-century *Daresbury*, had their names carved into the bow and stern. Draught marks were carved in as well. There is one photograph of George's Dock, Liverpool, about 1890 showing a flat with a multi-pointed star carved in the aft face of the sternpost. Others have painted diamonds in the same place. The hawse timbers often had an inset panel. Even

The beautifully decorated transom of Leeds & Liverpool short boat Joan, *owned by Thomas & William Wells, one of the last operators on the canal. Note the camber of the deck.*
E. W. Paget-Tomlinson

the last flat, *Ruth Bate*, had a chain of three diamonds carved into her top strake – this was a design carried by all of Bate's flats.

These simple designs are echoes of earlier, more elaborate carved features. The Liverpool Ship Register between 1787 and 1789 contains entries for flats with figureheads; for example, the *Happy Return* built at St Helens in 1785 had a 'knee figurehead'. The most elaborate painted decoration was found on the boats of the Leeds & Liverpool Canal: the square-sterned short boats had red panels with chamfered corners outlined in white at the bow: these also appeared on the wooden chimneys of the Yorkshire versions, the rudder post, rudder, dog kennel, provender tub and water barrel. The gunwales fore and aft might be painted with small connecting triangles of red, white and blue, called 'dragon's teeth'. The upper part of the stern carried the boat's name to port and the owner's to starboard on decorated panels; below there were panels on each side of the rudder with scrolls, flowers or bunches of fruit. The registration number was painted on either side in black letters on a white panel.

Finally, every flat at sea or on the estuary carried a cock boat. Incidentally, this is a term for a tender that goes right back to the Middle Ages. Humber keels have their 'cog boats'; the name which obviously has the same root and is a reminder perhaps of the medieval cogs of northern Europe. The Clwyd Record Office has a document about an inquiry into the drowning of men at Greenfield on the Dee 'by the oversetting of a cockboat' in 1722. One retired flatman, Mr Colley of Birkenhead, told me that they were called punts in Liverpool and Birkenhead. 'Cock boat' may be a Weaver term – just as the flatmen of that river were known as 'watermen'. The flat's boat was invariably carvel built because it was stronger and could take more knocks. One built by Yarwood's in 1913 measured 13 ft 6 in. (4.1 m) long, with

5 ft 3 in. (1.6 m) beam and 1 ft 11 in. (585 mm) depth. Manchester Ship Canal work boats which were modelled on the cockboat and built until within the last thirty years measured 16 ft (4.9 m) 5 ft 8 in. (1.75 m) by 2 ft 9 in. (838 mm). The latter had larch planking $^7/_8$ in (22 mm) thick. They had eighteen frames, mainly of oak, in them and three thwarts, and the transom was knotched to take a sculling oar for propulsion. The *Fox*'s boat of 1792 was equipped with four oars; but that may have been unusual. When a boat at the (Manchester Ship Canal) Runcorn Yard was built, the keel was fixed securely to the trestles and the stempost and stempost with transoms fastened to it. Midway along a mould or 'feather' was fixed and six flexible battens were fastened round each side to make the shape. Next the floors were put in and then the shape of the short frames (top timbers) was taken off the battens. There were two cant frames forward and one aft. Planking proceeded with the four top 'rubber' planks, the bottom garboard strake and finally the two bilge planks. Apart from acting as a lifeboat in emergencies the cock boat was in constant use for running lines to move the flat in and out of dock or for moving berths. Sailing flats usually towed them astern when under way.

Sculling a cock boat to the powder hulk Swallow. *The 'hoy' is* No I Bebington *(see chapter seven).*
Frank Rogers

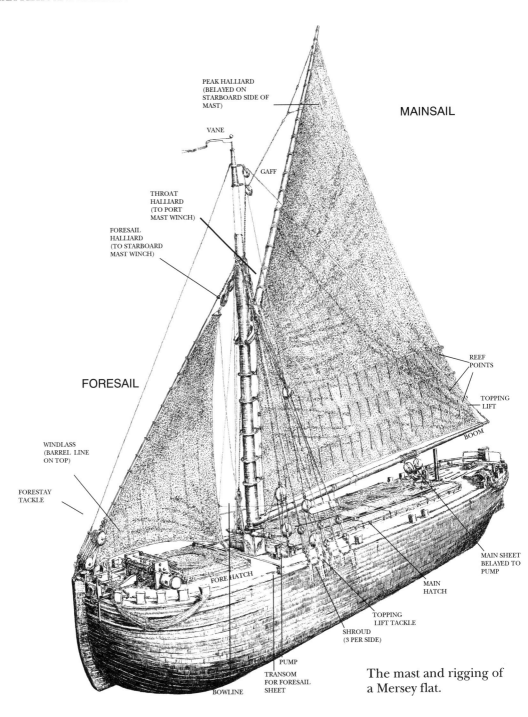

PEAK HALLIARD
(BELAYED ON
STARBOARD SIDE OF
MAST)

VANE

MAINSAIL

GAFF

THROAT
HALLIARD
(TO PORT
MAST WINCH)

FORESAIL
HALLIARD
(TO STARBOARD
MAST WINCH)

REEF
POINTS

TOPPING
LIFT

FORESAIL

BOOM

WINDLASS
(BARREL LINE
ON TOP)

FORESTAY
TACKLE

MAIN SHEET
BELAYED TO
PUMP

FORE HATCH

MAIN
HATCH

TOPPING
LIFT TACKLE

SHROUD
(3 PER SIDE)

PUMP

TRANSOM
FOR FORESAIL
SHEET

BOWLINE

The mast and rigging of
a Mersey flat.

40

Rigging and Sailing   3
the Flat

The flat rig was a foresail and high-peaked long gaff mainsail and boom generally reaching over the stern. Like the hull the mast sails and spars were on a heroic scale. Richard Hart, the skipper of the *Edward* (the *Big Ned*) in the early nineteen-thirties recalled that the *Ned*'s boom was almost fifty feet (15.24 m) long and twelve inches (305 mm) in diameter. Yet flats were handled by a crew of two or three and by all accounts were handy if not speedy vessels. The flat rig with a short gaff was already in use on the Mersey in the late seventeenth century and early eighteenth century. The gaff seems to have been gradually lengthened and rigged at a more acute angle. Mid- and late eighteenth-century views of Liverpool show flats at a half-way stage, gaffs longer than the Bucks' but shorter than and rigged at a less acute angle than the nineteenth-century version. The gaff sail seems to have superseded the square sail directly without any intermediate steps. John Leather in his standard work *Gaff Rig* (second edition, 1989), suggests that the sprit rig evolved from the square sail, developed into the half-sprit or standing gaff with a loose-footed sail and then finally into the lowering gaff with a boom to spread the foot of the sail. The Bucks' view of Liverpool shows one such vessel with a brailed mainsail but a raised poop. The small open boats of the Mersey and the Dee such as the salmon and the gig boats were rigged with spritsails to within living memory. There is no documentary evidence to link flats with sprits, but the famous engraving of the great Sankey viaduct that carried the Liverpool & Manchester Railway of 1830 over the Sankey Canal does show a sprit-rigged flat. It is likely to have been a piece of artistic licence imported from the Thames. The shipping Registers do not mention sprit sails and are quite specific about rigs: flat, sloop, dogger, galliot or schooner. On the other hand the barge is flat shaped and the mast and sail are of a size that suggest that this was a dumb flat used only in the canal with a small temporary mast and sail for fair winds. The Liverpool Museum guide (1935) stated that the sprit sail was common in flats into the nineteenth century but I can find no evidence for this. Square-sail flats co-existed with gaff rig during the eighteenth century. The two square-rigged flat-hulled ferries in the Bucks' view did not require the more elaborate rig because they were on a short cross-river run and could work with the strong tides. The square sail was considered suitable for the Douglas and the Ribble. The flat *Success* of twenty tons' cargo capacity carried coal from the Wigan collieries for transshipment at Tarleton to coasters or to Ribble creeks such as Freckleton. The account for her repairs in October 1765 shows that a new yard and square sail were bought for her. In October 1797 Brockbank's at Lancaster contracted to build four flats for the Douglas and Ribble trade for Gregson and Company The hulls – fifty-eight feet six inches (17.8 m) by fourteen feet (4.3 m) by four feet six inches (1.4 m) – were 'to be completely finished with Iron, Joiner and Painter work and one mast and Yard made and fixed for the sum of £327'.

John Harris's *South West Prospect of Manchester and Salford* of 1736 shows a flat sailing close-hauled with a square mainsail and a jib; five years on Casson and Berry's map has an illustration of a similar flat with a bowsprit. The account in the *Manchester Mercury* of the opening of the Bridgewater Canal's aqueduct over the Irwell at Barton in 1771 suggests that small square-rigged flats also persisted on the Mersey & Irwell. The centre arch was thirty eight feet (11.6 m) high and vessels on the Irwell could sail through. This can be interpreted in several ways. First, they could literally sail through which meant that the flat could be no more than about thirty-five to forty feet (10.7–12.2 m) long if the height of the mast is about the overall length of the hull. Second, they could be going through with the sails down and the mast lowered (quite likely). Third, the large river-going fifty-six foot (17 m) barges lowered their masts and rigged a temporary sail to assist passage in fair winds. This was common practice on the Thames with barges shooting the London bridges and there is some evidence for the same practice with flats. When steam tugs were introduced in the eighteen-thirties, the Mersey & Irwell's own flats were unrigged and given a square sail to help the horse on the passage inland from Runcorn. Small square sails were found on the Leeds & Liverpool, especially on the Rufford branch to Tarleton – the successor to the Douglas – according to Clarke. J. Corbridge's *Pictorial History of the Mersey and Irwell* (1979) includes a photograph of two flats with very light masts and gaffs at the Runcorn terminus of the Mersey & Irwell. These would not have been capable of beating down the estuary but would have been good enough for fair weather inland.

Flatmen were great traditionalists and knowledge was passed from generation to generation, so there may be an echo of earlier practice in the many dumb flats that were sailed around Liverpool docks round about the Second World War. Mr Albert Caldwell, once skipper of the *Mossdale*, recalled that flatmen used to earn extra money by shifting flats without a tug. Nelson dock was always an obstacle because there was a change of water level between the deeper North Docks and the shallower Central Docks. To avoid delays flatmen would move their flats out of the Salisbury entrance just before the gates were closed at the top of the tide and pole them along to the next entrance. Sometimes a small square sail would be rigged to get up to the Canada Dock entrance. Some flats had properly made square sails set on their light masts, and some improvised with a ladder and tarpaulin.

The flat's mast was positioned about a third of the length from the stern. In the nineteenth century it was usually made from pitch pine and was from twelve to fifteen inches (305–381 mm) in diameter. It was approximately the same length as the overall length of the hull. It was rebated at the hounds to receive the shroud collars and its top section was tapered and painted white. Later flats had coloured bands to indicate who owned them – rather like funnel colours; the Liverpool Lighterage Company's flats, for example, had two blue bands. One view of the River Mersey in the nineteenth century shows a flat with a red spiral which makes the top of her mast look like a barber's pole. The main part of the mast was varnished (as in the case of the *Keskadale*) or treated with linseed oil. Some flats had masts that could be lowered to pass under fixed bridges. The major obstacles such as the bridges at Warrington on the Mersey and the Weaver at Frodsham could be avoided after the opening of the Runcorn & Latchford and the Weston Canals. But others remained, particularly the bridges in the centre of Warrington on the actual River Mersey and those on the Bridgewater Canal, the bridges in the centre of Northwich and the Barton aqueduct which carried the Bridgewater over the Mersey & Irwell Navigation. The Northwich bridges were replaced by swing bridges in 1893, but the Hartford bridge between there and Winsford remained fixed (though rebuilt) and this meant the Winsford packets were equipped with lowering masts and funnels right up to the end of the traffic.

As steam towage became the norm on the Weaver and the other inland canals, flats were 'barged' and became 'cut flats'. The later sailing flats had no arrangement for lowering their masts because they worked the Mersey and coastwise. By 1900 there seem to have been only a few flats with lowering masts. The knowledge of how masts were lowered has disappeared and this has led to a debate about how it was achieved. At first sight the logical way would be to mount the mast in a tabernacle on deck in the same way as on a Thames barge, and this in fact was the case on the Weaver packets and for the light masts of dumb flats. However all the evidence for sailing flats points to the mast pivoting on the keelson. The *Daresbury*, built in the seventeen-seventies, had this arrangement in her later role as a derrick barge on the Weaver. She survived afloat until about 1958. Although she had been repaired many times, I think that her mast fitting was to the original design. She had a three-sided mast case, with the aft side open and fixed onto the keelson at its base. The heel of the mast – which had a groove in it – pivoted on a heavy iron bar fixed just above the keelson between the two sides of the mast case. To back this up, the archives

Daresbury *of 1772 with mast lowered.*
E. W. Paget-Tomlinson

of the Boat Museum, Ellesmere Port, contain a description and sketch of a similar arrangement, provided by an 'old flatman' to the British Waterways engineer at Northwich. It states that this was the usual means of fitting and lowering a mast.

The model of the flat *Wesley* is the most important piece of evidence. This model, which is in a private collection was built by a flatman in about 1863. It may be based on the *Wesley* built at Northwich in 1861. The hull seems to be rather too deep for its length but this is because the model was built to be sailed. On the other hand it has a wealth of convincing detail. Much of this can be checked for accuracy against other sources such as photographs. The cabin, the pump and the rigging are three examples where I can be sure the *Wesley*'s builder got it right and on this basis I would go on to assume that the mast pivoting arrangement is correct. The *Wesley*'s mast is pivoted on a bar just above the keelson as in the *Daresbury*. The heel of the mast is notched to fit over the bar and reinforced with two iron straps. There is an iron latch at the top of the mast case which can be unhooked when the mast is lowered. With this latch released and by releasing the tackle on the forestay the mast could be lowered. Lowering the mainsail was presumably an essential preliminary step. But the problem, looking at this operation in hindsight without the benefit of the knowledge of a flatman who had performed mast lowering, is that the main hatch boards are in the way. The mast can only be lowered if the boards are removed and a gap left in the cargo at the foot of the mast. This seems cumbersome but just about possible since the cargo was usually in bulk. The arrangement – as far I can work it out – was that the mast was lowered onto the deck beam or 'no man's land' in the centre of the main hatch.

An early picture of flats at Bromborough mill with masts lowered shows a chock mounted on the deck beam to take the mast. This meant that only the first four or five hatch boards would need to be removed. Shifting boards on either side of the keelson would ensure that there was a clear slot into which the mast could be lowered. Indeed, this odd arrangement probably dates back to the 'open flatts' of the eighteenth century. These had no hatch boards at all. Another possibility was to lift the mast, spars and sails off the boat and leave them on the bank for voyage up the Weaver. Sailing was difficult on the narrow reaches except with a fair wind and there were men and, later, horses available for towing. Humber keels certainly left their masts ashore and were towed on inland canals. The flat's standing rigging could be readily unhooked from its chainplates – a feature

Bromborough mill about 1860. The flat in the foreground has her mast lowered onto a chock on a beam across the main hold. For the history of trade to Bromborough see chapter seven.

that persisted in the later flats with fixed masts. The print of the Weaver at the Old Bridge, Northwich, about 1800–20 shows two unmasted flats and another with her mast lowered. There is also a large crane on the quay. Another mast-lowering method is shown in Strickland's plan of a Mersey & Irwell flat. This has its mast pivoted just below the boom. The heel swings forward in a narrow slot in front of the mast case, as in a Norfolk wherry. Strickland is quite specific that this is an existing flat and not a proposed design. Perhaps this was one of the 'fly-boats' that could deliver a consignment from Liverpool to Manchester in fifteen hours. There are many detailed differences from the 'normal' flat in the rigging. For instance, the main sail is sheeted right aft instead of to the aft end of the main hatch, and the foresail sheets have two single blocks – one of which is hooked into an eyebolt in the deck. There are only two shrouds and the peak halliard has an additional tackle.

The normal flat's mast had three hemp cable-laid shrouds on each side. The leading two were paired and all three were parcelled and served at the hounds. The starboard pair were fitted first. Dead-eyes and lanyards set up the shrouds and the lower deadeye was

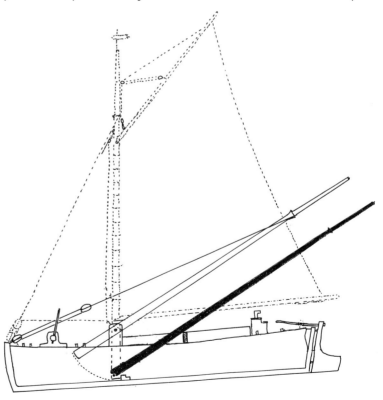

Mast-lowering arrangements of flats. The unshaded mast shows Strickland's plan for a Mersey & Irwell flat and the shaded one the arrangement on the model of the Wesley (see chapter eleven). The hull and sail plan are drawn from Strickland's plan.
Trustes of NMGM

Northwich Old Bridge,
early nineteenth century,
with open flats – one with
a lowered mast. Note the
horse and its harness on
the left. See chapter six for
the salt trade.
British Waterways Archives

hooked into the chainplates. Some jigger flats also had a topmast shroud as well. The lower block of the forestay tackle was hooked into a large forged ring bolted to the stem. The top block was attached to the forestay by a series of three chain links. The stay itself was usually a one-inch (25 mm) diameter iron rod. Its upper end was U-shaped and attached by a shackle to a stop around the hounds. The top mast stay was attached to the uppermost mast band by a shackle and its lower end was attached to the ring on the stem by a set of small dead-eyes and lanyards.

The size of a flat's sails called for heavy running gear, and purchases and winches to enable the two-man crew to work them. The large wooden blocks with their large-diameter free-running wooden sheaves were a characteristic feature and would have eased the work. The hand winches were fitted on each side of the mast case. The foresail was raised by a halliard with a single purchase tackle to the starboard mast winch, and this could be raised by the mate on his own. Its tack was secured by a single rope which led through an iron ring on the aft side of the stempost through to a cleat on the windlass knee. This was released when the sail was furled so that it could be hauled clear of the windlass. The sheet was shackled to the clew of the sail and was lashed round an iron ring on the horse (the transom) across the deck. The downhaul for use if the halliards jammed was a single rope from a small loop in the head of the sail; when not in use it was belayed to a diagonal cleat on the forward side of the mast case. The bowline was attached to the leech and led through a fairlead on the fore shroud to a cleat on the shroud. It was important because the sheet was not adjustable. Frank Ogle remembered, 'The adjustment of the bowline was quite critical. I remember Capt. Beswick in the *Olivet* going to, what seemed to me, a lot of trouble to get it just right, even though we were moving a short distance.' (*Sea Breezes*, 1971, pages 882–9)The jib had eight cloths in it with a large roach and cut away at the tack if a pair of mast lowering blocks were fitted. Some flats had a short spar at the head of the jib. Coasting flats, including jiggers, carried topmast staysails and these were stowed aloft well clear of the deck.

The mainsail was hoisted by two sets of halliards which were often made of chain. The peak halliard started with two strops around the gaff linked by a chain span with a sliding iron ring. The halliard itself was led from the ring to a single block shackled to an eyebolt on the mast. There was then a single purchase and the lower block was shackled to a ringbolt on the headledge of the main batch. Its fall was belayed on a diagonal cleat on the starboard side of the mast case. The throat halliards were shackled to the upper side of the gaff jaws and led through a single block suspended from a strop at the hounds, passing down to a larger pair of double blocks. Like the peak the lower block was shackled to the headledge and belayed to a diagonal cleat on the port side of the mast case. Both were in easy reach of the mast winches. The topping lift supported the boom when the sail was stowed. It was led from the end of the boom to a single block at the top of the mast on the same iron strap as the forestay eyebolt; from there it went to a large single block on the starboard side. One end of the fall was hooked onto a chainplate between the second and third shrouds and the other was seized to the upper of another large pair of single blocks. The lower of these was shackled to a chainplate between the first and second shrouds and the fall was led through a ring bolted to the deck and then up to a cleat lashed to the second starboard shroud. Some flats' topping lifts had a small tackle hooked onto the upper block to the hounds. This – apart from taking the weight of the block – must have helped with the trimming of the lift tackle. There was also a tripping line tied to the gaff to help control it as it was raised or lowered and this was tied off on the boom.

The mainsail sheets are led through three large single blocks and belayed to a cleat on the pump. The head of the mainsail was lashed to an eyebolt on the underside of the gaff, the clew to a short strop and an S-shaped iron at the end of the boom and the tack to an eyebolt in a slot cut in the top surface of the boom. It was loose footed but laced to the gaff, and there were four or five mast hoops made out of cane. There were fourteen to sixteen cloths in the sail, all sewn with flat seams. According to Mr Worthington, who worked for Greig's, the Runcorn sailmakers, sails were hand stitched with best tarred twine at a rate of four stitches to an inch. Flat skippers would test the stitching by stretching it over their backs. Much skill went into the cutting of cloths to give due allowance for the stretching of the canvas with age. This was especially important on the leech where the weight of the boom stretched the sail. The sail would be tight and would split if it was not puckered when new. Attaching the heavy bolt rope (soaked in Stockholm tar) called for skill. This was one inch (25 mm) in circumference on the foot, two (51 mm) on the luff and the head and four (102 mm) on the leech, all joined by rat-tailed splices. Making grommets for sail lashings by hand called for experience and dexterity. There were also two or three lines of reef points and some flats had an additional single row on the jib. Jiggers had a single row on their mizzens. The Strickland plan shows a bonnet laced on to the jib, but I think this was unusual. The *Phebe* of 1813 painted on a flagon made by the Herculaneum Pottery, Liverpool, shows a mainsail bonnet laced to the luff, which is almost the same size as the mainsail itself. As the *Phebe* was owned by the pottery for hauling coal and clay, there is every likelihood that the artist painted in the correct details. To preserve them sails were tanned with a mixture of red ochre and fish oil – a mixture that attracted wasps in summer. According to Lou Atkin who sailed on the *Keskadale*, the crew were responsible for this and a stock of ingredients was kept in the store forward. Some flats carried a small jib-headed topsail and jigger flats had topsails on the main and mizzen. At the beginning of the nineteenth century, the ship registers have many entries for flats with bowsprits. In March 1831 Arthur Barron of Woolden Hall owned three flats: the *Comet* (1805) and the *Amy* (1800) had standing bowsprits and the *Mary Jane* (1826) had a lifting one. Others had sliding bowsprits which, like the lifting version, would be useful in crowded docks. The *Lively*, built by Brockbank's in 1789, had a bowsprit thirty one feet (9.4 m) long, nine inches (229 mm) in diameter at the heel and eight feet six inches (216 mm) at the head. The wind vane which was sunk into the top of the mast was both practical and decorative. It was made of sheet copper with the name or a design pierced into it and perhaps a seagull or some other emblem on the top. There were a couple of yards of red bunting to show the wind strength and a small ball as a truck.

There were some other rigs for flats. Sloops must be mentioned. Many craft in the late eighteenth- and early nineteenth-century records are referred to as sloops. Some were not flats and those built in North Wales, for example, tended to be shorter and deeper, with a counter stern, topmast and bowsprit. Two craft demonstrate this: the sloop *Darling* was built at Barmouth in 1781 and measured 42 ft 8 in. (13 m) length, 14 ft (4.3 m) beam, 7 ft (2.1 m) depth of hold, burden variously 38 to 44 tons and net tonnage 33 tons. The *Prosperity* was built at Aberdovey in 1842, 32 tons, 42 ft (12.8 m) long, by 14 ft (4.3 m) beam and 7 ft (2.1 m) depth of hold. The difference between sloops and sloop-flats was recognized in the early nineteenth-century editions of *Lloyd's Register of Shipping*. At least three sloop-flats are listed: the *Beby*, *Hannah* and *Hannah and Martha* between 1808 and 1815, all sailing between Liverpool and Dublin. Sloops that were built at flat building centres appeared in the Liverpool Ship Registers. Most have identical dimensions to flats built at the same place. For example, an analysis of flats and sloops at St Helens between 1760 and 1800 shows there was no difference in dimensions. The difference seems to lie in the rig. The sloop rig was recognized as separate because it had a topmast and sometimes square sails for running in fair weather and a bowsprit. The spars of the flat *Mite* of 1830 built by Brocklebanks' at Whitehaven, measured:

Mast, deck to hounds	40 ft (12.2 m), 13 in. (330 mm) diameter
Bowsprit outside stern	20 ft (6.1 m), $11\frac{1}{2}$ in. (292 mm) diameter
Main boom	$41\frac{1}{2}$ ft (12.6 m), 10 in. (254 mm) diameter
Gaff	28 ft (8.5 m), $6\frac{1}{2}$ in. (165 mm) diameter

and when altered to sloop rig:

Mast from deck to hounds	39 ft (11.9 m), $14\frac{1}{2}$ in. (368 mm) diameter
Head	$10\frac{1}{2}$ ft (3.2 m)
Topmast	$24\frac{1}{2}$ ft (7.5 m)
Topsail yard	$25\frac{1}{2}$ ft (7.8 m)
Top gallant yard	18 ft (5.5 m)
Crossjack yard	34 ft (10.4 m)

What a splendid sight she must have been, running before the wind with three square sails set! One of the flats in Rooker's *Prospect of Liverpool* of 1770 has a yard for a light weather square sail, as does the flat with a bowsprit photographed at Bank Quay, Warrington, in about 1860. I suspect that sloops were intended largely for coastal work and that solid bulwarks – as against rails – might be another feature that marked them as different from flats. Two of the St Helens-built sloops show this. The seventy-three-ton sloop *Raven* of 1788 was owned in Bangor, North Wales, and carried slate coastwise; and the *Green Linnet* of 1786, seventy-six tons, carried copper ore from Anglesey to the refineries sited on the banks of the Sankey Canal at St Helens.

The late eighteenth- and early nineteenth-century galliot was a ketch rig with the addition of a square topsail on the main mast, very similar to the east-coast billy boys. They were built in small numbers compared with the standard flat. In the Liverpool register between 1786 and 1804 there were seventy-five new flats and only fourteen galliots including two 'galliot flats'. There were also three doggers: the *Mary*, 1786, 92 tons, built at Frodsham; and the *Olive*, 1786, 86 tons, and another *Mary*, 1778, 80 tons, built at Liverpool. All three were beamier than a flat, but I suspect the hull design was similar although the rig was not. The dogger, according to Falconer's dictionary of 1780, was 'ketch rigged' (a main and a mizzen) with two square sails on the main and a standing gaff on the mizzen. There were schooner-rigged flats too. In some cases flats and sloops were re-rigged as schooners. The *Raven* of St Helens was re-rigged as a schooner in 1817 and the *Samuel Dixon* of Bangor was built in 1848 and altered in 1854.

The *Liverpool Mercury* for 11th January 1865 advertised:

For sale
Flat *Rose Ann*
of Warrington, 60 tons register carrying 120 tons of grain on a light draft of water, it is now lying at Old Quay Dock, Runcorn. Built of English oak and diagonally bound with iron. It is in first rate condition and well found with sails, ropes and all requisite materials and *be easily made into a coasting schooner.*

Sometimes these schooner-rigged flats were over-masted and given too much sail. Their big hatches made them more vulnerable than ordinary coastal schooners. For a regular coastal trader this was still a sensible rearrangement of the sail plan: the main boom of a sloop measuring sixty feet (18.3 m) overall would have been over forty feet (12.2 m) long and could be difficult to control when going about in a good wind. Splitting the sail area into two not only made the sails easier to control but in bad weather the crew could snug down to mizzen and foresail alone.

I will not write anything about the rig of the 'Barrow flats' since they have been covered in detail by other authors, particularly in the writings of Basil Greenhill and David MacGregor. The rig was a handy one for long distance coastal work with its combination of square and fore and aft sails. It also brought with it much more complex rigging to control eight or nine sails as against two in a basic flat. The same applied to the galliot with its square sail or sails. Around the middle of the nineteenth century the square sails of the galliot were abandoned along with the separate topmast. Such sails could have been seen as expensive to maintain and as not contributing enough to the overall performance of the vessel to justify their retention. What survived was the jigger flat, a ketch. Jiggers as well as 'Barrow flats' were built right into the twentieth century. The last were the *Eustace Carey* and the *Santa Rosa* in 1905 and 1906 respectively. Some single-masted flats were also converted: the *Livadia* of 1873 became a jigger in the eighteen-nineties. The mizzen was a scaled-down version of the main mast set in a mast case without the winches and with two shrouds. Both masts were fixed and the normal deck fittings of a flat were retained. Some, like the *Protection* and the *Sarah Lathom*, had steering wheels and bulwarks, which must have helped considerably on rough passage in the Irish Sea.

Since the disappearance of the sailing flats, there has been much debate about their sailing qualities. The lack of a centreboard or leeboards has raised the question of how they managed not to be blown to leeward, especially when light. Expert flatmen said that they were not. This must have been in part due to the crews' experience in

Jigger flat Santa Rosa *with all sails set at her builder's yard at Sankey Bridges in 1906. Note the topsails, some single masted flats carried one too.*
E. W. Paget-Tomlinson

handling a flat in local waters. Flatmen were born flatmen; son followed father and there was an inheritance of expertise in getting the best out of a flat with all her limitations, and in spite of the river and its tides. It is also important not to apply the performance of modern yachts, for example in getting to windward, to traditional craft such as flats.

Getting underway varied; often it involved warping with the barrel line from the berth and into a lock. If you were lucky you might get a tow from a passing steamer. Richard Hart, skipper of the *Edward* remembered that in the Liverpool North Docks:

We'd get the North End hoppers [hopper barges] to give us a pull off. At that time you could slip them a tanner. Well between three or four of you and a couple of bob or half a crown used to be a lot of money. Even the gateman, he'd always throw a line down and you'd slip a tanner in the rope. You got a big favour done by that way. As soon as you'd got a pull off, course they'd let go the rope. You'd be away then and you used to race up the river . . .

Flatmen talked about 'rigging a flat', not setting sail. The mainsail was raised first; some skippers hauled the peak and some the throat halliards first. Lou Atkin, mate of the *Keskadale*, recalled, 'To rig a flat they slack everything off and took off the stops [ties] off the mainsail . . . the peak halliards were hoisted first by all the crew and the last few feet hoisted by the winch attached to the foot of the mast. When the peak was nearly up the heavy throat halliard was hoisted.' Richard Hart, on the other hand, said:

> You raised the throat first. Say you was pulling off same as we used to do at Birkenhead, you'd get the throat up. . . you might be able to get part way up before they let go. It all depended on what kind of wind it was. Soon as they let go you'd have it up in no time, set. Down with the helm. The mate could raise the foresail then.

In light winds the topping lift would be slacked off and the boom lowered, which meant that the cabin chimney had to be taken down. Although flats did not carry leeboards, tacking was not considered a problem. John Brown said, 'You had to drive a little before you tacked.' The foresail would be pulled across with the bowline to help the head round. By all accounts, flats were quite handy in going about. Many flatmen ascribed this to their large rudders, which in fact were about seven per cent of the immersed area of the hull. The keel, the hollows at the bow and stern all assisted grip in the water. Mr Arthur Warburton of Sankey Bridges who was eighty-seven when I met him in 1976, was a keen yachtsman who took an interest in the local flats. He remembered flats being able to tack in the confined and bending waters of the Mersey above Runcorn. Skippers would use the cushion of water between the bow and the bank to help the head round. On particularly tight bends they would steer close in and the mate would go forward with a boat hook and push the head round to help get her on to the opposite tack. With the tide and a good wind flats could go faster than the steam packets and the local yachts, making New Ferry from Fiddler's Ferry in one and three-quarter hours. This is borne out by many other reports. Strickland reported that the Mersey & Irwell flats 'sail very fast and are capable of contending the most boisterous weather'. John Sutton, who owned the *Protection*, claimed to have got eight knots out of her under sail and motor. This was exceptional and probably near the theoretical maximum speed from a flat's hull. Most flats probably sailed at well below this rate, even in optimum conditions.

Flats tended to go about more slowly when loaded. Jiggers would also use the mizzen to get the stern round when tacking. When tacking in the confined Rock Channel off the Wirral between the Mersey and North Wales, skippers would let them go close into the sandbanks when tacking to use the cushion of water to help the head round. The tide above all else governed sailing. A loaded flat probably had a fair chance of beating to windward with the tide, but would only reach or run against it. All sailing on the Mersey was with the tide. If the wind did not suffice or was a 'dead muzzler', flatmen would make progress by 'springing' their flat. It was a skill that was widely practised in other parts of the kingdom. In the West Country it was known as 'dredging'. A flat drifting with the tide would quickly let go her anchor with sufficient cable just to stop her. She would swing head to the tidal stream, her rudder would be put hard over in the required direction and the cable raised clear of the bottom. Then she would move stern first, with the tide. Richard Hart said, 'It was a case of drop the anchor quickly. You'd swing head to tide and once you'd settled in and got the tide running past her, then you'd hand over your helm and spring her off, and up anchor at the same time. There was no messing about . . .'

'Springing' a flat.

Flow of tide

54

Lou Atkin added, 'The flat spun on the anchor when springing and when you were dragging which every way you put the tiller the tide would steer you the way you wanted. You sometimes had to spring her four or five times to West Bank [Widnes] from Eastham.' Springing had to be carefully timed and there was no brake on the windlass, only a fork or devil's claw to hold the chain. He continued:

> You had to pull two turns of the chain on the windlass barrel over to the port side. The chain would walk along the barrel and you had to fleet it [out on deck] to make sure it was on the right side. The other turn of chain was pulled on to the foreside of the windlass and laid on deck in straight lines. As soon as the skipper rounded up and shouted 'Let go' you put your weight on that chain and that put enough slack in it to fetch the fork out. The anchor dropped pulling out the chain on deck. The skipper would then say 'Give her a bit' or 'Fetch it up' and in the latter case you had to fetch it up from the foreside and throw it over the windlass. You had to be careful because two turns would not hold and the chain could be snatched off you.

Entering docks under sail from the river with its eddies and restricted water was a hazard that could be tackled with the right knowledge. Richard Hart recalled:

> I reckon it was the worst river in the British Isles to navigate. If you were in fog, coming out of Langton or anything like that, there was always traffic in the river and there was always a big black buoy off the south end, just below Garston. The tide would always set you there; if you didn't sail and let her go down, she'd always take you to that buoy.

Flats could carry a lot of weather helm, 'hard mouthed' and difficult to steer: 'Then you had a steering rope in a sheave in the rail and that was fastened to your tiller. That gave you leverage. You'd heave on it and take a turn', continued Richard Hart.

Going down the Mersey was more trouble than coming up. Going up, the tide was lifting all the time and the biggest banks were all covered. The north bank had a lot of exposed rocks and the south banks had sandbanks. They were just as hazardous. If a flat grounded, silt would form on the lee side and the suction could make it difficult to float off the next tide. Flats could also be swept across the banks, which would strain them and cause leaks. Runcorn railway bridge was especially dangerous on big tides because the peak had to be dropped to get underneath. This called for nice judgement for if the peak were dropped too soon the flat lost way. Richard Hart described the process:

> Soon as you got through, heave it up quick the skipper would have to let go the tiller, run and you'd be hanging on and he'd give you a hand . . . soon it was up, he'd back at the helm. . . . But if you didn't watch yourself you got in the Cheshire deep . . . you'd be in a mess. . . . It was a hard river to navigate, but once you was used to it, you took no notice of it really.

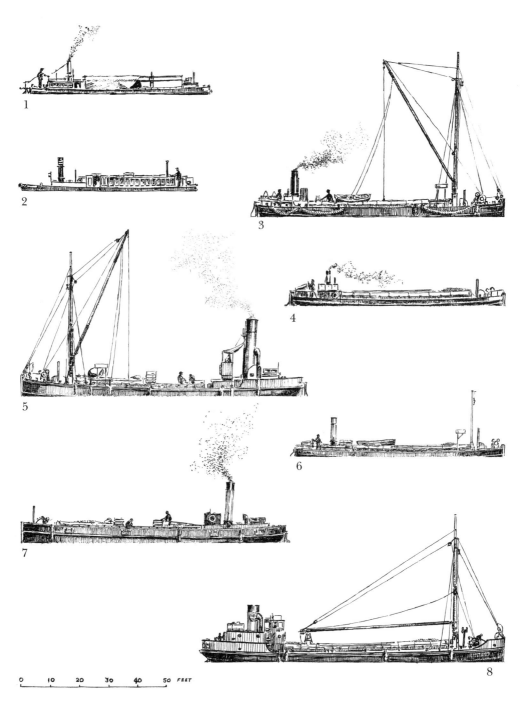

1

2

3

4

5

6

7

8

0   10   20   30   40   50 FEET

Towage and Steam Power   4

Sailing flats probably spent no more than a third of their time under sail. For the remainder they were in dock loading or discharging or under way in the docks by barrel line and boat hooks or inland, sails furled under tow from a gang of men, a horse or a steam tug. A great deal of the crew's time was spent shifting small distances, especially in the Liverpool docks.

The barrel line on the windlass was a very important means of propulsion over short distances in dock. The cock boat would be sculled across the dock carrying the line. This was attached to a quay bollard and the flat could then be hauled across to a new berth. The photograph of the *Dauntless* in Canning Dock illustrates the process. She is lying just off the end of the dry docks. The mate is climbing back on board from the boat while the skipper is on one of the handles of the barrel winch. Richard Hart remembered:

> You used the barrel line out in dock, fifty fathoms in a reel. You'd put the line in a little boat, scull it off to where you wanted, hook it on and we always had a knack of being able to throw it. You could all throw a line and get it on a bollard without getting out of a boat. Or if you were passing a barge you would always throw it on one of his bollards and then you'd heave and heave against the wind. Perhaps you'd have to go through three lengths of locks, if you had a part cargo.

Flats would be poled along the quays using the boat hooks and dumb flats' crews would frequently have to work their flats to the entrance walls of the docks to await the tug that would tow them up river. Similarly, on the return trip they would be cast off just by the entrance and would work their way through to their destination. If they were lucky there would be a passing tug or packet to give them a tow. Flatmen were also paid for moving without a tug.

John Leather, in his book *Sailing Barges* (1984), mentions the use of sweeps when there was no wind. I have not found any evidence for this in the later flats but it is quite possible. Many coastal craft, including the Liverpool pilot cutters of the 1766–1850 era, carried them and they would have been easier to work with the flat's low freeboard than on some other vessels. The boat hook was also a useful tool for moving over short distances; well after the end of the sailing flat, flatmen were adept at using them to work through the Liverpool dock system. Flats were also poled on the upper Mersey reaches around Fiddler's

Opposite page: *Steamers – all to same scale*

1. *Leeds & Liverpool canal steamer, c1910.*
2. *Bridgewater Canal 'little packet' steam tug, 1876.*
3. *Salt Union packet* Vale Royal, *1873.*
4. *Rochdale Canal Co.'s* Treat *c.1905.*
5. *Brunner Mond packet* Frances Poole, *1929.*
6. *Wolverhampton Corrugated Iron Company's* Ellesborough.
7. *Ryland's (wire works at Warrington) and later Bishop's Wharf Carrying Company's* Nonie, *1909.*
8. *ICI motor packet* Wincham *1948.*

The Dauntless *(1870) of the Liverpool Lighterage Company in Canning Dock between 1897 and 1910. The mate, having taken the barrel line across the dock, climbs back on board from her cock boat. The skipper is at the winch. Note the diamond decoration on the top of the rudder and the name and registry port carved into the planking.*
Williams Collection,
Trustees of NMGM

Ferry to Sankey. This is mentioned in a court case about diversion of water from the river which was heard at Lancaster in 1827. Kedging with an anchor was common practice. If there was not too much tide it was possible to move a flat with a kedge anchor lashed to the barrel line. Lou Atkin recalled that it was no joke sculling the cock boat across the tide with a kedge on board and the skipper shouting at him to hurry up.

Inland navigation – where masts and sails would not be much use except in fair winds – depended on men or horses. The canalization of rivers such as the Weaver in the early eighteenth century entailed building locks, dredging shallows and perhaps making new cuts on the tightest of the river bends. A towpath for horses raised problems for the promoters. It was not simply a matter of the cost of making one; local landowners were not enthusiastic about losing their field boundaries. Indeed, many landowners actively campaigned against the improvement of the Weaver and defeated parliamentary Bills in 1711, 1715, 1718 and 1720 before the Act of 1721. The undertakers for the Weaver had built a towing path for men by 1733, but a full horse towing path was not built until the seventeen-nineties. On 23rd June 1753 the cost of two men hauling the flat *Expedition* on the Douglas from Wigan to Tarleton was five shillings (25p). At the end of the eighteenth century, the charge for a round trip from Winsford or Northwich was fifteen shillings (75p) for a horse and five shillings for a man to lead the horse. If bow haulers were employed they charged five shillings each; from two to six would be needed, depending on the state of the wind and the current. J. A. Picton in his *Memorials of*

Liverpool (1875) stated that six to eight men abreast yoked to a rope were used to tow flats on the Sankey.

Hauling seems to have been a separate and casual occupation. The flat haulers were among the witnesses called to give evidence in a case tried at Lancaster in September 1827. The mayor and council of Liverpool brought a case against the Mersey & Irwell for causing a nuisance by diverting water from the River Mersey at Woolston to the detriment of navigation on the Mersey. Those called were asked to testify on the state of the river. Thomas Higham was forty-four and a former flatman who now worked hauling 'open flats' on the Sankey Canal; Thomas Williamson who was a former flat captain and Thomas Moors, who had worked in flats for twenty-five years in the employ of Dudley & Blackburne, were both flat haulers. It is difficult to judge whether hauling was a job for older men or perhaps more likely done by those who had been dismissed or were down on their luck. Haulers seemed to have been linked with heavy drinking. The new extensions to the Sankey and the Weaver in 1804 and 1810 which brought the two navigations right down to the wide part of the estuary reduced the scope for manual hauling. Horse towage seems to have become the predominant method of moving flats on inland canals in the early nineteenth century. The 1831 edition of Priestley's *Navigable Rivers, Canals and Railways* reported that horses had taken over from manual haulage for flats and were cheaper and less troublesome than bow haulers who were paid a fee and tipped with a drink. The railway guide of 1837 stated: 'Great numbers of boatmen were formerly employed in the dragging of vessels between Winsford, Northwich and Liverpool. Within the last few years, horses have been employed for the purpose . . .'. Maintenance men on the Sankey hauled their boat right up to the nineteen-twenties. when the St Helens section was all but closed. One maintenance man's memories are reported in Charles Forman's *Industrial Town* (1978) and they have echoes of old bow hauling days, including the perks of the canal bank:

> There were four of us pulling the boat on a long rope. It was like walking in a sling. You used to saunter along. You'd start off the boat from the canal bank, the captain would push off with a pole. The speed of the boat was called the way – a chap would say 'We've got a good way on it'. The canal was full of waterlilies and rushes and all sorts of wild fowl. I've seen twenty swans at a time, shelduck, anything you care to mention. . . . I brought a few eels home from the ditches, nice too! I've had a few ducks. Fellows used to be out shooting and they'd give you one!

It is not known how exactly the earlier flat haulers performed their task but canvas slings round the chest were used for other craft, such as the Humber keels.

The position at which the towline was fixed on the flat was critical for bank haulage, whether by man or horse. If it was too far forward the flat's bow went into the side; too far aft, it ran into the opposite bank. Slightly forward of amidships it would tow true but would be easily deflected by cross-winds (which were certainly a consideration both on the upland Pennine sections and the flat Liverpool end of the Leeds & Liverpool); slightly more forward, the flat will tend to pull into the bank but be fended off by the cushion of water that she built up between herself and the bank to which she was running parallel. Lengthening the tow reduced the sideways pull, but was difficult to manage on bends.

The towing of a sailing flat by a horse was from the mast. One arrangement is shown in the famous print of the Barton aqueduct; a masted flat is shown with a towline attached to a tackle from the hounds. This print is something of a puzzle because the fixed bridges of the Bridgewater would have prevented a flat with its mast raised from crossing the aqueduct. On the other hand, the details of the boat have undoubtedly been taken from a flat. Rochdale Canal flats had a 'towing mast' just forward of midships. It was mounted in a kind of tabernacle called a lutchet which was slotted into the top of the keelson and secured to the mast beam across the hold. The actual mast or 'neddy' was seated in a socket in the top of the lutchet. The Leeds & Liverpool boats had more complicated arrangements. Two round iron towing masts were fitted at either side of the forward end of the hold, and these projected about thirty inches (762 mm) above the deck. A lutchet fixed in the centre of the forward cross-beam provided a third towing point. Its mast could be raised or lowered according to the height of the cargo and when the boat was loaded or unloaded. The mast nearest the towpath was normally used, and the lutchet came into use when working through locks and in strong winds because its position made steering easier. Fly-boats always hauled from the mast in the lutchet.

The horse was a major mover of boats on inland waterways well into the nineteen-thirtiess, in spite of the tugs and steamers and eventually motor craft on the Leeds & Liverpool, the Shropshire Union, the Sankey and the Rochdale. There was no particular breed of canal horse. Almost every type of horse was represented. Cart horses were much used on the Bridgewater. Most measured between fifteen and seventeen hands and most were mares or geldings, stallions being rare. All had to be broken to boat haulage. To move a loaded boat a horse had to hang forward in its collar until it broke the boat's inertia, straining until it could take another step. The Bridgewater in the Duke of Bridgewater's day had mules because they had plenty of stamina. Mr Arthur Warburton recalled an old character on the St Helens stretch of the Sankey who scraped a living by helping haul flats with a donkey. It was generally reckoned to take two horses to haul a fully loaded ninety-ton flat on the Bridgewater between Runcorn and Preston Brook. The towline, which had to be light and elastic to save straining the horse, was normally a cotton rope of about six

*Bow hauling the Leeds &
Liverpool long boat* Robert
Arthur *with the last coal
cargo for Westwood power
station, Wigan, 1972.*
Liverpool Echo

pounds and was attached to the swingletree hook by a spliced eye in
its end. The swingletree in turn was hooked into the two side ropes.
These were threaded with hardwood bobbins or leather tubes to prevent them from chafing the horse's flanks. The side ropes hooked into
the hames on either side of the horse's collar. The horse wore a bridle
and blinkers, while the reins were led back to the swingletree. The
horse's gear could be highly decorated. Horses were valuable and had
to be looked after and fed with care. The big companies had regula-
tion rations and extensive stables.

The Leeds & Liverpool boats carried a proven tub on deck in
which to keep their feed. Boatmen, whether they had a company
horse or their own, took great interest in its welfare. There were however occasional prosecutions for cruelty. If, like the Alty family (on the
Leeds & Liverpool), they worked for themselves, the well-being of a
valuable animal that provided the family income was a matter of great
concern. Horses tended to work from about five or six in the morning
to seven or eight in the evening. Many did not stop to feed but were
given a nose tin on passage. They were stabled at night at canalside
pubs. They had to be treated for horse ailments, usually with special
boatmen's remedies. Their shoes – which had a special cross bar to
provide grip, especially on the steep stone paved slopes of bridges and
lock sides – had to be renewed about every two weeks.

A well trained horse was a great asset because it would know all the right places to stop and start. The Altys hired their boat but owned their horse. On one tragic occasion, recalled in the *Maghull Advertiser* on 1st September 1977, the horse fell in near Litherland lift bridge:

> in no time at all he was in the middle of the canal and the 'nostin' [the feeding tin] filled with water very quickly. The poor animal was kicking and struggling and there was nothing we could do about it. He would not let us go near him and sadly his life soon came to an end. A passing steamer gave us a tow to Bootle and we pulled the horse behind.

The beloved animal was left at a knacker's yard in Chisenhale Street and the same day Mr Alty went to Clucas's horse sale in Liverpool and bought a replacement for forty pounds.

> Now we had about forty-eight tons of manure and first when the horse took the strain he appeared to be what was known as a little cold-shouldered, which means he did a lot of dancing about and not a lot of pulling but after a few yards he started to take the strain and after about a mile father said: "This chap will do. He is going to make a good one."... When we had travelled about ten miles, father took the reins off the horse and let him go on his own and to our surprise he went quite well.

Pulling a sixty- or seventy ton boat out of a lock required a lot of effort from the horse. On the Rochdale and the Leeds & Liverpool a

'West Country keel' Emily, of similar design to a Rochdale Canal flat, under tow on the Rochdale Canal.
R. Wood

tackle was used which provided a two to one reduction. The ingenious way in which this was used is described and illustrated on page 30 of Clarke's book. Empty horse boats were expected to give way to loaded ones and fly-boats working to a timetable had precedence over all. The operators of the latter needed a large number of horses and stables at regular intervals to allow changes of horses in order to keep to the schedule. Before railway competition closed them, there were also horse-drawn passenger boats. Samuel Curwen left a description of one on the Bridgewater in 1780:

> The boats employed in carrying pasengers are about fifty feet long and fifteen wide and capable of holding more than a hundred persons and drawn by a single horse, guided by a lad mounted and one man at the helm needed ... the rope to which the horse is tackled, fastened to a stump rising about eight feet above the gunwhale and about a quarter of a boat's length from the bow.

The Weaver and Mersey & Irwell kept a large number of horses; in 1832 the former had over eighty. The Mersey & Irwell's 'Old Billy' had his portrait painted. He lived for fifty-seven years; having been trained for the plough in 1767, he retired from flat towing in 1819. This is a record for any working horse. His portrait and his skull are preserved at Manchester Museum. There are a few surviving stable buildings. The Boat Museum has restored the Shropshire Union stables at Ellesmere Port, complete with a shire horse.

Steam power first made its appearance in flat territory with a certain Mr Smith's steam boat on the Sankey in 1797. This must have been some form of experimental paddle steamer because nothing more was recorded about him or his steam boat. Two years later the *Bonaparte*, a stern paddle tug, successfully towed a train of narrow 'mine boats' from Worsley to Manchester on the Bridgewater, but at a speed slower than horse traction. After the trial the tug's machinery was converted to a stationary pumping engine. The Duke of Bridgewater expressed an intention of buying eight tugs following the demonstration of the *Charlotte Dundas* on the Forth & Clyde Canal in 1802. However he died the following year and the matter was not pursued. Waterway owners were apprehensive about steam towage because of legitimate fears of bank erosion. When the Bridgewater finally introduced tugs above Runcorn in 1874, they had to undertake a major programme of strengthening the canal banks.

Such considerations did not matter on the wide Mersey estuary. The first steamers on the Mersey were employed as ferries, starting with the *Elizabeth* in 1815. The ferry *Etna* was built in 1817 from two flats with a single paddle wheel between the hulls. She was designed to carry carts and carriages as well as passengers and as such must have been the first roll-on roll-off ferry. The design must have been reasonably successful because other boats were built to the same design, including the *Vesuvius*, and the *Etna* herself lasted until about

1832. The *Elizabeth* had been useful as a tug on her regular service from Liverpool to Runcorn, but the *Eagle* was probably the first boat to be used regularly for Mersey towage. In 1824 she was employed towing flats from Queen's Dock, Liverpool, to Runcorn from where the barges were moved by horse along the Bridgewater to Manchester. Steam offered the opportunity to provide regular services and expand traffic. Another five steamers were added to the Runcorn route by 1830, chiefly for passenger traffic. By 1830 specialized steam towing was being offered from Runcorn by the St George's Steam Packet Company. The following year the Mersey & Irwell decided to build three steam tugs rather than relying on hiring from others. Two were supposed to be in service with one in reserve and they were intended to assist the company's sailing flats. Flat captains were instructed not to anchor and wait for the tugs and to use them only in contrary winds or calms. Steam towing proved successful, except for the tug *Mallory* which was a hasty conversion from a flat. She was unreliable and soon scrapped. In 1833 the Bridgewater began using the *Alison* and the *Blanche* on the estuary. Not much is known about these early tugs. They were wooden-hulled paddle steamers, with low-pressure boilers (about six pounds per square inch) and side lever engines. The latter were a maritime version of the tried and tested stationary beam engines. Paddles made them very manoeuvrable. But they were not very powerful and they burned a lot of coal.

Estuary towage took a major step forward with the building of a flotilla of large paddle tugs for the Bridgewater in the late eighteen-fifties. The first, the *Earl of Ellesmere* of 1857 was built of iron of 114 tons and had improved boilers and side lever engines. She was about the same size as contemporary tugs for handling deep-sea ships, and was capable of towing up to twenty flats in two lines. She and her sisters were double ended, with a rudder at each end. They could lock one rudder and move backwards and forwards with equal efficiency. The wash from the paddles kept the two lines of barges separated from each other and so made steering easy for the flatmen. They were heavy on fuel, consuming about three tons of coal on every tide. The introduction of these tugs, followed shortly afterwards by Falk's steam packets, doomed the sailing flat for virtually everything except estuary and coastal trades. The Mersey & Irwell had unrigged many of their flats before their takeover by the Bridgewater in 1844. The Bridgewater followed suit. By the time of the introduction of the Canal Boat Registry scheme, which started in 1878, all the Bridgewater flats were unrigged, and by 1896 there were no more than a dozen sailing flats on the Runcorn register.

Screw propulsion which was pioneered in the eighteen-forties by ships such as Brunel's *Great Britain*, offered more power than paddles but less manoevrability. Screw-propelled tugs were built in small numbers at first and only became the accepted type in the eighteen-eighties. Screw tugs for towing flats first started in the eighteen-fifties with trials on the Leeds & Liverpool and the Weaver. The Leeds & Liverpool connection with screw populsion went back to 1843, when John Tayleur of Liverpool was allowed to experiment on the canal with boats propelled by an 'Archimedian screw'. Two years later his experiments were promising enough for him to receive twenty-five pounds from the Leeds & Liverpool Canal Company, who wanted to try steam power. This is very early in the history of screw propellers – Brunel was still completing his *Great Britain* at Bristol. Tayleur was probably related to Charles Tayleur who was both a shipowner and engineer and had set up a locomotive building factory – the Vulcan works – at Newton-le-Willows and a shipyard for building iron ships at Bank Quay, Warrington. In 1852 there was a proposal to introduce screw tugs to tow coal flats from Wigan to Liverpool and there were extensive experiments the following year. As a result the tugs' speed was restricted to two miles an hour because of their wash. However, in 1858 – despite this limitation – the Leeds & Liverpool Canal Steam Tug Co. Ltd was formed. Most of the shareholders were colliery owners or coal merchants with a stake in the Liverpool trade. Four tugs were built with horizontal engines connected by bevel gears to the propeller shaft. They pulled up to six boats at two miles per hour on the canal, or five on the Mersey. They worked between Appley lock (the first between Liverpool and Wigan) and Liverpool. A round trip cost fifteen shillings (75p) per boat. The company had plans to expand its fleet to twenty tugs, but after only a year and a half they

Bridgewater flats at Morpeth entrance, Birkenhead. Three flats in the foreground are being worked into the dock using boat hooks. The paddle tug (possibly the Dagmar) *is about to tow five flats upriver to Runcorn. Note the shape of the transom stern of the nearest outward bound flat.*
Trustees of NMGM

65

failed. There are hints that the canal company took the tugs over for maintenance work, but steam towage was seen as a failure. There was another unsuccessful experiment in 1870 with catamaran tugs, twin hulled with a paddle in between like the ferry *Etna*. Steam power was not finally established on the Leeds & Liverpool until 1878. The *Firefly* was tried out on the Weaver in 1857. She appears to have been built in 1856 as a screw-propelled tug with a two-cylinder simple 'high-pressure' engine. Unlike the Leeds & Liverpool tugs, she was a success and was joined in 1862–63 by two more tugs operated by the Weaver trustees.

The 'high-pressure' engine implied an improved design of boiler. The early boilers had been designed with large flat-sided flues to cope with the scaling-up caused by using salt water. The development of a surface condenser meant that the exhaust steam (condensate) from the cylinders could be kept separate from the salt cooling water and could be condensed back to water and reused with safety. In the early steamers the condensate was mixed with the cooling water, enabling salt water to enter the boiler and cause scale, which meant loss of heat and the risk of blockages in the flues. By the eighteen-fifties there had been striking improvements in the design of high pressure boilers for railway engines. Unlike the conventional flat flue marine variety these were cylindrical to withstand the extra pressure and had large numbers of small tubes through which the hot gases of the firebox were drawn. This multiplied the heating surface in contact with the water in the boiler several times and made it possible to raise more steam to a higher pressure. By the late eighteen-fifties locomotive boiler pressures had increased to over a hundred pounds per square inch. Marine engineers were more cautious, but men like the Liverpool engineer Alfred Holt – who had trained with the Liverpool & Manchester Railway – were beginning to experiment with high pressure multi-tubular boilers in combination with compound engines. Compounds utilized the higher steam pressure by using the steam twice, first in a small high pressure cylinder and then as the steam expanded in a bigger lower pressure cylinder. Compound engines using higher pressure steam of sixty pounds per square inch (in Holt's ships) were far more economical than simple engined equivalents. It enabled Holt, for example, to build steamships which were sufficiently economical to compete with sailing ships. This may seem a long way from a humble steam tug or flat on the Mersey, but the success of Holt's ships led not only to the expansion of his Blue Funnel Line but to the establishment of many other Liverpool based steamer lines.

This expansion of Liverpool's trade in turn put pressure on the inland waterways to provide more tonnage and faster deliveries. The waterways also had to compete for traffic with the growing network of railways. Steam propulsion offered the possibility of at least holding their share in the bulk traffics such as coal and salt. The compact multi-tubular boiler made it possible to build towing vessels that could also carry cargo. The costs of building any steamer were far higher than for a sailing craft and the possibility of carrying cargo to help offset the investment was attractive. This was first tried on the Aire & Calder Navigation in 1852. A decade and a year later the first cargo-carrying steam packet was launched into the Weaver at Winsford in December 1863. This was Falk's iron hulled *Experiment* which was followed the next year by the *Improvement*. The *Warrington Guardian* of 20th July 1864 mentions her launch and describes her. She could carry two hundred tons of salt on the Weaver, but 240 if fully laden – unfortunately the river was not deep enough to permit this. Her engine was a two cylinder horizontal, but it is not clear how the cylinders were arranged, possibly opposed to save space. The boiler was tubular and with the engines as far aft as possible to give maximum cargo space. In 1881 new engines and boilers were fitted to the *Improvement* and the *Experiment* was lengthened, re-boilered and re-engined in 1885. These craft set the pattern for the Weaver steam packets and other salt producers took note of Falk's success and began buying or building steamers. Not only did the packets speed up delivery of salt exports but they also broke the power of the flatowners to charge high rates.

Thomas Higgins of Winsford, Winnington and Anderton bought the Forth & Clyde iron steam barge, *Ariel* – built at Maryhill, Glasgow – in 1859, apparently for carrying fish from the Forth to Glasgow. She was sixty-five feet (19.8 m) long, a limit imposed by the Forth & Clyde locks, but Higgins had her lengthened and indeed widened at Thompson's yard, Northwich. She arrived there in early 1864 from Leith under the command of a Northwich man, James Cross, who had her after her rebuild. She was launched in July 1864, a few days before Falk's *Improvement*. The *Warrington Guardian* of 16th July 1864 describes her new appearance. 'She was 82 feet 6 inches long by 18 feet 4 inches wide with a depth of hold of 8 feet 4 inches. She was expected to carry 135 tons of salt on a 7 feet draught and tow two or three flats'. A second *Warrington Guardian* article on 6th August 1864 describes her trial trip and gives hull and engine details. To resist salt corrosion, the iron hull was coated inside with Portland cement and wooden ceilings were laid across the bottom and up the sides of the hold. This was normal practice on the packets – to coat both iron and wood in the holds with a cement and lime wash. The engine was two cylinder – 10 in. (254 mm) bore x 12 in. (305 mm) stroke) – diagonal, presumably arranged in a V; the boiler was a vertical tubular, and a donkey pump provided the feed, also acting as a bilge pump. Both boiler and engine were right aft, separated from the hold by a bulkhead 16 ft (4.9 m) from the sternpost. The bunkers, also aft, contained 8 tons of coal, the living cabin was forward and 54 ft (16.5 m) of the vessel's length remained as hold. The propeller was

4 ft 6 in. (1.4 m) in diameter, and the paper mentions the *Ariel*'s fine stern lines, her easily managed helm and her light tapering mast. A water ballast tank forward compensated for the weight of the engine and boiler. Her launch and trial trip seems to have aroused a good deal of interest. The *Ariel* was later owned by J. & J. Hind of Liverpool and eventually by the Salt Union, who took the engines out of her. Local legend says they converted her into a sailing flat, but I think it is more likely that she was dumb. She was still afloat in 1923.

While Falk was building iron craft, William Cross built the wooden *Excelsior* at Winsford in 1864. Some owners thought wood was a better material than iron for salt-carrying packets because it was resistant to salt corrosion. She had a vertical engine made by Edward Booth and Company of Manchester and a horizontal tubular boiler, but a bunker capacity of just two tons. She was expected to tow flats and her owners were Cross & Blackwell of Winsford, salt producers, who also had the *Standard* built in 1865.

Between 1871 and 1897 the Weaver was modernized for steam navigation. The locks were reduced in number to four large pairs that could accommodate a packet-towing dumb flat. The number of steam packets increased over the same period. The Winsford firms who had started their development continued to use much the same boiler and engine designs. Mechanical simplicity, reliability and making full use of the hold space were all important factors. Boilers were fitted athwartships with the funnels offset. This saved space but created problems on bad weather days on the Mersey because when the packet started to roll, the top of the combustion chamber could be left exposed without water. This could result in not only a loss of steam but distortion of its plates. Boilers had two furnaces. There was no separate stokehold, the engine came right up to the boiler. The bunker held ten tons and was to port, balanced by a feedwater tank to starboard. The engineer-cum-stoker used a long narrow shovel to put coal into the furnaces. It was important to have the fire burning evenly across the grate, neither too 'black' nor too 'bright'. Clinkers and ash had to be broken up and raked out using a longer poker with a blade on one side – a slice – and a rake with a solid end. The ashes fell into the ashpan below the furnaces, which had to be cleared out regularly. They were loaded into an ash-bucket and hoisted on deck by a davit and tipped over the side. When the boiler was cold, the stoker had to sweep out the boiler flues with a long tube brush.

The bearings of the engine, pumps and the cylinder lubricators had to be kept topped up. Water went into the boiler via a pump driven off the crankshaft. There was a second pump working off the same crank for pumping the bilges. There were also bilge ejectors fore and aft in the hold. Condensers were not generally fitted because enough water could be carried and the steam was exhausted directly into the atmosphere via the feedwater heater. Steam pressure was about

Combined boiler and engine room of the steam packet Vale Royal, *1873.*

seventy to ninety pounds per square inch. The engines, though high pressure, were two cylinder simple, not compound. They could be positioned either in a V formation or inverted and in line, in accepted marine fashion. Cylinders measured 10–12 in. (254–305mm) bore by 12–14 in. (305–356 mm) stroke. The crankshaft revolved at about 120 revolutions a minute and the four-bladed propeller was up to 6 ft (1.8 m) in diameter. The valves were worked by Stephenson's link and the shaft counterweight was set high up at the back of the engine just under the cylinders because of the need to put the reversing lever on deck. The steam valve was fitted at the aft end of the boiler casing to enable the steerer to control the machinery from the steering position. The engine was not separated from the boiler room. It was at a slightly higher level to improve access to the engine when oiling it, and to give a level floor over the thrust bearing and propeller shaft. On the starboard side there was a bench with a vice and an oil tray for the oil cans and a rack for spanners behind. There was also a drum of steam cylinder oil and a large cupboard aft of the engine to hold spares with a fixed bench below it. There were exceptions: the *Nil Desperandum* of 1870 was the first compound and her boiler pressure was higher, 100–120 pounds per square inch. Some, like the Clyde puffers, had vertical boilers and others had boilers fore and aft. The *Albion* of 1887 had a triple expansion engine, while the *Dolphin* of the same year had a four cylinder two-crank compound, with two low pressure cylinders below two high pressure ones.

The engines aft cargo carrier-cum-tug was copied by others on the Mersey. The Warrington based carriers, Bishop's Wharf Carrying Company and the Warrington soapmakers Crosfield's were good examples. The big chemical manufacturers changed to steam because of its great reliability. A packet could make two or three trips to Liverpool in a week. Some placed more emphasis on cargo carrying than towage, and some packets were built which were far more seaworthy than the Winsford variety, with raised bulwarks, a good sheer and increase in size and bigger engines. The chemical manufacturers Brunner Mond of Winnington, near Northwich, were particularly influential. Established in 1874, they initially employed chartered barges and tugs. Then in 1888 John Thompson of Northwich built them the wooden-hulled *Shamrock* to carry finished soda down to Liverpool for export. The 'Brunners' had two-cylinder compound engines and surface condensers. The high pressure bore was thirteen inches (330 mm), the low pressure twenty-six (660 mm) and the stroke for both was eighteen (457 mm). The 'Scotch' boilers were set for and aft, except for the small *Caledonia* of 1904. This set the pattern until the building of the last three in the nineteen-forties, the *Anderton, Barnton* and *Davenham.*

I have written about the packets at length because they are the main example of steam powered development of the flat. However, the Weaver was not the only waterway to use self-propelled cargo carriers. Steam tugs were successfully introduced on to the Leeds & Liverpool in 1878, and in 1880 the directors decided to order four steam fly-boats. They were round sterned and at thirteen feet (4 m) beam narrower than the horse boats. The boilers were vertical with Field water tubes projecting into the combustion space. The engines were of the V type and compounds. Most of the later fly and long distance boats had four-cylinder tandem compound engines. Cylinders were six or eight inches (152 or 203 mm) stroke and propellors three feet three inches (991 mm) diameter for working at low revolutions. The boiler and engines took up ten tons of cargo space leaving thirty tons capacity, and most steamers generally towed two or three dumb boats. Engines were non-condensing with the exhaust steam heating the boiler feedwater before going up the funnel. Coke was usually burned and working pressure was 150 pounds per square inch. The steerer controlled the steam valve and the reversing gear from the deck; while the engineman looked after the fire, the water level, lubrication, ash disposal and cylinder drains. Because of tunnels and bridges the funnel was hinged and could be quickly pulled down by a rod.

The Bridgewater, which took over the Mersey & Irwell in 1844, did not follow the Weaver's example. An experimental tug, the *Result*, sixteen horse power, successfully towed five flats on the canal at three miles an hour in 1859. However, this was not followed up. There were also trials with cable towage in about 1872 which proved too complicated. In 1875–76 the engineer and general manager Edward Leader Williams the younger, who had planned the modernization of the Weaver, ordered six fine-lined tugs to tow existing flats. The 'little packets' – of which another 20 were built – ranged between 59 ft 3 in. long to 61 ft (18.1–18.6 m), with a beam of between 7 ft 7 in. and 8 ft 9 in. (2.3–2.7 m) and a draught of 3 ft 9 in. (1.1 m). Various builders were employed, which accounts for the variations. All except the wooden *Runcorn* were constructed from Low Moor iron. Propulsion was by a single cylinder horizontal engine of 12 in. (305 mm) bore and 16 stroke (41 mm), with a right-angle bevel drive to a 4-bladed propeller, 3 ft 6 in. (1.07 m) diameter, turning at 200 revolutions per minute. Steam came at 80 lb per sq. in. from a locomotive boiler set close to the bow, with bunkers on either side. There was no condenser and no tanks, for water came in direct from the canal by means of a brass ram pump on the port side of the engine. There was an injector fitted on the starboard side to pump the water via the feedwater heater into the boiler. In the early days the 'little packets' were divided between the Bridgewater and the Mersey & Irwell Navigation and they probably helped with the building of the Manchester Ship Canal by towing flats loaded with spoil from the excavations after the latter took over the two older navigations in 1887. Four loaded flats was the usual tow on the Bridgewater, and six in two lines on the ship canal. The trip to Manchester could take between six and eight and a half hours, depending on the load and the weather conditions.

The volume of towage on the Mersey reached huge proportions by the eighteen-eighties and nineties. Dumb flats outnumbered sailing flats. Although the opening of the Manchester Ship Canal hurt this traffic, it continued at an impressive level until the Ship Canal Company gave up their Mersey towage service in 1948. The tugs of the Bridgewater trustees and their successors had offered a public service, and small lighterage firms would use their tugs on the river instead of going to the expense of owning their own. The nine large paddle tugs owned by the Bridgewater handled most of the work to Runcorn. They were inherited by the Ship Canal Company and the *Earl of Ellesmere* (1857), *Brackley* (1859), *Helen* (1860), *Dagmar* (1863) and *Alice* (1864) were not broken up until 1926–27. A second service was provided by the screw tugs of the Weston Point Towing Company. This seems to have been established about 1873 with the *Gladiator*, 78 gross tons,

71

Sixteen empty flats under tow by a Manchester Ship Canal tug in the Mersey and passing a steam packet about 1935.
W. Leathwood

completed at Northwich in that year. Later tugs included the *Liberator*, 79 gross tons (1877); *Emulator*, 106 gross tons (1885); and *Aviator*, 66 gross tons (1876). The last named was rebuilt in 1911 and was still operating under Abels' ownership in the late nineteen-fifties. The Salt Union Combine, besides operating packets towing flats, owned the original eighteen-fifties *Firefly* and the *Waterfly* built at Winsford in 1901 of 49 gross tons. The latter two ended up in Abels' ownership.

Cooper's had an interesting tug for work around Widnes – short jobs to the Ditton Brook, for example – called the *Duke of Northumberland*. She had been built as one of the few steam lifeboats for the Royal National Life-boat Institution in 1890. She was 'jet propelled' by a steam pump and was stationed at Harwich, Holyhead and New Brighton. When she was sold out of the service in 1923 with the introduction of motor lifeboats she was bought by Cooper's, who blocked up the jet nozzles, removed the steam engine and boiler and fitted her with a propeller and a motor. George Wharton, who worked for Cooper's, recalled that she was fitted with a paraffin tractor engine which was unreliable, then a Hispano Suiza – 'which must have held the world record for petrol consumption' – and finally a seventy-horse-power Thornycroft Atlantic petrol-paraffin engine which proved highly satisfactory. George was her skipper for the trips to take a flat loaded with tanning raw materials for the Calder Mersey factory on the side of the Ditton Brook. She was also used as a salvage tender and the directors used her as a pleasure cruiser at weekends. She was laid up because of lack of engine spares in 1942 and her remains are buried under a pile of concrete and rubble at Widnes West Bank.

The various Liverpool tug companies also had small barge tugs for handling flats – including Rea's, who had a substantial coaling business, and Liverpool Lighterage, who normally had two tugs at any one time in addition to steam packets. Their last, the *Kerne*, became the last steam tug to work on the river. She was sold in 1971 to a group of enthusiasts who have kept her steaming to this day. The Shropshire Union also had tugs for their flats. They owned two in 1870 and these were replaced by three large tug-passenger tenders of 175 gross tons between 1903 and 1904: the *Ralph Brocklebank, W. E. Dorrington* and *Lord Stalbridge*. They all had twin screws and compound engines, and could carry passengers between Ellesmere Port and Liverpool as well as tow flats. They were bought by the Ship Canal Company. The *Ralph Brocklebank* was converted into a director's yacht and still survives as the *Daniel Adamson*, laid up by the company at Ellesmere Port.

Six hours, three before and three after high tide, were busy for river tugs. At low water they would lie alongside, dried out, at the Albert Dock river wall. Having raised steam, a typical tide-time duty – according to Bill Leathwood, who served on the Bridgewater tugs – would be to pick up flats from one of the main dock entrances. The flatman would have worked them out to the river wall. One tug could tow up to sixteen flats in two lines using four-inch (102 mm) tow ropes. There was usually a mixture of different owners' flats for various destinations. Once picked up, they would be towed up stream to Weston Mersey lock via the 'main deep' and the access channel. The train of flats would be dropped off at the entrance and the flatmen would steer for the outer wall of the canal. It would be taken in tow by one of the smaller Bridgewater tugs which in turn had brought another group of flats for onward despatch to Liverpool. These might be all for one dock entrance or they might have to be dropped off at various entrances on both sides of the river. Towing of any description is quite an art and towing a train of flats on the Mersey into a north-west gale called for both seamanship and toughness for most of the tugs had open wheelhouses until the nineteen-thirties.

Internal combustion engines first made their appearance in 1891. Two Bridgewater flats, the *Forward* and the *Humber*, were converted to 'petroleum engines'. The first was destroyed by fire three years later. It is not known how successful they were. The first diesel Weaver packet was the *Egbert*, built in 1911 for Brunner Mond. She was

quite small, 75 ft (22.9 m) long by 17 ft 6 in. (5.3 m) with a capacity of 130 tons, and was designed to serve the soapworks at Widnes on the Sankey. She had an eighty brake horse-power Gardner diesel engine, a 10 cwt derrick and a compressed air winch. A further three were built in 1913 and at about the same time the Leeds & Liverpool experimented with an ex-steamer. About 1920 the *Ina*, a short horse boat, was given a 13-horse-power Kelvin engine and a round stern to improve the flow of water to the propeller, together with a water ballast tank to keep it immersed. In 1921 G. E. Ramsey of Shipley began to specialize in motor craft, fitting a 30-horse-power Widdop into a short boat owned by the Burnley Brick & Lime Company. This early Widdop was a semi-diesel; later a full diesel of 24-horse-power by Widdop's became the standard power unit for Leeds & Liverpool motor boats. Motors took less space than steam engines and increased the cargo capacity to 45 tons. They usually operated singly but were also capable of towing. In 1934 the newly formed Canal Transport Company embarked on a programme of building steel motor boats with Widdop engines.

Other flat operators converted steamers to diesel and some of the jigger flats and 'Barrow flats' – such as the *Pilot*, the *Protection* and the *Sara Lathom* – were fitted with motors to make them more efficient at a time of severe competition from road transport and Dutch motor coasters. The 'little packets' were also converted. But the Winsford salt packets stubbornly resisted the new engines until the closure of their trade in 1958. Steamers also persisted on the Leeds & Liverpool to about the same year. After the Second World War the last seven 'Brunners' were all diesel powered, as were the new Bridgewater barges. The last steam packet, the *Davenham*, was converted to diesel in 1972 after some years as a dumb barge. Other Brunner steamers had their careers extended by conversion. (Barge tugs on the Mersey tended to be steam powered until the Clean Air Act forced the Mersey tug owners to re-equip with diesels. The last barge tugs still work for the maintenance department of the Manchester Ship Canal.)

Steam and diesel engines extended the use of the flat from its sailing form. Dumb flats towed by tugs or packets in their hundreds enabled the port of Liverpool's inland distribution system to cope with the huge growth of trade after 1850. But such was the strength of tradition and the versatility of flats, they carried on many of the design features and practices of their predecessors. I always think it is a great pity that none of the original wooden steam packets survived long enough to be considered for preservation.

Opposite page: *Old Quay Wharf, Runcorn on the Manchester Ship Canal, about 1903–05 with MSC tug* Cornbrook, *United Alkali flat* John *and topsail schooner beyond. The two bridges in the background spanned the Mersey and the canal. The railway bridge's piers were a hazard to flats. The other bridge is the road transporter bridge.* P. Dunbavand

*Flat ready for launching
from Abels' Castlerock yard,
Runcorn, about 1915. The
owners and the work-force
can be distinguished by
their bowlers and caps
respectively.*
J. Abel

The Flat Builders 5

The flat builders were numerous and widely spread throughout north-west England. The inland yards tended to specialize in flats; the coastal ones normally built a wider range of vessels, schooners, brigs, barques and ships. Repairs and maintenance were the bread and butter of many businesses. New building was often intermittent and followed the cyclical patterns of the general shipping business. Eighteenth-century yards could be temporary. A master shipwright could built one or two flats at a suitable site and then move on. In the nineteenth century many building and repair yards were run by flatowners and manufacturers. Wooden flats were built for the whole of the 'flat era' down to the *Ruth Bate* of 1953. Sailing flats – apart from jiggers – were scarcely built after about 1880, but the volume of Mersey and canal traffic needed a good supply of dumb flats and steam packets. There had been tentative experiments with iron hulls in the early nineteenth century. Iron or steel packets and flats were built in increasing numbers after Falk's *Experiment* in 1863. However, some owners such as the Salt Union still preferred wood because of its cheapness, ease of repair and resistance to corrosion by salt cargoes. Flats were not only built on the Mersey and the Weaver but all along the coast from North Wales to the Scottish border. A survey of ship registers of Liverpool, Preston, Lancaster, Whitehaven, Carlisle, Chester and Beaumaris between 1786 and 1823 identified 203 registered flats. They were built as far north as Lancaster and Milnthorpe, ten and three flats respectively, and as far south as Chester, seven flats. Small numbers were built on the Ribble at places such as Ashton, Fishwick, Freckleton, Tarleton and Preston, and on the banks of the Leeds & Liverpool and Bridgewater Canals. Northwich on the Weaver launched the biggest number by far with sixty-nine and Liverpool contributed thirty-four, St Helens on the Sankey Canal fifteen and Frodsham eleven. The Northwich total may be even higher because not all flats working inland were registered.

Moving on to the mid-nineteenth century, *Marwood's Register of Liverpool Shipping* published in 1854 shows that Northwich builders were still dominant: out of 217 flats listed, 115 were built there. Winsford, which had only one in the previous survey, was second with twenty-seven. St Helens was third with fifteen, Liverpool and Sankey Bridges built thirteen each and Frodsham and Runcorn nine each. As before, the 'outer fringes' of the flat area contributed single vessels including one from Conway. Sixty years later, in the 1914 Mercantile

Navy List, Northwich was still top with 190, Winsford second with 109 and the remainder had small numbers only. The main concentration was on the upper Mersey and the Sankey canal: seventeen from Fiddler's Ferry, thirteen from Sankey Bridges, six from St Helens and five from Widnes. Again the outer ports contributed a few: Chester produced five and Rhyl three. Liverpool was the biggest shipbuilding centre in the North West until the rise of Barrow-in-Furness in the second half of the nineteenth century. Its shipbuilders produced a wide range of deep-sea ships and even in the late eighteenth century building flats was a minor activity. In 1786 thirty new ships were added to the Liverpool Ship Register, all products of local yards, with a total tonnage of 3,758 tons. There was only a sloop of fifty-one tons and a dogger of eighty-six tons; the rest were deep sea vessels. Northwich, on the other hand, launched three flats and a galliot and no doubt more flats which were not covered by the Ship Registers. Northwich was the pre-eminent flatbuilding centre and the town's skills were put to good use by sending master shipwrights to other yards and ultimately by building a wide variety of inland waterways craft for export to every continent.

Ship and boatbuilding was carried on at Liverpool from at least the sixteenth century. Town regulations of the time noted the need to keep the shore end of Water Street clear of boatbuilding work. The seventeenth- and early eighteenth-century views show vessels on the stocks on the shore at the end of James Street and later to the south of the new dock. I have already mentioned the *Concorde* built at Wigan in 1742–43. Thomas Holland, who built her for the proprietors of the Douglas navigation set up 'a yard' at Miry Lane, Wigan – the terminus of the Douglas – and built at least eleven flats there. No trace of the Miry Lane 'yard' remains for this, like other small wooden shipyards, did not need major plan or buildings. The building stocks on which the keel was laid would have been heavy baulks laid parallel to the bank of the Douglas. On the narrow waterways flats were launched sideways rather than stern first. There would also be a sawpit for working a big two-man saw for cutting planks and frames, a steam box for bending timbers and a small building to store tools and materials such as oakum, paint and iron spikes. Timber was stored outdoors in stacks and most of the work took place in the open. With a few exceptions – like Rathbone's at Stretford and the Shropshire Union dock at Chester – this remained the practice right down to Abels' Castlerock at Runcorn, the last building yard.

The selection and purchase of good timber was a crucial responsibility of the master builder. Thomas Holland had to spend time travelling to buy suitable timber. For example, he had to ride to Liverpool to buy a mast, boom and bowsprit for the *Concorde*. Timber supplies were critical and even a relatively small vessel like a flat used large quantities. Supplies of 'crooked' oak for curved frames and long straight lengths for keels, keelsons and spars were difficult to obtain. Liverpool was the centre of timber imports, especially from North America, and large baulks of pitch pine could be readily purchased there. Oak was purchased from local estates. Speke Hall just outside Liverpool was a noted supplier in the eighteenth century. Between 1789 and 1822 John Brockbank, who built flats as well as deep-sea ships at Lancaster, travelled extensively to buy timber and other materials. According to his day books, which are deposited in Lancaster Library, he would travel away from his yard about six times a year on average. Some purchases were close to home:

April 1794, John Boothman's Oak Timber at Ribchester, pay'l Mich'as 1794. I bid 16d. to take what I chose del'd here, he asked 17d. I told him Sh'd take more of it at 16d. and left it unsettled till I go, say Sunday next 13th April. He offers the follow'g to be del'd at Mch's. Pay £400 then rest Christmas:

Oak tim'r wet 1/5	£200
60ps. Floors 15 to 18 and 13 upw'd 1/6	£100
50 beams 18 to 25 ft 2/-	£120
20 roods plank	£210
	————
	£630

He is at home every Sunday, I am write to him end of July.

Most of the timber seems to have been delivered by water. In the same year he bought a large quantity of oak, including treenails and knees, at Chepstow and noted the cost of delivering timber from Uxbridge to Liverpool by canal. From Liverpool it would have presumably been delivered to Lancaster by one of the regular packets sailing between the two ports. He also noted the prices of Canadian timber arriving at Liverpool and the departure and arrival of Lancaster ships going to Memel, the great Baltic timber port. On 16th August 1801 he sent a bolster, wheels and steering wheels valued at £11 5s (£11.25) to Rhydland (Rhuddlan) in North Wales on the *Dove*. This was to fetch timber from the woods for shipment to Lancaster. In April 1789 he used the flats *Mary* and *William and Nancy* to load timber at Chester. The cartage cost him between 1s 3d (6p) and 1s 5½d (7p) a ton and the labour 7d (3p) and 10½d (4½p) a ton.

Flatbuilders were principally assemblers of the wooden hull; other materials such as iron spikes would be bought in and specialist subcontractors would supply such items as ironwork, blocks, sails and anchors. Some yards had a blacksmith's and a sailmaking shop but more complicated equipment such as anchors or castings were usually made by outside specialists. Bryan Blundell, who mentioned flats in his journal in 1702, supplied tar and pitch for the *Concorde* and Benjamin Robinson, sailmaker of Liverpool, made the sails. The compass, price 7s 10d (39p), was probably made by one of the town's instrument makers.

Miry Lane contrasted with the flat and boatbuilding yard that the Duke of Bridgewater established for his own fleet at Worsley near Manchester in the seventeen-sixties. He employed about two hundred men, with specialist trades such as blacksmithing all in one works. Today the surviving nineteenth-century covered dry docks and workshops which are still used are an impressive reminder. The nineteenth century Shropshire Union works at Chester were similar. The company operated a large fleet of wooden dumb flats on the Mersey and the Ellesmere Port to Chester section to Nantwich, together with narrow boats for its Welsh and Midland routes. The yard, which still survives at Whipcord Lane, was sited in the basin just above the locks that connect the canal with the River Dee. It has a covered dry dock and two large covered slipways. These could be used either for repairs or for building, and there were a stable block, saw mill, blacksmith's shop and a large wooden shed for joinery work and building small boats. The gable of one of the sheds also contained a drawing office, for later flats were constructed to plans. The Shropshire Union employed over two hundred men there. In 1921 they gave up carrying and the yard was leased to Taylor's who continued repair work as well as building several floats for the Wolverhampton Corrugated Iron Company, salmon boats and pleasure craft. It is still in use, but no flats have been repaired there since the Second World War.

Shipyards constructing flats in iron and steel needed more buildings to protect valuable machines. At Pimblott's near Northwich the building berths were still in the open, as was the fitting-out quay. There was a large corrugated iron shed for plating where the steel plates were shaped and punched for riveting, this had an upper floor laid out as a mould loft for making wooden patterns for marking out the frames. These were bent on a bending block, a large cast-iron grid into which clamps (dogs) could be fitted to make a shape round which the frames could be bent after they had been heated in the adjacent furnace. There were also blacksmith's, machine and joiner's shops, stores and an office. In later years a shed for gas cutting and welding was added. Yarwood's nearby had a foundry for casting iron and brass work including engine cylinder blocks and beds.

The flatbuilders worked in a traditional craft trade. They had to serve an apprenticeship lasting seven years. Sons frequently followed fathers. In Liverpool shipwrights had to become freemen of the town before they could work. As freemen they had the right to vote in parliamentary elections and the various shipwright's associations exercised political influence and power to restrict membership and to negotiate with the shipyard owners about pay. Most were not in such a privileged position and surviving accounts for the eighteenth and early nineteenth century suggest that they were employed casually by the day – or the week. In 1790 John Brockbank of Lancaster paid his foremen, journeymen, shipwrights and boatbuilders 15s (75p) a week;

joiners, painters, 'treenailers, carters, labourers and chippers' 9s (45p) or 9s 6d (47p); and apprentices 5s (25p). Whether the apprentices' pay was in addition to board and lodgings – which were supplied for them – is not clear. The sawyers were the highest paid at £1 a week in the summer and 19s (95p) in the winter; by 1791 this had gone up to £1 1s (£1.05p), a summer rate. In 1798 he advanced the joiners 6d (2p) a day out of their wages and allowed them a half day's travelling time for working at Glasson Dock. It is not clear whether Brockbank paid a daily or a weekly wage in 1790–91. These calculations may have reflected the average 'take-home' pay of his employees at the time because on 24th June 1806 he noted that his journeyman shipwrights had gone on strike to advance wages by 4d (2p) from 3s 4d (17p) to 3s 8d (19p) a day. They returned to work on 3rd July at the old wages. Deakin's at Winsford were paying 4s 2d (21p) a day for shipwrights, 4s (20p) for sawyers and blacksmiths and 1s 6d (8p) for boys in 1861; and Hodson's at Whitebirk on the Leeds & Liverpool paid their men 5s 6d (27p) a day in 1878.

There was no formal teaching or examination except in latter years. Hodson's sent men to Liverpool Nautical College to learn naval architecture. It was chiefly a case of being taught on the job. Experience was all important: a shipwright's 'eye' for whether a timber was true or a hull fair often counted far more than measurements. The

Heating and bending frames for a steel barge at Pimblott's new yard at Hartford, about 1906. The straight iron was heated in the furnace at the back of the shed and bent with the help of heavy hammers round a former on the bending block.

flatbuilders' tools were the standard kind for wooden shipbuilders: adze, side axe, pin maul, drawknives, chisels, augurs, hand saws, planes, caulking mallet and irons. There was an unusually long augur with a large two- to three-inch (51–76 mm) bit which was used to cut the bore of a wooden pump. The ability to work with these hand tools to produce complicated curved components was important and this again came down to plenty of practice. Knowledge of how to care for and sharpen tools was another essential. Apprentices not only learned from the older men but were often given tools by them to start their own kit, for everyone used their own and jealously guarded and cared for them. Surviving tools such as the ones given to the Warrington Museum by the late Mr Domville, who worked for Clare & Ridgeway at Sankey Bridges, were stamped with the owner's name. Some of his tools were stamped with two or three names demonstrating how they had been passed down. Although tools might be made locally, perhaps by the local blacksmith, toolmaking became a specialist business and the majority were made in Sheffield. Some were stamped with the tool merchant's name, such as Ross & Alexander of Liverpool.

Measuring equipment was basic: a folding wooden rule and a bevel for measuring angles were the essentials. Four or five moulds at critical points and ribbands outlined the shape of the hull; and pieces of scrap wood were used for bevel boards, which were used to record the angles of the curved frames at different heights.

Flatbuilding was labour intensive, even after the introduction of machine tools such as the band saw with an adjusting table to cut bevels; and yet an experienced team could complete a flat in about two months. Brockbank's at Lancaster wrote in the contract and specification for the *Fox* on 11th January 1792 that she was to be launched on or before the 15th March 1792. The ironwork, joiner, plumber and painter's work plus fitting out was to be finished at the same time. The price was £537, which worked out at £7 a ton. In March 1803 the price for the flat *Lark* had gone up to £10 5s (£10.25) a ton, making her total price £1,075. The accounts for Deakin's at Winsford show they launched three new flats between 14th December 1861 and the end of January 1862. This seems remarkable because the work-force was only eight to ten men. Specialist work such as blacksmithing was sent out. The new flat *Hannah*, laid down on 15th January, contained:

1300 ft	(396 m)	oak	at 3s	a foot
650 ft	(198 m)	deal	at 6d	a foot
200 ft	(61 m)	oak	at 1s	a foot
260 ft	(79 m)	elm	at 7d	a foot
320 ft	(97.5 m)	pitchpine	at 9d	a foot
90 ft	(27 m)	ash	at 2s	a foot
40 ft	(12 m)	elm	at 2s	a foot
60 ft	(18 m)	poplar	at 1s 9d	a foot

Her account included £387 5s (£387.25) for wood; ironwork and castings cost £61 13s 6d (£61.67) pitch and oak were £10, blocks £32, canvas £18 6s 8d (£18.33), ropes £28 16s 4d (£28.82) and painting £3 17s 6d (£3.87). The total building cost was £653 12s 7d (£653.63) and the price charged to John Hough & Company was £800, giving Deakin's a profit of £146 7s 5d (£146.37). They made even more on the *John*, £216 15s 8d (£216.78), and the *William*, £183 13s 2d (£183.66). I have the suspicion that Deakin's profits may have been higher than average. This was a time of growth in the salt industry. Payments were usually made in three or four stages: the first on laying the keel and the final one after the launch. For comparison, the price of a Leeds & Liverpool boat built by Hodson's was £215 in 1877, and a Shropshire wooden flat, the *Dart*, cost £575 in 1890. Neither of these had any rigging – which was expensive and could amount to a fifth of the total cost. The hull price continued to advance; the *G. R. Jebb*'s hull cost £895 in 1913 and the *Oakdale* about £2,000 in 1950.

Launching was always celebrated to wish the flat good luck. The completion of the *Concorde* in 1742 called for expenditure of £1 10s (£1.50) for rum punch. In the nineteenth century launching ceremonies were quite elaborate and reported in the local newspapers. The launch of the *Edith Mary*, built by Hill & Grundy at Fiddler's Ferry, was fully reported in the *Warrington Guardian* of 11th June 1879. A large number of people gathered to witness the event

The sideways launch of the jigger flat Santa Rosa *at Clare & Ridgeway's yard, Sankey Bridges, 1906. Note the crowds watching: the launch of a new flat was a major local event. This was the last sailing flat built.*
Warrington Museum

83

and the flat was 'gaily decked with flags and bunting' with 60 or 70 people on board, 'chiefly men and boys with a sprinkling of the fair sex'. At one o'clock twenty hands under the instruction of the foreman Mr Roughley:

> commenced driving home the wedges and in a few minutes the boat which was launched sideways and parallel with the canal slipped from her position on the blocks and moved gently down the prepared grooved ways into the water amid the cheers of the spectators. The vessel named *Edith Mary* is calculated to carry about 170 tons and is intended for river traffic in Liverpool such as coaling, loading and unloading steamers. After the launch . . . the men employed in the works and the captains of the numerous flats owned by the proprietors adjourned to the Ferry Inn where they were joined by Messrs. Hill & Grundy and about half a dozen friends from Liverpool and to the number of about 50, they sat down to a substantial dinner consisting of 'Old English fare' such as rounds of beef, legs of mutton, etc. and the usual plum puddings, the cloth having been removed, the usual loyal and patriotic toasts were heartily given.

Many shipwrights seemed to have remained loyal to their employers, gaining a wealth of experience and taking immense pride in their work. However, work hours were long and usually included Saturdays. The *Warrington Guardian* for 4th March 1854 noted:

> We believe that Mr. John Clare has kindly permitted the carpenters, blacksmith and sawyers in his employ to leave work an hour earlier on Saturday afternoon. We are happy to see that the custom of finishing work earlier on a Saturday is gaining ground in this part of the country and we hope this example will be followed by other firms.

Facilities were basic. The urinal at the Chester yard was no more than three sheets of corrugated iron on the edge of the canal basin. At Pimblott's shipwrights created an ingenious shelter with a stove from offcuts of steel plate, with scarcely a straight piece in it. It deserved to be preserved as a work of art. At the ship canal workshops at Old Quay, Runcorn (the old Mersey & Irwell yard), there was a small corrugated shed finished with no more than a wash basin, a couple of benches and a coal stove. Work was either out in the open or in unheated sheds. With large baulks of timber and metal being moved about and lifted, furnaces and moving machinery, there were always dangers.

Scaffolding was wooden stagings which could give way and yards were often cramped for space which made working difficult. The *Warrington Guardian* reported one such accident at Clare & Ridgeway's shipyard in the edition for 26th June 1867:

> A youth named Thomas Roughley 19 years of age was carrying a cauldron of pitch along a staging in the dry dock when his foot slipped and he fell a depth of seven feet breaking one of his ankles and scalding himself in the face. He was taken home to Bank Quay where he was attended by Mr. Starkie Smith. The poor young fellow had a narrow escape with his life.'

Day-to-day maintenance, including regularly tarring the hull, was carried out by flat crews. Repairs could be carried out on any convenient beach. In the accounts of the *Success* there is an entry of 1s 2d (6p) 'for expenses of docking at Freckleton Marsh' on 28th January 1761. Perhaps there was a 'grid iron' of heavy timbers on which to dock the *Success*. At Lathom, near Burscough, an eighteenth-century dry dock survives in working condition. It is no more than a stone-lined pit capable of taking two boats on stone blocks, with stop planks for a gate. The water can be run off via a large drain to a stream below the level of the main canal. This arrangement was common to many inland dry docks such as those at Winwick, Sankey Bridges and Chester as well as the original 'graving docks' at Liverpool. 'Graving' referred to the process of scraping off all the accumulated marine growth from the underwater part of the hull.

The 'patent slipway' or marine railway was invented in the first part of the nineteenth century. This consisted of a set of rails sloping into the water. On them heavy carriages could be lowered down and the flat floated over them. The carriages were then winched up the slope supporting the flat. These were often worked by hand, but the slow, burdensome process was mechanized at some yards. The Liverpool Lighterage yard at Northwich had a Foden steam engine to take

Steel dumb flat Monkey Brand, *photographed immediately after completion at Pimblott's old yard in the centre of Northwich in 1900. A second flat is nearing completion on the stocks. Note the steam winch, which was powered by a boiler in the fo'c'sle and the wheel instead of a tiller. She was owned by Lever Brothers, the soap manufacturers of Port Sunlight, Bromborough.* Trustees of NMGM

85

the strain and this and one of its carriages is preserved at the National Waterways Museum, Gloucester. Yarwood's and the Weaver Navigation had similar slipways at Northwich. Stubb's and Abels' at Runcorn, Cooper's at Widnes and Burton's at Bromborough were other examples.

I have the impression that repairs did not pay as well as new building. The amounts involved were much smaller, except where flats were completely rebuilt. There was no such thing as an average bill. The highest in Hodson's books from Blackburn on the Leeds & Liverpool between 1876 and 1877 was £68 16s 6d (£68.82), the lowest 4s 8d (23p). It is worth quoting from the largest bill to give an impression of the nature of repair work. John Hodson was repairing boat *No. 6* belonging to the Dunkenhalgh Colliery Company in April 1879:

$9\frac{1}{2}$ feet oak timber for stem and transom at 3d	£ 1	8s	6d
18 feet of $3\frac{1}{2}$ inch oak plank at 1s 2d	£ 1	1s	0d
184 feet of 2 inch oak plank at 9d	£ 6	18s	0d
77 feet of $2\frac{1}{2}$ inch elm plank at 9d	£ 2	17s	0d
485 feet of 2 inch pitch pine plank at 6d	£12	2s	6d
47 feet of $1\frac{1}{4}$ inch pitch pine board at $4\frac{1}{2}$d		17s	$7\frac{1}{2}$d
22 feet of $\frac{1}{2}$ inch pitch pine board at 2d		3s	8d
Two knees at 3/6, 3 timbers at 5/6	£ 1	3s	6d
24 timbers at 3/6 one mast 4/6 one tiller	£ 4	8s	6d
Sawing stem, transom and timbers		10s	3d
Repairing rudder pin, stem and bend plates		3s	6d
Two new bend plates	£ 1	1s	7d
Three new ring bolts and two new pump boxes and spears		5s	0d
9lb screwbolts at 4d 181lb of bolts and spikes	£ 2	15s	$9\frac{1}{2}$d
25lb plate nails and 5lb of small nails		12s	11d
65lb of oakum, paint, pitch, tar, varnish	£ 2	11s	8d
$17\frac{1}{2}$ feet of pine for keelson, use of ships, tallow, wedges etc	£ 3	9s	6d
Wages 7 men, total $118\frac{1}{2}$ days work, 4 at 5s 2d, 1 at 4s and 1 at 3s per day	£23	5s	6d

Flatbuilding, like any business connected with shipping, was subject to slumps; private yard owners could produce a few boats and then vanish into bankruptcy. Richard Bushell, for example, finished his apprenticeship and became a freeman shipwright of Liverpool in 1779. In 1784 he set up on his own building boats and shallops at New Quay. In March 1790 he launched a new boat for service between Wigan and Liverpool. In 1791 he had a new flat of sixty-two tons for sale along with various small boats. By 1794 his business had failed. Perhaps he had built the flat on speculation and could not find a buyer. Clare & Ridgeway, on the other hand, lasted for over a century. Their yard was established about 1807 on the inland side of the Sankey

Bridge carrying the Liverpool–Warrington road. The Clares had an interest in the St Helens coal trade. Investment in a shipyard was a logical step because transport by water was the key to the coal business. From 1807 to 1846 they repaired their own flats and built twenty new ones on their own account. There were some years when no flat was launched. Four were built between 1807 (the *Hannah*) and 1812 (the *Royal Oak*). The *John Clare*, the next one, was not launched until 1822 and after that they built one at about two year intervals. After 1846 they built for outside owners as well as themselves. Production was not continuous; only two – the *Adelaide* and the *Jane* – were built between 1847 and 1859. Another eighteen were completed by the end of the building in 1913. Customers were all local: the *Jane*, 1857, was for Fairclough's, the millers at Bank Quay, Warrington; the *Ellen*, 1868, for Joseph Cooper of Widnes. The last, the *G. R. Jebb*, 1913, was a flat hulled lightship for the Upper Mersey Navigation Commission. She was named after the general manager of the Shropshire Union and the chairman of the Upper Mersey Navigation Commission.

Clare & Ridgeway added a ropemaking business to the enterprise and their depot for building materials was on the opposite bank to the yard. Stone, slates and bricks were all brought in by water in their own vessels. This diversification of business can also be seen in John Brockbank's accounts. He owned property in Lancaster, undertook fencing and other agricultural work and from his notes he farmed some land as well. There was a celebration supper for the *Ellen*'s launch at Clare & Ridgeway on 14th November 1868; the eight shipwrights present were Messrs Abel, Pinnington, Richardson, Domville, Hatton, Prior, Palins and Warburton. There are hand tools belonging to the Domvilles and the Pinningtons in the Warrington Museum, no doubt handed down from father to son. Mr Ridgeway, who had become a partner in what had become Clare & Ridgeway, paid tribute to their work and loyalty. 'He then thanked all employed by the firm for the way they had worked for its benefit and it was always a pleasure for a master when he could look back on the past and find all had worked amicably together.' That the relationship between master and employees was close is supported by another event, on 17th June 1871. John Clare Ridgeway, who had just married a Miss Clare, laid on 'a sumptuous supper' at the Sloop Inn with Mr Bosworth's quadrille band in attendance for dancing. Clare & Ridgeway continued work on repairs after 1913, but by the nineteen-twenties the traffic on the Sankey was so small that the firm closed. The last flat to be dry docked was the jigger *Protection* about 1929.

Relations between men and master were not always quite so harmonious. The eighteen-forties saw much industrial action in the Liverpool yards and John Brockbank had no hesitation in dismissing the shipwrights whom he considered were the ringleaders of the strike in 1803. 'June 24th 1806 Philip Pym and Jos Bee having raised a disturbance some time ago about not being employd on a wet day, and being considered as ringleaders – discharged. Ed. Cooper came back on Wednesday but being also considered as a ringleader having offered money to a man to stand out, was told I had no occasion for him.'

There were other yards on or around the Sankey; various builders launched at least fifty-six flats, galliots, schooners or sloops between 1765 and 1854; and at Fiddler's Ferry Wilkinson's built sixteen flats for Rea's coal-bunkering business at Liverpool between 1859 and 1885. A second yard, Hill & Grundy, added another three between 1877 and 1880. Flats, 'Barrow flat' schooners and packets were built at Widnes. The 'Barrow flat' schooner *Maude* of 1869 was the most notable Widnes built vessel. She lasted in the coastal trade until about 1947 and much of her stout hull still remains on the beach at Appledore. Gandy, the last Widnes builder, continued repair work until Cooper's – who had a large sand and lighterage business – bought his repair yard at Spike Island and improved the slipways and facilities to maintain their wood and steel flats.

Runcorn was the main building centre on the south bank of the Mersey. The Mersey & Irwell and the Bridgewater had repair yards

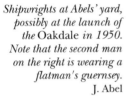

Shipwrights at Abels' yard, possibly at the launch of the Oakdale *in 1950. Note that the second man on the right is wearing a flatman's guernsey.*
J. Abel

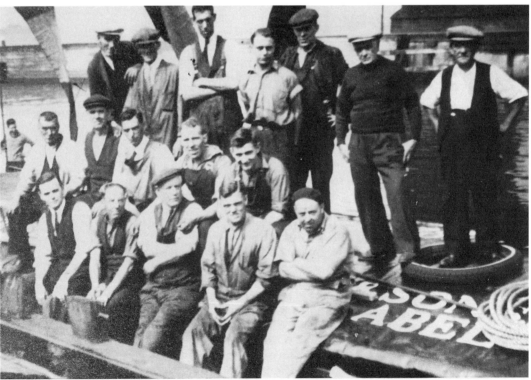

where their flats passed from the inland waterways into the estuary and there were shipyards on the Mersey shore inland of the Runcorn Gap. The earliest recorded launch was in 1778 and at least two-hundred were completed, finishing with the flats by Abels' between 1950 and 1953. From 1778 to 1887 seventy two flats, sloops, galliots and jiggers and fifty-four schooners were built. The last named were employed chiefly in the coastal trade, especially the china clay trade from Cornwall to Runcorn. The *Snowflake*, built in 1880 by Brundrit's, the main builders, was employed in the Newfoundland fish trade across the Atlantic, which is a testimony to the sea-going qualities of a 'Barrow flat'. Abels' took over Speakman's Castlerock shipyard at the foot of the Runcorn railway bridge as a repair base for their own fleet. It was closed down when they were taken over in the nineteen-sixties. Further along what is now the south bank of the Manchester Ship Canal, the Old Quay yard still maintains the ship canal's vessels, although the original Mersey & Irwell buildings were demolished in 1976–77. The Sprinch yard on the inland level of the Bridgewater had bought the Mersey & Irwell in 1844 and both company's flats were looked after at the Old Quay yard. This was inconvenient with the building of the ship canal and in 1890 a new yard – the Sprinch – was built by the large basin at the top of the locks leading down to the Mersey. Facilities proved to be some of the finest in the country, with four dry docks, a boiler shop, fitting shop, wheelwright's shop, saw mill, shipwright's shop and blacksmith's smithy in addition to spacious offices and stores. This yard was to service about 250 craft and employed about fifty staff. Only three 'Duker' flats were built there: the *Coronation, Empire* and *Carrier*, all between 1911 and 1913.

Frodsham was also an important if smaller centre. Fifty-nine vessels were completed there between 1728 and 1862, out of which thirty-five were flats and five sloops plus one galliot and one dogger. The Weston Canal diverted traffic away from Frodsham but it retained its yard, which seems to have enjoyed a late boom with three flats and a hundred-ton schooner launched in 1858.

There were many yards inland. Thornton's and Mugg's at Manchester and Rathbone's at Stretford docked the Bridgewater and Rochdale flats. The Leeds & Liverpool Canal Company's official hand-book for 1935 had advertisements for nine builders and repairers along its length, from William Rider at the Canal Basin, Leeds, to Robert Lund of Lydiate, near Liverpool. Most of them combined the canal business with other work, particularly sawing and selling timber. John Tyrer at Lathom had a blacksmith's and wheelwright's business and Mayor's at Tarleton repaired and stored yachts. Mayor's also operated the company's Wigan yard between 1932 and 1959 and launched the wooden boat the *Darlington* from there in 1951. There were many more docks in the nineteenth century. One firm that did not advertise – J. W. Parke – had a depot and maintenance yard at

A general view of Abels' yard, Runcorn, about 1960. Note the flat on the patent slip and the clutter of buildings.
J. Parkinson

Syren Street, Bootle: it was that firm that built the last four wooden Leeds & Liverpool boats in 1954–55 – the *Bruno, Leo, Mario* and *Murillo*.

Winsford came to prominence in the mid-nineteenth century and was notable for introducing the steam packets. It became the major centre for packet construction, with about six salt producers building and maintaining their own ships. Falk and his pioneer *Experiment* have already been mentioned and Deakin's were well known carriers in the salt trade; they became salt producers in 1846. They had their own yard and turned out wooden packets. In 1888 the yard became the centre for all the work for the newly formed Salt Union. Repair work continued until 1952. In 1897 they built the

Monarch, the largest packet ever built on the Weaver, 121 feet (36.9 m) long. She proved to be too big to be a successful packet and was sold as a coaster. She was the last packet to be built at Winsford.

Building at Northwich lasted much longer than at Winsford but with many changes in yard owners. William Okell's was an early one, between the two swing bridges in the town centre. Upstream of the Hayhurst bridge there were two repair yards, Cleghorn & Wilkinson, who had their own flats, and W. E. Bates. Both built marine engines as well. Nearby, Pimblott's occupied a small inlet next to Hayhurst bridge between 1847 and 1906. Surviving photographs show the yard was short of space and not surprisingly they decided to move a green-field site at Hartford up river from the town near Hunt's locks. Although they built mainly steel craft for export, they also completed the splendid wooden jigger *Pilot* for T. J. May of Liverpool in 1894. Between 1934 and 1936 they built nine steel motor boats, all named after rivers, for the Canal Transport Company for work on the Leeds & Liverpool Canal. After the Second World War they completed four diesel barges, three canal tugs and three steel dumb flats for the Bridgewater Department of the Manchester Ship Canal plus the motor barge *Iris Abbott* for the family owners, F. J. Abbott & Sons, in 1947. The yard closed in 1971 and some of the yard's machines, including a frame bender and a compressed air hammer were acquired by Merseyside Maritime Museum. Liverpool Lighterage took Pimblott's old yard in the centre of Northwich over and stayed until closure in 1972. They repaired their own flats and latterly ex-Weaver steam packets. The premises remained virtually unaltered until the end with a large frame bending block, plate rolls (now preserved by Merseyside Maritime Museum), cross-cut saws, blacksmith's and sail-maker's shops. To the west of the town centre, Gibson's had a yard at Witton dock in the nineteenth century.

The biggest yard at Northwich was Yarwood's. This was crammed in beside the Cheshire Lines railway viaduct. It started as John Thompson's, later becoming Woodcock's, and in 1896 W. J. Yarwood – who had a boiler works in the town – took it over. After 1896 the yard built up a big business, not only in flats but also in tugs, river steamers, dredgers, coasters, lighters, buoy tenders and survey launches for home and overseas customers. Their early work was chiefly for local Weaver carriers, notably Brunner Mond and Company, but expansion came with the First World War and Admiralty orders. Between the wars they mingled large orders for canal craft, including many narrow boats for the Grand Union Canal Carrying Company, with barges and steamers for West Africa. Although they survived the Depression and continued building into the nineteen-fifties, closure came in 1966 with the rationalization of the parent company's business. Not a trace of the yard remains. However, examination of the shipyard lists and photographs held in Cheshire Record Office show what a remarkable business it was. They took over an unfinished packet from Wood-cock's, the *Hibernia* – built of wrought iron – and delivered her to Brunner Mond. Almost all their packets had engines and boilers built on the premises. The last set was supplied for the Clyde puffer *Storm-light*, in 1957. Their last packets were for ICI, successors to Brunner Mond, in 1946-48. Earlier they had built one of the biggest of the dumb flats, the *Gowanburn* of 1902, which could carry 260 tons of salt for H. I. Thompson of Marston. The composite packet *Scotia* followed in 1903 for Griffith's, the Chester corn millers, and the *Petrel* for W. J. Dutton, suppliers of animal feed of Nantwich. Brunner Mond took delivery of several wooden flats for dumping lime refuse from their works, all prefixed, 'Wood' – *Wood Lark*, *Woodwren* and so on and the Rochdale Canal Company ordered a series of steel-framed wooden planked flats. By 1914 eighteen had been delivered. Six steel Leeds & Liverpool long boats were completed for J. Parke between 1910 and 1914. There were also steel flats for the Wolverhampton Corrugated Iron Company of Ellesmere Port, including nine dumb flats in 1920–21, a steam flat in 1924 and two motor ones in 1925–27. The following decade saw the completion of twenty steel boats for work on the Leeds & Liverpool: twelve for the Canal Transport Company, seven for B. I. Transport – a subsidiary of Rank's, the millers – and seven for Ainscough's of Burscough. Between 1948 and 1957 they built two motor and sixteen dumb barges for the Bridgewater Department.

One of Leeds Co-op's coal boats in Rider's dry dock, Leeds about 1960. Her coamings were a Yorkshire feature that was not found on the Leeds & Liverpool boats carrying coal in Lancashire. Note also the wooden cabin chimney, another Yorkshire feature.
J. Parkinson

There is no greater testimony to the craftsmanship of the flat-builders than the longevity of the products. Wooden flats that lasted fifty years were not uncommon and several achieved a century or more. The *Daresbury* of about 1772, though rebuilt was still afloat in 1958. The *Chester* of 1827 lasted until about 1930 carrying stone for the Dock Board. The *Jane* had a most interesting career. She was built by John Crippin at Runcorn in 1800. She was probably used on the Weaver and the Mersey as far as Liverpool because she was not registered until 1842. In 1847 she was sold to B. J. Nowell and others, contractors, of Menai Bridge and in 1859 she was bought by a Captain Smart of Bridgwater, Somerset. She spent the next sixty-five years in the Severn coal trade. Her rig was changed to a ketch and in 1925 she became a mastless coal hulk for a Bristol brewery. Finally, in 1938, she was no longer fit even for this lowly job and she was towed round to Lydney and sunk to protect the harbour bank from the fierce Severn tides. The same quality of workmanship was to be found in later metal hulled vessels. The *Decempedes* of 1879 was not broken up until 1969, having been a steam packet, sailing flat and motor vessel.

Flat Trades – Coal and Salt 6

There are many good books in print which chronicle the history of commerce in north western England and I propose to do no more than sketch in the essentials of the economic background and a few key figures for the volume of flat trades. Freight rates will be covered in chapter eight. The main aim will be to examine what flats carried and from where, and how the cargoes were handled. Almost any commodity that came into the port of Liverpool either as an import or an export would have been carried in a flat. The high point of sailing flat traffic was in the eighteen-fifties. This was before the spread of tugs and the introduction of steam packets, when the flat could still hold its own against the railways. Braithwaite Poole, the goods manager of the London & North Western Railway, wrote *The Commerce in Liverpool* (published in 1854) in 1852 to record the volume of trade and highlight the shortcomings of the port. He was critical of the coal and grain-handling facilities and the lack of rail access to the docks, and this meant he included a great many useful facts about the work of the flats.

Flat traffic can be split into three types: short distance lighterage between the docks, cross river or to anchored vessels, up river and canal for a twenty- to fifty-mile radius; and coastal traffic. The last was the least important for flats; the bulk of it was short haul to the Dee and North Wales. The 'Barrow flat' schooners, which were mainly owned on the Dee, in Runcorn and in the north Lancashire ports were engaged in comparatively long hauls. They were common traders to the West Country ports such as Fowey and Par with coal, bringing back china clay; and the Irish east coast was a regular destination. It is impossible to put a figure on total flat traffic at any particular date, but to provide some idea of the scale of operations I have inserted figures for key traffic at certain dates. These need to be considered in the context of the trends in Liverpool's trade, with rapid expansion up to about 1850–60, continuing expansion at a slower rate up to 1914 and decline thereafter. The recent revival of the port need not concern us because all the flats and their successors have been eliminated.

Lancashire had large coal deposits and the seams in the St Helens and Wigan areas were both rich. A cheap and plentiful supply of coal to produce heat for industrial processing to raise steam to power machines and for export was one of the key factors in the Industrial

Opposite page: *Jigger flat* John and William *discharging on the beach at Sunderland Point near Lancaster, about 1900. Scenes like this were common all along the coast where no harbour facilities existed.*
Lancaster City Museum

Revolution which transformed Britain from a nation of agriculturalists to the leading industrial power in the world. Coal was of no use unless it could be delivered inexpensively and in bulk to where it was needed and in the eighteenth century that meant water transport.

The major aim of the promoters of the Weaver, Douglas, Mersey & Irwell and Sankey Navigations was to provide water access to collieries. The Duke of Bridgewater's first objective was to build a waterway to supply Manchester from his mines at Worsley and the Leeds & Liverpool meandered its way through the major cotton towns and coal fields of Lancashire. As the preamble of the enabling Act for opening up the Douglas put it, it would be 'convenient for the Carriage of Coals, Cannel [a type of very hard coal which burnt with a bright candle-like flame], Stone, Slate and other Goods and Merchandize'. Notice how coal is the first item mentioned; that proved to be appropriate.

The surviving accounts for the Douglas flats for 1752–55 and 1764–68 show coal to be their major cargo. The *Expedition* in 1752 worked only on the Douglas as far as Tarleton, where her twenty-ton cargo was probably transshippped into coastal vessels. Her owners also had three other flats. They delivered coal to Ribble creeks, and cinders (coke) cannel to Poulton on the Wyre and to the Furness peninsula. On at least one occasion, in 1754, coal was delivered to Dublin. The round trip took about three weeks to Poulton and six to Furness. Return cargoes included timber, hides, kelp, soap ashes, barley, beans and limestone. On the river the *Expedition* took about a week for the round trip to Wigan with either men hauling – who were paid sixpence to a shilling (2p–5p) a day – or a square sail – made by Luke Bradley out of 203 yards (210 m) of canvas at threepence (1p) a yard – in fast winds. These four flats paid dues which work out to reveal a total delivery of coal of about 1,800 tons a year. The 1764–68 accounts are for the *Success*, which worked mainly from Wigan to Freckleton, Savick Pool and Preston. There was a warehouse at the head of the creeks at Freckleton where the *Success* discharged coal for a Mr Cowburn and loaded limestone for Tarleton. The operations on the Douglas were small scale and did not have much effect on a growing coal shortage at Liverpool. After 1700 domestic consumption had grown with its expanding prosperity; sugar boilers processing raw cane sugar from the West Indies needed coal, as did other industries such as glassmaking as well as potteries and the new salt works established by Thomas Blackburne. Coal came from the Prescot collieries by road; supplies were expensive and insufficient. Liverpool Corporation and Liverpool merchants were the promoters of the Sankey; their main purpose was, 'the better supplying this town with coals which of late years are become scarce and dear and the measure greatly lessened, to the great imposition and oppression of the traders, manufacturers and inhabitants of this corporation'.

In November 1757 the Sankey was advertised as being open 'for the passage of flats to Haydock and Parr collieries'. Apparently three mines had already opened. Early in 1758 Mrs Sarah Clayton announced that she would load her coal at 4s 10d (24p) a ton and that she had built a wagon road and other conveniences to load a flat in a few hours. The Parr collieries overlooked the Sankey valley and a tramway ran to Broad Oak Basin cut out of the side of the canal. This was excavated in 1977 as part of a campaign to improve the derelict canal. The quays were red sandstone blocks and midway along its main length were found the sandstone foundations of a coal chute projecting out into the basin – clearly one of Mrs Clayton's 'other conveniences'. Coal tips became a feature of all flat waterways and the wide hatches of the flat fitted in with the tipping of coal in bulk from railway wagons. The one at Wigan, nicknamed 'the pier', first became famous as a music-hall joke and is now the foundation of a new tourist industry for the town. I have referred to 'open flatts' when discussing the whys and wherefores of lowering masts and no doubt the many flats that carried nothing but coal did not need hatch covers. The Leeds & Liverpool long boats bringing coal from Wigan down to Liverpool in the nineteen-fifties and coal 'lighters' on the Bridgewater did not have hatch covers or tarpaulin, and this was probably true of many of the eighteenth-century flats on the Sankey.

The Sankey and the Douglas both had one major drawback, and that was lack of water. It is noticeable in the accounts of the *Success* that much of her carrying was seasonal and that there was a lull in the summer months. The same applied to the Sankey – or rather not to the Sankey Canal proper, but from the point where it entered the Mersey at Sankey Bridges. The upper Mersey suffered from silting, frequent changes of channel and a high tidal range. Neap tides could leave flats stranded for days. It was a highly sensitive issue because of the disruption to the coal supplies. The 1827 court case brought by Liverpool Corporation against the proprietors of the Mersey & Irwell about the waters of the upper Mersey which I mentioned in connection with flat haulers produced all sorts of evidence for and against a change in the river.

John Hill of the flat *Mary*, who had worked the river for twenty years, told the court that the flat did not have the same room to sail. They had to use poles instead of sailing and poling was increasingly difficult because the bottom had become 'slutchy'. Thomas Brock, forty-eight years old and flat skipper of the *Young Tom* from Northwich, had sailed with his father as a boy and been neaped (stranded by the tide) for seven or eight days. He had never heard anybody claim the river had deteriorated in his time. Some flatmen had difficulty tacking because of lack of water, or perhaps lack of skill: 'I have known in my time Sir, some old flatmen had had to shift against the wind and not had room to turn down and I have not done that during my lifetime . . .'. Other flatmen pointed out that the flats had become bigger and deeper, especially in recent years, that there were more of them and that the recent dry summers were a prime cause of delay. John Leigh, river pilot, balloonist and ex-Mersey & Irwell flatman, said 'it reeks up in summer according to the dryness of the season. Flats can tack as well as they could forty years ago.' The extension of the canal down river to Widnes in 1833 helped to solve the problem. The same year also witnessed the opening of a dock at Widnes that was connected to the St Helens collieries by the St Helens & Runcorn Gap Railway. After a poor start coal traffic on the railway increased but did not supplant the amount carried by water and much of it was loaded into flats for delivery down the estuary. In 1771 ninety thousand tons had been carried down the Sankey; in 1836 this had increased to 170,000 tons by canal and 130,000 by rail.

Although the Sankey met some of the ever rising demand for coal, it did not satisfy it, nor did the Bridgewater – for most of its coal deliveries went to Manchester and the Liverpool line tended to specialize in general cargo.

The Leeds & Liverpool canal between Wigan and Liverpool was finished in 1780. It superseded the Douglas and gave Liverpool much improved access to coal supplies. By 1800 over two hundred thousand tons were delivered and about fifty thousand of that was then trans-shipped and exported to Ireland. The drawback of the Liverpool terminus was that it did not have a direct connection with the docks. The coalyards were very extensive with many basins close to the centre of the town. Not a trace remains except for a small Georgian house next to St Paul's Eye Hospital on Old Hall Street, which was the coal office of the Wigan Coal & Iron Company. After the Leigh branch connected the Bridgewater and the Leeds & Liverpool in 1820, flats would go to the Wigan pits via the Bridgewater to collect cargoes for ships lying in the docks. Although this was a longer route, it helped reduce the problem of the coal breaking up as it was shovelled from a flat to a cart and then on to a ship. It gave the Leeds & Liverpool a chance to compete with the Sankey and the Bridgewater, which had their own coal depots at the docks. The Sankey coalowners in fact offered discounts to encourage coals for shipping: 7s 2d (36p) per ton for householders and 6s 6d (32p) for ships in 1770.

By 1832 internal demand from the town of Liverpool amounted to four hundred thousand tons; this reflected the growing industrial demand as well as a population boom. Factories using steam power were built close to the docks or along the canal. These included the North Shore cotton spinning mills and various sugar refineries of which Tate & Lyle became the most important. The latter needed a continual supply because sugar boiling was a non-stop process. The Athol Street gasworks and those at Linacre Road, Bootle, were also major customers right up to 1964, when coal traffic to Liverpool ceased. At its height, according to Clarke's *The Leeds & Liverpool Canal, a History and Guide* (1990), 181 coal boats arrived every week at Liverpool including eighty-three from Crooke colliery, fifty-seven from Wigan and thirty-five from Douglas Bank. Coal handling became increasingly mechanized to handle such bulk and most shoreside works had grab cranes, including a huge overhead gantry spanning the canal at Barton power station and a suction system for small coal at Athol Street. The earlier method of unloading was the No 10 shovel.

In his reminiscences Robert Alty recalled that when his father discharged coal for the distillery in Vauxhall Road, he would hire two or three of the casual labourers who hung round hoping for work to help discharge the boat. At its fastest a horse boat could do as many as three or four trips a week. Bulk cargoes included ashes and cinders and manure from the many stables. Farms near the canal bought large quantities of both. Robert Alty recalled in the *Maghull Advertiser* of 1st September 1977:

> At Plex Lane, Halsall, I have known as many as six boats unloading at the same time. One captain would shout to the other 'What odds', which meant who would be unloaded first. One character who used to help unload from time to time was a man known as 'Old Slabs' from Weaver House, Bridge, Halsall. He was about six feet three inches and always called his fork his 'Overtaker' – a No. 10. He could make the man wheeling off [in a barrow] very hard.

By 1852 the total of coal arriving at Liverpool was over a million and a half tons; the majority came by flat, 730,000 tons being carried thirty-six miles from Wigan and 350,000 tons thirty-two miles from St Helens via the Sankey. Railways carried only 370,000 tons, but the relative costs were a significant pointer to the future. Flat coal cost between 2s 2d and 2s 6d (11–12p) a ton to deliver and the railways between 1s 6d and 2s 6d (7–12p). The London & North Western Railway, who were about to open a new coal dock at Garston, south of Liverpool, hauled 190,000 tons at the lower rate. Garston's coal traffic grew rapidly: its efficient coal tips and storage sidings for coal trains constrasted with the shambles at Liverpool docks. Braithwaite Poole, the LNWR traffic manager, said, 'the system of hoisting coals out of a flat and over the side of a vessel is destructive and bad and the correct principle is dropping the coal gently yet expeditiously out of the wagons which are sent from the pits, by leverage, direct into the vessel'. What was more, the cost of labour was higher and the pace of delivery slower. It took two to four men to shovel and whip four or five tons of coal into a ship depending on the difference in height between vessel and flat. A coal tip could handle 150 tons an hour with three men. High-level coal drops were built at Bramley-Moore and Wellington Docks about three years after Poole published his criticism. These and the coal tips for railway wagons at Garston, Widnes and Runcorn reduced the amount of inland coal traffic for flats.

However, sailing flats found employment at the dockside coal tips as bunkering barges. The number of steamships steadily increased. By 1832 they took a hundred thousand tons and the figure rose steadily, especially after 1870 when steamers began to take on an increasing share of the long-distance deep-sea traffic. Much of the coal was delivered in flats either from Garston or the High Level coal railway at Bramley-Moore Dock. A great deal was transshipped to ships lying in the river. A large liner might take a thousand tons, which took quite a lot of flats and coal heavers. The coal bunkering business appears to have kept many flats under sail up to about the outbreak of the First World War. Edward Smith and Company, owners of the *Elizabeth*, and

Coaling flat Elizabeth *being loaded from coal wagons on the High Level Coal Railway, Wellington Dock, 1894. Note how the hatches are stacked on deck and the beam across the main hatch.*
Trustees of NMGM

Rea and Company were noted for their fleets of bunkering flats in the late nineteenth century and the trade was continued by the Wadsworth Lighterage & Coaling Company into the nineteen-thirties. In 1934 they had six 'derrick barges' and seven dumb ones including four ex-Weaver packets: the *Excelsior, Social, America* and *Hettie*. With the exception of the *Hettie*, they were all fitted with tall derricks for hoisting tubs of coal aboard the deep sea steamers. The main reason for the success of the Wadsworth business was that it enabled vessels to receive the coal supplies while discharging or loading at general cargo quays. On finishing cargo operations the steamer was ready for sea without having to waste time and money in shifting to the coal tips at Canada, Bramley-Moore, Herculaneum, Birkenhead or Garston Docks.

The actual bunkering operation was undertaken by casually employed coal heavers. They worked by the half day and were hired at one of two 'stands': at the 'Gardens', a group of five trees at the junction of James Street and the Goree Piazzas, and at the Dock Road near the Canada Dock. There were six diggers in a gang to shovel coal into tipping tubs. A filled tub was then hauled up by the derrick and steam winch and swung over the bunker hatch and tipped by two more heavers. Three tubs were used: one filled ready to swing, one being filled and the third on its way to and from the vessel. Each tub held sixteen hundredweight of coal. An older and alternative method was with hand baskets. This was used by small steamers such as the Isle of Man boats tied up at the Landing Stage.

Eleven men were needed for baskets. A steel bracket would be hooked over the coamings of the flat and a plank would be fixed to it. Four men filled each iron shod basket which could hold about half a hundredweight, and handed it up to the man standing on the plank. He would then hand it on to a man standing on the deck of the barge who would then pass it through a coaling door in the side of the ship. The third heaver would shoot the basket along a steel plate which had been laid on the ship's wooden deck, and it would be caught by a fourth who emptied into the bunker. The empty basket was returned down the line while other members of the gang trimmed the coal in the ship's bunkers. A tubbing gang could shift at least a hundred tons in a half-day and the basket men sixty tons. The largest vessel bunkered from flats was the White Star liner *Laurentic* in 1937, which took three thousand tons. Wadsworth's were clearly employing the methods of coal handling used on the sailing flats.

Flats moved coal coastwise, delivering it to small havens, creeks and every open beach along the North Wales coast, as far south as Aberdovey. North of the Mersey many small creeks received coal by flat, especially from the Ribble. At the newly built Lytham Dock at the mouth of the Ribble, two of 'Worthington's flats' discharged sixty two tons of coal on 25th June 1916.

In the eighteen-fifties the *Sarah* and the *French* were regular traders to the Dovey estuary, bringing in coal and carrying away lead ore from the local mines. On 25th August 1857 the *Sarah* loaded a bulk cargo of twenty-one tons of lead ore – dues 3s 6d (17p). In *Brief Glory* (1948) D. W. Morgan recalled not only the coal-lead trade but the flats' special qualities:

> The Mersey flat, I have heard say, sailed like a witch, on any point of the wind – beating, running, going free – and when aground stood as upright as a church steeple. This speediness combined with shallow draught, were excellent qualities in any craft requiring to negotiate a maze of sandbanks on her passage to inland waters and up-river ports such as Derwenlas. Both ships [the *Sarah* and the *French*] were owned by Merseyside merchants who found it profitable to dispatch a fleet of these handy craft with coal or general stores southward bound, returning home with slate, pitprops, timber or lead ore. . . . Mostly they went to no further south than the Menai ports.

The port of Amlwch on the north coast of Anglesey was important for the coal trade at the end of the eighteenth century. The discovery of a huge lode of copper ore at the Parys and Mona mines in the seventeen-seventies brought an upsurge in coal traffic. Copper ore was partially smelted there using coal from St Helens and then shipped to the two copper refineries on the banks of the Sankey Canal. Demand for copper was increasing because of its use for bolts, spikes and copper sheathing for ships, especially those of the Royal Navy. The trade was dominated by Thomas Williams, an Anglesey solicitor who owned not only the Sankey refineries but ones for copper and brass-making at Holywell and Flint on the Dee and others elsewhere beyond the north west. A variety of ships were employed including square riggers like the brig *Eagle* of 1786 which was no bigger than a flat – in fact, beamier and deeper: 54 ft (16.5 m) length, 18 ft 6 in. (5.6 m) beam and 10 ft (3 m) depth of hold, registered tonnage 76. Welsh-built sloops (as against sloop-rigged flats) were also regulars. The *Portland*, built at Pwthelli in 1778, 54 ft (16.5 m) by 19 ft (5.8 m) by 10 ft (3 m) and 83 tons was typical. Then there were flats owned by John Jackson, a Liverpool merchant and Michael Hughes, the manager of the Sankey and also of the Williams operation. These included the *Mersey*, the *Union*, the *Happy* and the *Miner*.

There was also a coal field on the edge of the Dee with collieries close to small harbours such as Bagillt, Flint and Connah's Quay. By 1845 the collieries around Flint were yielding 1,500 tons a week. Coal was connected with the widespread industrial activity along the south bank of the Dee, which included lead mining and smelting around Holywell (6,000 tons in 1845), papermaking, cotton spinning in the Greenfield valley, brickmaking and potteries inland from Connah's Quay and production of ferro-manganese at Mostyn. Flats with their shallow draught proved very useful in the Dee, the approach to a

Flats at Bagillt about 1880; note the narrow 'gutter' from the main Dee channel.
Welsh Industrial and Maritime Museum

'port' such as Bagillt was no more than a tidal gutter and the wharf at its head had to be kept clear of silt by releasing water penned in a flushing reservoir at low tide. In spite of the difficulty there was still sufficient trade to justify rebuilding the wharf in 1894. The Mostyn Coal & Iron Company owned the steam packet *Temple*, built at Trefiw in 1874 and acquired in 1894 to unload manganese ore from tramp steamers anchored in the Mostyn deep. Ore and steel were also carried from steamers berthed at Liverpool by the jiggers of the Liverpool Lighterage Company. They had the sailing flats *Doon* and *Mary* too. The remains of all three are still visible at Mostyn. Coal was often delivered to places without harbour facilities. For example, the Lleyn peninsula had no railway beyond Pwthelli and coal was delivered by water. At beaches such as Porth Or a vessel would be run ashore and the local farm carts would come down at low water to collect the coal. These are a few representative examples of coal trading by flats. The last commercial coal traffic was on the Leeds & Liverpool Canal in long boats to Wigan power station. This finished in 1973.

Saltmaking is an old industry in Cheshire and was centred around Northwich, Middlewich, Nantwich and Winsford. 'Wild brine' from natural springs was traditionally evaporated in shallow lead pans fuelled by wood or charcoal. In the seventeenth century larger iron pans were constructed; these were heated by coal from Staffordshire or Lancashire. By 1682 Northwich, the chief producer, was boiling 12,214 bushels (about 300 tons) of salt a week. Apparently the coal was taken by pack horse from the pits to Hale on the north bank of the Mersey and shipped to Frodsham or further up the Weaver to Pickerings, where it was transshipped to carts. A ton of coal was needed to produce two tons of coarse salt and two for three tons of fine salt. Transport was more expensive than the coal, which was three shillings (15p) a ton at the pithead. The cost of moving it to the nearest saltworks was 18s 10p (94p). In 1670 William Marbury of Marbury found deposits of rock salt on his land when prospecting for coal. It was cheaper to move the rock salt to meet the coal on the Mersey than vice versa. A rock salt refinery was believed to have started at Frodsham in 1694, and two more were set up shortly after this: one at Dungeon near Hale and one at Liverpool on what was to be the site of Salthouse Dock. The new rock salt refiners incurred the opposition of the existing producers, especially after a new salt excise tax introduced in 1694 favoured them. The opening of the Weaver for navigation in

Loading salt in bulk at Anderton.
K. Done

1732 was followed by a rapid expansion in salt production. Shipments totalled fourteen thousand tons in the first year of navigation. Salt was in great demand as a condiment, for preserving meat and fish, in cheese making (a Cheshire speciality), for curing hides, glazing pottery and for chemicals, and was used in soapmaking, bleaching, tanning and glassmaking. It was also an important export cargo for ocean traders at Liverpool. Fine bagged salt was carried to West Africa along with other barter goods such as cloth, guns and brandy to buy slaves for transport to the British plantations in the West Indies. By the end of the eighteenth century John Holt wrote, 'The salt trade is generally acknowledged to have been the Nursing Mother and contributed more to first rise, gradual increase and present flourishing state of the town of Liverpool more than any other Article of Commerce.'

Salt production stood at about 150,000 tons annually by 1800. That huge increase depended on a ready supply of coal. Many flats plied on a triangular route: salt down to Liverpool for export, light or possibly with manure or general cargoes to the Sankey, and back to the Weaver saltworks with coal. The rate of expansion was even faster in the first half of the nineteenth century. Shipments of white salt down the Weaver stood at 196,433 tons in 1808; fifty years on the total had trebled to 647,347 tons. Poole gave a very detailed report of the industry in 1852. Seventy-nine out of a total of ninety-seven saltworks in the kingdom were situated on the banks of the Weaver. They made 700,000 tons of salt out of the nation's total output of 800,000. The bulk of their production was exported via Liverpool. By 1846 flats carried 539,302 tons down the Weaver. Coarse salt was sent to the east-coast fisheries, the Baltic, the Netherlands and North America, and refined salt also went to those destinations and further afield to West Africa, India and Australia. Poole stated there were about four hundred flats on the Weaver.

The flats were loaded directly from the works on the banks of Weaver. In the nineteen-thirties there were still fourteen works at Winsford alone and that was after the great consolidation of the Salt Union in 1885 and the disappearance of the many small family producers. Coarse rock salt was loaded in bulk after the hold had been cleaned out and every particle of the previous coal cargo removed. This was hard work using a sailing flat's hand pumps. Steam packets had a steam ejector to get rid of water used for hosing the hold clean. Once dried, any rusty ironwork would be painted with whitewash. It was very important to keep the bulk salt clean. Salt was checked for lumps and stray pieces of scale from the sides of the pan. A few hundredweight extra were loaded over the bill of lading to allow for contamination whilst discharging at Liverpool. Bulk salt was loaded down chutes from storage sheds. There were also chutes at Anderton where the Trent & Mersey Canal ran parallel to but fifty feet (15 m) above the Weaver. Narrow boats from Middlewich would transship here into flats. The procedure was retained even after the building of the famous Anderton boat lift in 1875. Flats unloaded directly alongside ships in dock using steel tipping tubs. Sailing flats had derricks which were rigged on the mast with the gaff and boom swung clear of the main hatch. One of these can be seen in the photograph of the bigger flat discharging at Sunderland Point. Steam packets had a permanently rigged derrick worked from the steam winch at the bow, which also handled the anchor, and the arrangement can be seen on the photographs of the *Monkey Brand* and steam packets in Salthouse Dock, Liverpool, and in the drawing of the *Vale Royal.*

Bagged salt came in several varieties and had to be treated with even greater care. 'Wet' salt, such as coarse salt, had to be kept clear of dry 'stoved' salt and there might be several consignments for different destinations or different ships. Salt bags were stowed in tiers with the bags lying fore and aft. A tier could go up to the coamings, depending on the type of salt. Vacuum salt, or 'light Boston' might weigh ten tons to a tier. 'Lagos salt', exported to West Africa, was lighter – it would weigh two tons less. The bottom of the hold was laid with straw up to the bilges. Sacking was laid over the staw to protect the bags. This was especially important with the white calico Lagos bags. For these additional sacking was hung round the side of the hold and canvas covers were placed over the stack before the hatch covers were put on. Lump salt for cattle had to be separately wrapped and in a packet it would be stowed aft close to the boiler to keep it dry. The trimmers had to wear canvas bags over their boots so that they did not dirty the salt. Every bag had to be counted as it came on board. Cheshire Record Office have a tally book for a Northwich works running from 14th June 1843 to 29th January 1844. It shows that bags were checked in fives with eight hundred bags for one flat on a six foot three and a half inch (1.9 m) draft. On average one flat was loaded a day. The busiest day recorded was 16th June 1843, when the *Phoebe, Captain, Jane* and *Speculation* were despatched. The packets took about a day to load.

The flats carried between eighty and 120 tons of salt and completed from fifteen to fifty voyages to Liverpool annually. The number depended on whether the flat was owned by the saltworks or was hired in according to need. A fair average for a flat was estimated by Poole to be two voyages every three weeks, all the year round. A packet took about eight hours without delays and with the right tides from Winsford to Liverpool, and averaged about two trips a week. If the cargo was to be discharged directly into a ship, the dockers would usually use the ship's derricks. Loads would each be up to half a ton of bagged salt and would be lifted with a rope or in a canvas covered rope sling. The bulk salt would tend to be worked with the packet's own gear. The crew might have to operate the winch and whether it was bags or bulk they had to tally or count the cargo out of the hold and

Salt Union steam packet
Vale Royal, *built at*
Winsford in 1873. See also
the drawing of the packet's
engine and boiler room.
The funnel as well as the
mast could be lowered.

ensure that the total agreed with that of the tally clerk keeping count on the ship. This is only a summary of packet working in the salt trade. Tom Lightfoot's book, *The Weaver Watermen* (1982) gives a detailed account which cannot be bettered of all the workings of the Winsford packets on the Weaver, on the Mersey and around the docks.

Returning to the salt trade itself, although the introduction of packets had enabled the Weaver salters to keep pace with demand and reduce the price of carrying, the industry was approaching a crisis in the eighteen-seventies. Salt producing firms had always come and gone as small producers (often owner-flatmen using their accumulated capital) gambled on making their fortune. Competition had grown and prices had fallen. As a result of over-production in the mid-eighteen-seventies, prices had dropped to a point where most producers were making a loss. H. E. Falk proposed an amalgamation of all United Kingdom salt interests to control production and raise prices. The Salt Union came into existence in 1888 and claimed to control ninety per cent of British salt production. Financially it was not a success because there was much squabbling among its members. Foreign competition especially from the United States and Germany, led to a decline in demand for Weaver salt. Total shipments stood at over one and a quarter million tons in 1880–81 and by 1892–93 this was down to just under seven hundred thousand. Most of the Weaver

The Salt Union's Persia *built at Northwich in 1867, and another steam packet discharging salt into a deep-sea sailing ship in Salthouse Dock, Liverpool. Note the steel tubs on the stern deck of the* Persia. Trustees of NMGM

based producers joined in the Salt Union, including Falk, Evans, Verdins, Stubbs's and Higgins together with the packet owners Deakin's and the Mersey–Weaver Carrying Company. Rail transport and brine pipelines, the first of which was completed in 1882, took traffic away from the flats as well. There was a great rationalization of fleets and dockyards and it is likely that the last sailing flats working the Weaver gave up at this point and were stripped of their sails and 'barged'.

Though salt production declined and with it coal shipments, chemicals saved the Weaver traffic. Alkali was needed in the form of soda for making soap, bleaches (essential to cotton and paper manufacture) and glass. Originally this was made from wood ash (lye) or kelp, but in 1822 Muspratt established a Le Blanc process works to make soda ash from salt and sulphuric acid at Liverpool, close to the canal. The resulting chemical reaction gave off clouds of poisonous gas and there was much protest from local residents. As a result the whole operation was moved to Widnes at the end of the Sankey Canal, where it expanded. By 1875 the Widnes Alkali Company, the British Alkali Company, Holbrook Gaskell, Henry Deacon, J. L. Muspratt, Pilkington's Mersey Chemical Company, Hutchinson's and Gossage's were chemical makers based around Widnes and the lower part of the Sankey. Two other firms, Golding Davies and J. Vickers, used the Widnes West Bank Dock, which opened in 1864. All these chemists chose waterside sites for the factories to receive coal and raw materials and to deliver their products for export from Liverpool.

During the eighteen-sixties the Solvay process, another method for making alkali, was gaining ground. This depended on the treatment of ammonia saturated brine with carbon dioxide. Large quantities of salt were needed. In 1874 Ludwig Mond and John Brunner established alkali production on the Weaver. They bought a riverside site at Winnington below Northwich. They used the railway to bring raw materials, especially coal and limestone, and the Weaver for exporting their soda products down river to Liverpool. The ammonia was brought in by water either as 'bone liquor' or 'gas water'. The former was made by the rendering down of cattle bones. Liverpool was the centre of the live cattle trade from Ireland and the United States with huge slaughterhouses at Woodside, Birkenhead. Gas water which is also rich in ammonia, was a by-product of making town gas. At first dumb flats were fitted with tanks to carry these liquids; then in 1880 four new purpose built tank barges were completed. The first packet for shipping soda to Liverpool was the wooden *Shamrock* built by Woodcock's at Northwich in 1888. Brunner Mond went from strength to strength, offering severe competition to the Le Blanc producers. In 1883 the latter tried to establish a cartel of all the Lancashire firms to maintain prices and resist competition. It did not work, and in 1890 the United Alkali Company was formed incorporating forty-eight

factories across England, Scotland and Ireland, including the Widnes plants. The new combine rationalized and modernized with a new works, the Castner-Kellner factory, Runcorn, producing soda and bleaching powder from brine by a new electrolytic process. They retained flat transport and it was United Alkali which ordered the last two sailing flats: the *Eustace Carey* and the *Santa Rosa*. They were launched in 1905 and 1906 by Clare & Ridgeway and were among the best looking of all the flats with good sheer, sharp bow, a fine run aft and jigger rig. They were designed to carry limestone from Flint to the firm's soda works at Fleetwood. They continued under sail into the nineteen-twenties. Frank Ogle recalled in *Sea Breezes*:

> They were a fine pair of jigger flats and always smartly kept by their crews. I remember one morning in 1917 coming out of Saltney [on the Dee] in a tug which had been built there; we passed these two flats coming loaded out of Flint and they looked magnificent with gleaming paint and varnish and gorgeous red sails. After all this time I still recollect the scene with pleasure.

1926 saw the merger of United Alkali and Brunner Mond as Imperial Chemical Industries in an effort to withstand world competition. The Salt Union joined ICI in 1937. All the different sections continued to use water transport, they even had a few sailing flats such as the *Olivet* working out of Widnes until the mid-nineteen-fifties. Rail and particularly road competition led to a rundown of the packet fleet from the nineteen-fifties. The Salt Union packets finished in 1958. The last Brunners, the *Weaverham* and the *Wincham*, were both sold to Bulk Cargo Handling in 1971.

Opposite page: *'Brunner flat' steam packet* Madge *of 1913 returning empty from Liverpool on the Weaver.*

E. W. Paget-Tomlinson

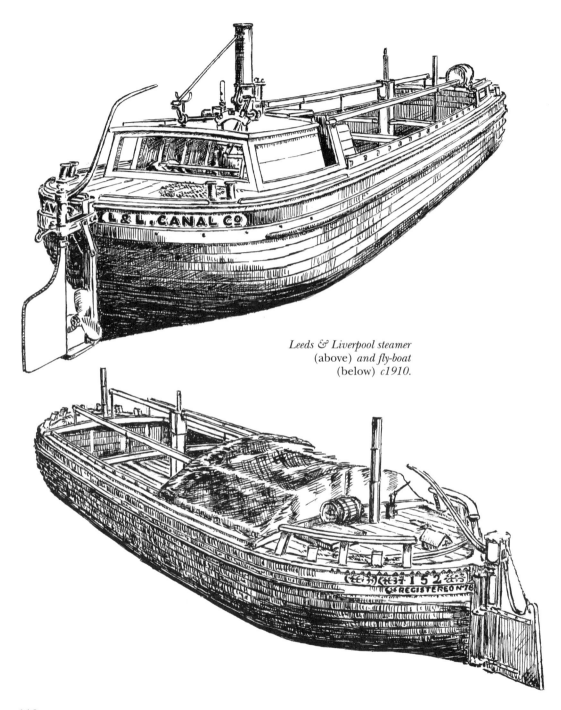

Leeds & Liverpool steamer
(above) *and fly-boat*
(below) *c1910.*

Groceries, Grain and Gunpowder – Other Flat Trades   7

Almonds to yarn, anchors to woollens; Baines's *History of the Commerce and Town of Liverpool* (1854) listed 194 different imports and 152 exports passing through Liverpool in 1770. These lists lengthened as new trading connections were made in the early nineteenth century. Flats carried not just coal and salt but a whole variety of goods. Water transport was the safest, most efficient method and in some remote places virtually the only one. The really valuable freights in small packages might be carried to timetable in 'packets' or 'fly-boats'. There was also a range of raw materials and foodstuffs carried in flats: stone, sand and iron were always staples and grain became of increasing importance because Britain became dependent on importing foreign grains to feed her growing population. Merseyside was a leading importer and centre of flour milling. Raw cotton and palm oil were two other essentials for north-western industries. Finally I have included gunpowder in this chapter because this was a very specialized traffic for flats.

Flats were probably carrying imports inland from Liverpool by the end of the seventeenth century when Thomas Patten's tobacco and sugar went by water to Warrington and Cheshire cheeses came down river. Huge numbers of cheeses were carried to London. Such was the value of the trade – chiefly from Frodsham in the early eighteenth century – that in 1708–09 the London cheesemongers raised objections to the dues they would have to pay the town of Liverpool for entering the Mersey. This was recorded in the bill for building a Liverpool dock. As the eighteenth century progressed Liverpool became the hub of a distribution network: merchandise came from inland and from the Irish Sea ports for export and imported goods – notably tobacco, sugar, rum and cotton – came from the West Indies and the North American colonies. The Dry Dock (later called the Canning Dock), which was the entrance basin for the first dock or Old Dock at Liverpool, became the centre of the 'packet' business. This meant carrying to a timetable. The seaward end was largely conducted in deep draught cutters and sloops that carried passengers as well as cargo. The inland end was worked by flats. The 1766 Liverpool Directory noted seventeen packets trading to London, five to Preston, four to Bristol and Chester, three to Milnthorpe and two each to Lancaster, Ulverston and Whitehaven. Then there were the flats: twelve Manchester flats for 'Old Key', including the *Manchester, Molly, Byrom, Betty* and *Patten* with John Davies as broker; the six 'Salford Key' flats with Peter Bankes as broker, three Warrington flats and ten Winsford flats with Richard Kent as agent. Finally, the directory notes, 'The Northwich flats are so numerous, it would take up too much room to insert them, but the undermentioned persons are Agents for the said Flats: John Pratt, John Maine and John Chubbard.'

The boats for regular services were called fly-boats, or fly-outs in the case of the Rochdale Canal. They took precedence over other craft and had permission to pass through locks at night. They provided the equivalent of a modern parcels service, loading and discharging at intermediate depots along the route as well as at the termini. They became widespread in the early nineteenth century and required a high degree of organization with regular changes of horses and double manning to keep the boat moving round the clock. The Leeds & Liverpool 'fly-boats' had canvas tilts to protect the cargo. They operated along the whole length of the canal, calling at company depots *en route* to pick up and deliver. Steamers took on the title and it was inherited by the new motor boats in the mid-nineteen-thirties. They, like the steamers, had the words 'fly-boat' painted on a white panel on either side of the stem and stern.

Flats carried passengers on the canals but for some services – for example, on the Lancaster Canal – narrow boats were preferred because they could achieve a higher speed. The earliest seems to have been on the Bridgewater Canal, on a service between Lymm and Manchester in 1769. The Leeds & Liverpool offered a similar service from 1776: Liverpool to Wigan, with the possibility of continuing on to Manchester via the Leigh branch after 1820. A surviving print shows the packet to have been a 'short boat' with a cabin built over the hold, pulled by one horse which would be changed at regular intervals at the company's stables along the way. Coaches also met passengers intending to take a holiday at the new resort of Southport at Scarisbrick Bridge. A second ran between Liverpool and Old Roan in the morning and evening for commuters, taking two hours. 'The Canal boat morning and night was the only public conveyance to Bootle and Litherland and not unpleasant', recalled Benjamin Blower in his *The Mersey, Ancient and Modern* (1878). Rail competition killed the service in the mid-eighteen-forties. The Mersey & Irwell started a service in competition with the Bridgewater in 1807 and there is an account of a trip from Manchester in 1839. The anonymous author travelled on a flat through to Liverpool. It was towed by a horse, but hoisted a sail in fair winds. It sounded a comfortable trip and at Runcorn, '. . . we partook of our evening meal in the cabin of our vessel. Those cabins though small were snug and comfortable and we had to wait until mid-night for the tide . . .'. From Runcorn the packet was marshalled with other flats and towed by steamer down to Liverpool. Some of the services lingered on into the middle of the nineteenth century, but more as excursions than essential services. Some of the Leeds & Liverpool ones had a reputation for being drunken and rowdy. The 1766 Liverpool Directory provided not just the names and desti-nations of flats but their agents too. This showed that there was some need for agents or brokers to find cargoes for flats and flats for cargoes. They would be particularly interested in 'general cargo' – that is, mixed cargo or anything that was not considered to be a bulk item such as coal. 'General cargo' could be anything from bales of cotton to puncheons of palm oil. It was more valuable than bulk cargo and therefore it had to be protected from weather and theft and the handling and documentation was much more complex than a single cargo of salt or coal. A bale of cotton or a cask of tobacco when discharged would have to be weighed and its distinctive mark and number checked against the bill of lading and for Customs duties before it left the quay. All the canal companies operating flats inland from Liverpool invested in depots to handle their general traffic. They also built inland depots at important towns and strategic transship-ment points.

The core of the general cargo trade was first the Liverpool–Manchester connection, Manchester being the booming manufactur-ing centre and Liverpool the port that brought in raw materials and foreign luxuries and exported finished goods. This was reflected in the traffic first on the Mersey & Irwell and then on the Bridgewater Canal. The latter was especially important because of its connection with the Trent & Mersey and Preston Brook, which gave access to the Midlands, London and the eastern half of the kingdom. Alf Hayman, an ex-Bridgewater manager, in his account of the Bridgewater in the Boat Museum's archives wrote, 'It needs to be emphasised that in the Duke's time to 1803 and during much of the 19th century general cargo grew more quickly than coal which only came into its own when steam, gas and eventually electric power plants were sited on the canal-side.'

The first known depot was the 'Manchester Key' on the Irwell. It is illustrated on Casson and Berry's map of 1741, which shows a stone quay with a crane, an enclosed secure yard with barrels and two ware-houses. The flats' first depot in Liverpool was at Mann Island, where a small tidal basin was dug out of the foreshore for the Manchester flats. This is shown in Lightoller's 1765 plan of the docks, complete with flats and two warehouses. In 1772 Henry Berry, the dock engineer and incidentally the man responsible for the building of the Sankey, was authorized to build a quay together with 'an engine . . . for the weigh-ing of coal'. Berry's work was probably an extension of the existing quay. In 1789 the corporation ordered the building of sheds and cranes 'for the accommodation of the merchants, dealers and others in the loading and unloading of the goods from flats employed in the navigation of the rivers Mersey and Irwell'. The Mersey & Irwell Navigation Company were offering a daily goods service between Liverpool, Warrington and Manchester with twenty-eight flats. Traffic to Liverpool increased in 1795 with the opening of the Ellesmere Port–Chester section of the Ellesmere Canal; this had a depot built for it next to the Manchester flats' basin, which became known as the Chester Basin. Both were tidal and both had warehousing and a resident manager's house. In 1813 the Manchester Basin became the Manchester Dock when it was extended and fitted with double lock gates enclosing an acre of water space.

In 1773 the Bridgewater Canal also set up a depot at Liverpool and, as on the Mersey & Irwell, general cargo proved to be the main constituent of the Bridgewater's Manchester–Runcorn–Liverpool line which was not finished until 1776 with the great lock staircase at Runcorn. Duke's Dock, opened in 1783, was separate and to the south of the corporation's docks. Large warehouses were built to house valuable and perishable goods, and there were cranes on the quay-sides for the fast loading of flats. The first warehouse at Duke's Dock was eight storeys high and ninety-three feet (28 m) long. It was built

Runcorn was an important point of interchange between the sea, river and wide and narrow canals. The large warehouses were used to store china clay and also finished pottery for export. This scene dates from about 1870 and includes two Bridgewater flats, narrow boats and a flat sloop (left) with raised bulwarks, bowsprit and square sail yard (see chapter three).
E. W. Paget-Tomlinson

between 1780 and 1783 and demonstrated the volume of the Bridgewater traffic. Food for the growing industrial towns was the key traffic, together with bales of cotton. The former included sugar, molasses, spices, salt fish and grain. Grain ships discharged in the adjacent King's Dock and the sacks could be stored in a huge new grain warehouse built in 1811. Its centre spanned the dock so that two flats could be loaded under cover. Duke's Dock developed as a mini-port in its own right, and when it was finally sold to the Dock Board in 1899 there were over 166 buildings, a half-tide dock, a main dock with four arms and a wide range of facilities including a shipyard, joiner's shop, smithy boiler and engine house, stables, dwelling houses and offices with storage for copper, coal and timber.

The Bridgewater also had the Egerton Dock for timber to the south of Duke's and by the eighteen-sixties a depot in the north dock system called Carriers dock. Other flat depots at Liverpool included Anderton and Eagle Basins in the south docks. The Leeds & Liverpool had a great range of warehousing off Leeds Street and Pall Mall for its fly-boat services. Even though the canal and all its basins have been filled in there is an impressive range of nineteenth-century canal warehousing along Pall Mall. The Manchester depots were concentrated mainly in the Castlefields area, and many of the buildings have been pulled down. Their complicated history has been admirably dealt with by V. I. Tomlinson in his article 'Early warehouses on Manchester waterways' in the *Transactions of the Lancashire and Cheshire Antiquarian Society*, volume 71 (1961).

In 1800 the overall traffic on the Bridgewater amounted to about three hundred thousand tons and two thirds of that was general. By 1830 it had gone up to three quarters of a million tons and by 1844 the combined traffic with the Mersey & Irwell was one and a quarter million tons. In 1875 the successor company, the Bridgewater Navigation Company, saw a peak of three million tons on both waterways. It is not clear how much was general and how much was coal or other bulk, but the figure of nine hundred thousand tons for general cargo carried on the Mersey between Liverpool and Runcorn in 1884 gives some indication.

Delivery time was important. As early as 1788 it was reported that the Mersey & Irwell flats left Manchester with goods at four o'clock in the afternoon and 'seldom fail to deliver them to Liverpool the second day'. In the late eighteen-twenties the promoters of the Liverpool & Manchester Railway made great play of the slowness, high tolls and poor handling of the existing canal services. Of course they were bound to do this because it strengthened their own case. The two waterways to Manchester held their own against the railways for at least fifteen years after the opening of the Liverpool & Manchester Railway in 1830. They were still carrying considerable quantities of valuable cargo such as cotton cloth and foodstuffs right into the twentieth century. In 1820 the New Quay Company plying the Mersey & Irwell offered an all-inclusive freight and toll charge – fifteen shillings (75p) a ton for cotton and twelve shillings (60p) for grain from Liverpool to Manchester. There was three weeks' free warehousing as well. Liverpool-bound goods –such as finished textiles – were collected free from the shipper's premises by the company's carts. The sailing time taken averaged between twelve to fifteen hours on either waterway. Loaded flats not only had their hatches covered with tarpaulins but also had them chained down to prevent pilferage.

The Manchester Dock at Liverpool found new users after the Mersey & Irwell had joined the Bridgewater in 1844. In 1872, this dock became a transshipment depot for the Great Western Railway. The GWR was denied direct rail access to Liverpool and much of its parcels traffic was transshipped at its goods station at Morpeth Dock Birkenhead into flats and carried across the river. The GWR shared the dock with the Shropshire Union flats from Ellesmere Port. Chester Basin was rented out to the Rochdale Canal Company. The Shropshire Union sold its flats in 1921, and the GWR went over to motor lorries. All traffic to Chester Basin and Manchester Dock had finished by about 1925. As their walls were prone to subsidence these once busy flat depots were filled in with spoil from the new Mersey road tunnel which opened in 1934. Only the GWR goods depot is left as a reminder. Fortunately, it has been restored as part of Merseyside Maritime Museum.

The transshipment of goods from flats to narrow boats was another facet of the general cargo business. Preston Brook, Ellesmere Port, Anderton, Runcorn and Weston Point were all important. The junction with the Trent & Mersey at Preston Brook gave Liverpool and the Bridgewater a link with the Staffordshire potteries, the Black Country, the Trent and eventually the capital. The biggest imports were for the Trent & Mersey – china clay and flints. At Runcorn in 1852 they amounted to about 44,000 tons of clay, ten thousand tons of china clay or stone from the West Country and about fifteen thousand tons of flints from Kent and Sussex ports. These were also brought into Ellesmere Port and Liverpool.

In return, a huge number of pieces of finished pottery – anything from fine Wedgwood to earthenware Staffordshire figures of George Washington – were delivered packed in pottery crates or barrels for export from Liverpool. In 1852 there were no fewer than 150 different works in the pottery towns exporting 54,013 tons – mainly to the United States, Canada, Brazil and the West Indies. The procedure according to Poole, was as follows:

> When an export order for earthenware is being executed, the manufacturers generally despatch the crates as soon as packed in small lots, by canal to the depots either at Anderton, Runcorn or Ellesmere Port, where they remain until the entire order is complete, when the merchant or shipbroker at his convenience either writes or sends a messenger directing the

whole to be forwarded alongside some outward-bound vessel then loading in Liverpool Docks. This is accomplished by flats or lighters, towed down the river.

There were also tropical imports such as cocoa brought back from Liverpool in 'Duker' flats. There was still a small amount of transshipping going on at Preston Brook, Black Shed into the nineteen-fifties and a well trained shire horse that worked the warehouse sack hoist was part of the establishment until its closure.

The flats' most important cargo in the nineteenth century apart from coal and salt was cotton, both imported raw in bags and bales and in finished 'piece goods' for export. The Lancashire textile industry led the Industrial Revolution and its new steam-powered factories clothed the world. In 1770 only 1,510 tons came in, but by 1852 Liverpool was the 'chief emporium for cotton in the world' with two and a quarter million bales imported and a thousand million piece goods exported. The rate of expansion was checked by the American Civil War (1861–65), but as late as 1931 Liverpool handled two thirds of all the kingdom's cotton imports and exports. Cotton was one of the major traffics that railways had aimed to grab from the flats; by 1852, 1,243,176 bales went by rail and 744,364 by water – 676,130 by the Bridgewater (which would have included the Mersey & Irwell and Rochdale traffic) and 68,234 via the Leeds & Liverpool Canal. After a period of bitter competition and falling rates the Bridgewater came to a sharing arrangement with the Liverpool & Manchester Railway in 1844, but this did not survive the merger of the Liverpool & Manchester and others into the London & North Western in 1846.

The flat operators did not give up their share without a struggle. For example, they offered rebates on the standard freight rate for cotton bales to mill owners outside Manchester who had to bring their cloth to there for dyeing or printing. The mill owners not only received a discount but the bales gave them a return load for their carts. The flats' share continued to fall for the rest of the nineteenth century. Nevertheless, Bill Leathwood of Runcorn, who used to run the Brunner packets on the Weaver recalled that there were still cotton shipments of both bales and piece goods in the 'Duker' flats in the nineteen-thirties. Rochdale was another major recipient of cotton and while it is not known what proportion went on the flats, many of the photographs of them show them loaded with bales stacked high above the coamings. These high loads of cotton bales required the substitution of an iron cranked tiller and a plank to stand on to see over the load. The Rochdale 'fly-outs' – or 'bale boats', as the locals called them – had ringbolts on the covering board so that tarpaulins could be lashed down over a high stack of bales. Stowage of bales was often a problem until bales with steel bands were introduced. It was a perk of the cotton traders in Liverpool to hack off every other one of the rope bands on an American bale. This destroyed its shape and made it more liable to dirt and wet and pilferage. In fact, the 'improper custom' led – according to Poole to – 'excuses and opportunities to men cutting and carrying off ropes of every kind belonging to anybody else to be sold; it induces other men also to do wrong and gives encouragement to places well known amongst the police as the chief receptacles for stolen property of this description'. Doubtless the flat's mooring ropes, tow lines and rigging were not immune from this kind of thieving.

After cotton, the iron trade was the most valuable of the Mersey nineteenth-century traffics with over a thousand tons a day coming into the port. Much of it was pig iron for further processing. In 1852, 85,000 tons of iron ore arrived coastwise, much of it from the haematite mines of Furness and Millom. The 'Barrow flat' schooners built by Hugh Jones of Millom and the Ashburners at Barrow were designed to carry this dense cargo. Iron ore was delivered to Runcorn and Ellesmere Port and also to the short lived Ditton Brook Ironworks at Widnes. Finished iron goods – anything from cast iron cooking pots to machine tools – were carried to Liverpool for export. The Ellesmere & Chester and its successor were especially prominent. In 1838 they carried 60,406 tons of iron to Liverpool, about half originating in Staffordshire and the remainder from Shropshire and North Wales. In 1903 and 1905 two makers of corrugated iron – Burnell's and the Wolverhampton Corrugated Iron Company – established factories at Ellesmere Port so that they had access to raw materials coming into Liverpool docks. Wolverhampton Corrugated Iron Company had a fleet of steam and dumb flats with the prefix 'Elles'. Unloading and loading at the works was performed by a crane with an electro-magnet and Mr Albert Caldwell, skipper of the *Mossdale* recalled: 'The iron was discharged day or night ... This was very noisy. I could not get home from Ellesmere Port and we had to try and sleep while they discharged'. Morton's ironworks at Garston also made corrugated iron and they shipped much of it down to the Liverpool docks for export from their own dock.

Shipbreaking provided another source of raw material for the steelmakers. Henry Bath – who broke up ships at Tranmere, including Brunel's *Great Eastern* – used flats to take away the fragments. There was also an important scrapyard at Dungeon Quay on the site of the old saltworks. Big ships such as the warship HMS *Glatton* could be floated up there on spring tides and beached. The *Fanny* and the packet *Progress* towing up to three flats each kept up regular scrap deliveries to the Monks Hall works at Atherton Quay, Warrington.

Erasmic, Doucil, Carbosil, Persil, Pagoda, Pyramid and *Pinkobolic* were some of the brands of soap made by Crosfield's at Warrington. Lever Brothers at Bromborough made *Monkey Brand, Big Ben, Lifebuoy, Omo* and *Sunlight*. These names were also the names of flats and steam packets owned by the two firms. Soapmaking became a major Merseyside industry because the main ingredients, soda and fat, were readily available. All the fats – including tallow, which came from the cattle trade and palm oil and coconut oil, which were brought from the tropics and particularly from West Africa – could be easily delivered to waterside factories. Equally the finished product could be cheaply sent to Liverpool for export. Crosfield's were about the first of the big operators and started in 1815. By 1852 there were sixteen soaperies at Liverpool and two at Runcorn – Wigg's and Hazelhurst's. Crosfield's relied on sailing flats to deliver goods to and from Liverpool and gave evidence against the proposed railway viaduct across the Runcorn Gap in 1860 because they feared it would interfere with navigation. In the mid eighteen-eighties they bought the 'screw steamer' *Ada* – probably second-hand – and used her to tow the sailing flats. After 1894, if the tides served, Crosfield's boats used the upper Mersey past Fiddler's Ferry, and otherwise they used the ship canal and locked out into the Mersey through Walton lock and down to their works, which straddled both sides of the river at Bank Quay. Apart from soapmaking materials, the packets brought up whole cargoes of sawn timber for making the boxes in which the bars of soap were packed. Crosfield's traffic lasted through to the nineteen-fifties with the motor barge *Doucil.* Their *Erasmic* was well known locally in Warrington because she had been built in Rotterdam in 1899 and at 168 gross tons was about the biggest vessel on this stretch of the Mersey. All the Crosfield pack-

This may be either Crosfield's Ada *or Monks Hall steelworks',* Progress *towing two flats on the upper Mersey near Warrington about 1910. All three vessels are fitted with derricks and foresails for steadying them.*
Trustees of NMGM

ets had lowering masts to clear Walton Arches and the Cheshire Lines viaduct. The mast was in a tabernacle on deck.

The Liverpool depot for the packaged soap was in the north east corner of Albert Dock. One of their letterheads for 1906 states that they ran a daily carrying service to Warrington in addition to carrying their own cargoes and that they owned six packets and four flats. The four flats – *Aileen, Aaron, Fairy* and *Industry* – were still under sail in about 1900 and the Warburton brothers recalled being taken for a sail on the river on the *Aileen* with Sam Lee. Their masts were retained after they converted into dumb flats and they were repaired at Clare & Ridgeway's yard. Gossage's, the Widnes soapmakers, were also flat-owners. The most important soapmakers were Lever Brothers at Port Sunlight. This was a 'greenfield' factory and industrial village erected in 1888. They used the Bromborough Pool – a tidal creek off the Mersey – to import their palm oil and other materials. Price's candle works on the south side of the pool also brought in their ingredients by water in their own steam packets. Lever Brothers had packets and dumb flats. The latter were mainly built at Pimblott's. Palm oil was at first brought in huge casks or puncheons but 'deep tanks' with steam heating coils were developed for cargo liners in the late nineteen-twenties, which meant the palm oil could be carried in bulk. Levers' eventually enclosed Bromborough to form a dock which was opened in 1931. This meant that deep sea ships could discharge direct at the works, but there was still a need to collect cargoes from Liverpool docks and a series of tank barges was built to carry palm and other fatty oils. They lasted into the early nineteen-eighties.

Hides and tanning materials with exotic names – valonia, myro-bolams, mimosa bark, divi-divi, shumac and cutch – as well as prosaic oak bark were shipped in from the Mediterranean and India. There were large tanneries at Litherland, Runcorn and Penketh which all received these products by flat. I have included a very good photo-graph of sacks of myrobolams or something similar being unloaded at Fiddler's Ferry for the Penketh tannery, showing the derrick and hand winch in use. Hides, especially 'green' uncured ones, were a particu-larly revolting, smelly cargo which left maggots in the hold. Guano and domestic rubbish were other unpleasant cargoes. Before mains sewerage was available for all houses, cities such as Manchester and Liverpool organized the collection of what was politely called night soil and this, mixed with domestic rubbish, was shipped out of the city centre depots by flat along with horse and cow dung. It was sold to farmers along the canals at a rate of four or five shillings (20 or 25p) a ton, and made a useful return cargo after delivering coal to Liver-pool. Robert Alty recalled how his father did a special trip to Leeds in the *Rose* on the Leeds & Liverpool with palm oil in casks, picked up coal cargo for Burnley and then bought a cargo of muck at Wigan and sold it to Thomas Sumner, a farmer at Melling, at a good profit.

Guano was sea bird droppings that had accumulated into large masses mainly on small islands off the South American coast. The first ever consignment was brought to Liverpool in 1841 and it proved such a good fertilizer that there was a guano boom. It was full of ammonia, very dusty, and rotted canvas and ropes. Timber on the other hand, might have a more pleasant smell but was difficult to stow, especially in the form of large logs. These were a local speciality, with long pitch pine baulks for spars coming from North America and mahogany logs from West Africa and the West Indies. This may account for the development of a subgroup of flats, the floats. They had no hold but carried their cargo on their decks. They were employed by the Wolverhampton Corrugated Iron Company for moving scrap and their sheet iron alongside more conventional flats. Floats were never common. The Bridgewater owned fifteen as against 206 flats in 1874. Taylor's at Chester built a couple in the nineteen-thirties and fortunately there is one surviving example – the *Cedar*, ex-Shropshire Union – preserved at the Boat Museum. Timber, like coal, was a universal commodity delivered and exported to small ports and large. In the case of the flats

Unloading a cargo of tanning materials for Penketh tannery at Fiddler's Ferry, using the barrel line winch. The flat was probably built as a sailing flat. Note the heavy blocks on the forestay for lowering the derrick mast and the rope fender.
Warrington Museum

123

this might mean collecting Welsh crooked oak from an upriver quay on the Conway for a Liverpool shipyard or delivering a consignment of Baltic or Canadian pine boards. Liverpool was a major centre of the business, especially from North America, and by 1852 served merchants within a hundred mile radius; that year 466 ships delivered 309,304 tons. Another ten thousand tons came along the coast or from inland. Fifty six per cent was shifted by river and canal and only twenty-three by rail. In 1839 the Bridgewater built Egerton Dock, which was a tidal basin to the south of Brunswick dock. This was a specialist timber dock and the land to the south of it was used for storing timber. Egerton Dock was bought by the Dock Board in 1875 and between 1875 and 1878 a branch timber dock for flats was created in its place on the eastern side of Brunswick Dock.

Grain became a major flat traffic at the end of the nineteenth century. Britain became a net importer of food because of her growing industrial population. Liverpool claimed an increasing share of the grain imports – North American, Argentinian and Australian wheat – which were milled in waterside mills. Indeed, the grain trade

was one of the major factors in keeping flats in business in the twentieth century. Before the big mills there was much small scale river and coastal business. On the Mersey there were watermills at Bootle, Garston, Wallasey Pool (which included an iron slitting works), Toxteth and Bromborough, together with others at Sankey Bridges, Runcorn, Frodsham, Warrington and the upper reaches of the Irwell. Jackson's tide mill at Toxteth was a major establishment, with two large pools to impound the tidal water to pass it through the waterwheels on the ebb. It had a quay for flats to deliver grain and take away flour. Liverpool Corporation paid the huge sum of £56,000 for it in 1827 so that they could build the new Brunswick Dock. This was the fate of all these small mills; they were either in the way of a development or they lost custom to the steam-powered mills. Bromborough mill was one of the most interesting. It was built at the head of Bromborough Pool, half a mile inland from the river, and consisted of a watermill, a windmill and eventually a steam engine. The mill was used until about 1910. The miller, Ned Briscoe, owned a flat called the *Brothers* which could carry two hundred sacks. She was poled down the narrow creek and could only come alongside the mill at high tides – she had to lower her mast to get under the bridge across the pool. Flour was also delivered by the *Brothers*. Other millers who owned flats included Griffith's at Chester and Fairclough's at Warrington. These two really fall into the category of the later steam mills although they have been in business longer than most. Fairclough's was one of the last to receive grain by water.

Poole was very critical of the primitive grain handling facilities in Liverpool in 1852. It took another thirty years to improve the situation. In 1869 the Dock Board opened the Waterloo Dock grain warehouses which had elevators for unloading and could hold thirty thousand tons. Shortly after they opened a second group of warehouses of 31,000 tons capacity with their own dock for flats at the East Float in Birkenhead Docks. The Dock Board experienced some problems in operating these warehouses and this may explain why a private company, the Liverpool Grain Storage & Transit Company, was set up in 1883. They built more granaries at Alexandra, Coburg and Brunswick Docks and had their own fleet. Large mills were built at the Birkenhead Docks: Rank's (1912) and Vernon's (1917); and inland at Ellesmere Port: King (1905), Imperial (1909) and Frost Mills (1910); and at Manchester, together with others such as Ainscough's at Parbold and Burscough and North Shore Mills on the Leeds & Liverpool. Grain, if not discharged direct, was normally unloaded over the side and indeed this was eventually made compulsory. Grain in bags had to be hoisted out of the hold, weighed and recorded on deck, and then the contents were tipped down wooden chutes rigged along the sides of the steamer or sailing ship into the flat below. The Grain Elevating & Automatic Weighing Company had floating steam ele-

Burton's motor Ellesweir
*(ex-Wolverhampton
Corrugated Iron Company)
at Sankey Bridges* en
route *for the Sankey sugar
works, about 1955.*
Peter Norton Collection

vators which lifted grain out of a steamer's hold, weighed it and discharged it into flats. They also owned the steam tug *Firefly* of 1903.

Flats were becoming too small for the increasing quantities handled, and larger steel barges were introduced from the nineteen-twenties. Four were built for the Liverpool Grain Storage & Transit Company by Chambers' of Lowestoft in 1921. These had a capacity of eight hundred tons each, so they could act as floating warehouses. The upriver mills such as Brown & Polson and the Manchester Co-op relied on deliveries from the Bridgewater by flats. Kellogg's, who were a late and welcome addition set up at Stretford in 1938. The *Mossdale*, of which there is more in chapter eleven, frequently carried corn there. The replacement steel motor and dumb barges built by the Bridgewater Department after the Second World War retained the flat's dimensions in order to pass through Hulme locks.

Sugar had been important since the mid-seventeenth century. By the nineteenth century most of the production was concentrated at Liverpool. Tate & Lyle's works straddled the Leeds & Liverpool canal. Outside Liverpool, Sankey Sugar Works at Earlestown was very import-ant to the flat's history because theirs was the last traffic on the Sankey apart from chemicals out of Widnes. Sugar still amounted to 35,000 tons in 1957. Burton's enjoyed most of the business and were still carrying in packets and flats until about 1960. Their wooden flats had been built in their own yard and they had also bought some of the steel flats belonging to the Wolverhampton Corrugated Iron Com-pany. It was a difficult trade because Burton's motor craft were under-powered and yet they were expected to tow up to three barges with about 110 tons of bagged sugar each. This called for great skill, especially as the full lines of the barges made them awkward to steer. It took a full day to work up to the sugar works, but the passage had to be timed so that the barges could work through the Widnes 'Wood-end' lock when the river was level with it. Each vessel had to be worked through individually. In 1959 Sankey Sugar decided to change to road transport, the canal trade ceased and one of the last fleets of wooden flats was put out of work.

Stone and sand were two long enduring trades. Stone was needed for building, paving and roofing. There were quarries around the Mersey, such as at Storeton for white sandstone – which had a tramway to Bromborough Pool – and at Runcorn and Weston Point for red sandstone. The latter was much used in the building of the eighteenth century docks. Large quantities of millstone grit came from the Pennines and lime was important as a fertilizer, an ingredient in mortar and cement, in iron and steelmaking and in chemical processes. North Wales supplied limestone, granite setts and slates. Stone was brought in from Ireland and Scotland from ports such as Annalong and Arklow. The dock trustees at Liverpool leased a granite quarry on the Solway at Kirkmabreck in 1830 to ensure a supply of good-quality stone for their dock building schemes. They had their own flats, including the *Wellington* (1815), the *Chester* (1827), the *Spitfire* and the *Canada* (both 1828); and their Trentham Street maintenance yard (now under the Albert Dock) built the remarkable *Oak*. Built like a flat and heavily rigged as a topsail schooner, the *Oak* was launched in 1836 and carried on her heavy trade to and from Kirkmabreck until sold to West Country owners in 1904.

Canning Dock was the centre of the nineteenth century Liverpool stone trade, first at Nova Scotia after the sailing packets had been displaced by steamers and then spreading to both sides of Canning half-tide dock. Where the Maritime Museum now proudly displays its maritime treasures the ground was piled high with huge heaps of crushed stone and a black painted transit shed (now demolished) held stocks of carved granite kerbstones. Deliveries came from North Wales – especially quarries such as Penmaenmawr – and from Irish ports. This was useful employment for schooners and jiggers right into the nineteen-thirties. Similarly, cargoes of North Wales slate were delivered to Sankey Bridges by the now auxiliary jigger flat *Protection*. The Warburton brothers of Sankey Bridges once sailed on her to North Wales and were bitterly disappointed that the skipper preferred to use his new Kromhout diesel engine all the way there, without setting sail once. She continued working for Clare & Ridgeway until laid up in 1936. In 1940 she was stripped of her masts and sails and ran as a motor vessel, eventually ending up – still in the stone trade – on the River Severn. Eleven flats, incidentally, had been sold to Bristol Channel owners in 1845 to carry stone for building the

Bristol & Exeter Railway. Their heavy construction would have been an advantage.

There were many of the 'Barrow flats' in the heavy bulk trades such as stone and iron ore, and it is worth examining their trading patterns, which were quite different from the average flat. Flats, even the coastal ones, tended to be on well defined routes; either they were owned by a company that needed a regular supply of materials or their owners had regular contracts with specific shippers – for example, Burton's working for Sankey Sugar and Abels' for North Shore Mills. 'Barrow flats' and other schooners tended to work more on a tramping basis, moving from single cargo to single cargo. A year's trading for the Ashburners' *James Postlethwaite* from May 1884 to May 1885 covered twenty-five voyages, starting with coal from Fleetwood to Plymouth, bricks to London, light to the Medway to load cement for Eriskay, light to Ayr for pig iron for Newport, then coal to Dundalk and from there to Whitehaven with timber and to pick up coal for London. In other words, the *James Postlethwaite* had made one and a half round trips of the British Isles in the first ten voyages.

I have not mentioned the sand trade because that will be dealt with in some detail in the account of the *Keskadale*. The 'gunpowder hoys' were peculiar to the Mersey and it is interesting to note how this old term for a sailing barge was used to describe a specialized kind of flat. The Liverpool Magazines Co. Ltd was founded in 1887 and took over an existing centre for the storage of explosives at Bromborough on the Cheshire side, well up stream from the docks. Previously the local magazines had been on the outskirts of Liverpool, but by 1768 they were moved to Liscard near Wallasey on the Cheshire side, then almost uninhabited. With the growth of Wallasey in the nineteenth century the magazines had to move again, to remote Bromborough. A little village of exceptionally solid houses (now demolished) was built on the shore for the workers and three old wooden ships were bought to store the powder. The last was the *Swallow*, a former steam river gunboat. She was painted a distinctive yellow. By 1913, the Liverpool Magazines Company had been taken over by Nobel's Explosives, which became a constituent of ICI in 1926. The explosives, mainly blasting powder, were latterly made by Nobel's at Ardeer on the Clyde and sent to Garston on the Mersey by rail. From Garston the consignments were taken to the magazine hulks by sailing flat. When it was required for export, flats took the powder to sea-going ships anchored in the powder grounds well down stream off Crosby. Most of the trade was to West and South Africa and the powder was loaded into ships belonging to Elder Dempster, the United Africa Company and the Clan Line.

There were four sailing flats, all built especially for powder carrying:

No 1. *Bebington*, 43 gross tons, built Northwich 1859
No 2. *Bromborough*, 28 gross tons, built Liverpool 1852
No 3. *Birkenhead*, 11 gross tons, built Liverpool 1861
No 4. *Eastham*, 16 gross tons, built Liverpool 1861

Because of the nature of the trade these vessels were exceptionally well built and all the fastenings were either brass bolts secured by copper washers or copper nails, to obviate sparks. No stove was allowed in the cabin. Deck fittings such as the foresail sheet transom were made of gunmetal. Their black hulls were surrounded by a five inch (127 mm) broad red band and a bold red diamond was painted on either bow, preceded by the boat's number, also in red. Also painted red were the rudder head and the top three feet (900 mm) or so of the mast. A red flag was flown. All in all, these flats were pretty distinctive. The mast was equipped with a lightning conductor. The mainsails of the *Bebington* and *Bromborough* had mast hoops, those of the smaller flats were laced to the masts.

Working the powder hoys required plenty of skill and local knowledge. The crew numbered two and they worked an 8 am to 5 pm day unless delayed by weather. Coming alongside at Garston was tricky although the dockers were quick at catching a heaving line. Berthing alongside the *Swallow* was equally difficult if there was a ronge on (a Mersey phrase for rough water) and the men on the hulk could stream a line on a copper buoy down to a flat if she failed to make it. The powder was packed in twenty-five-pound kegs which came down a chute from the quay, and were expertly stacked in tiers in the hold. Later on the explosives came in boxes which were more awkward to handle, the kegs having the ballistic qualities of a rugger ball. None of the powder hoys was allowed by the explosives regulations to load anything like to their full capacity, thus No 1 *Bebington* only loaded twenty-five tons, and No 3 *Birkenhead* ten tons; the *Bebington* could have carried about fifty tons and the *Birkenhead* about twenty. Before 1939 the *Birkenhead* was fitted with a seventy-five horse power Widdop diesel and all the fleet was unrigged. The *Birkenhead* acted from henceforward as a tug and the other three as dumb lighters. They all worked until 1945, the hulk *Swallow* lasting until the following year.

Before leaving the subject of flat trade, it is worth looking at the end of lighterage traffic; there was a rapid decline by the end of the nineteen-fifties and most wooden flats had been phased out except for the 'long boats' on the Leeds & Liverpool. In the next two decades their steel successors were all finished. There were many factors: the rationalization of the milling industry, closure of power stations and other waterside factories, industrial troubles in the Liverpool docks and more competition from heavy lorries all contributed. Ainscough's, the millers, withdrew their last horse drawn barge in 1960 and by 1969 Rea's were the biggest operators left. The manager's report for the year ending July 1969 gives a good summary of the barging activity on the Mersey in its last years:

Rea Limited continue to be the foremost Lighterage Contractors in the Port of Liverpool, although we have scrapped no less than 19 barges during the twelve months under review. Trade in the Port of Liverpool has been badly disrupted since the scheme for decasualisation of labour was put into effect in September 1967. The subsequent strike of dock workers, which lasted for six weeks and ended in the surrender of the Government to the workers' demands, opened the way for continued industrial unrest with strikes being called on the smallest pretext without fear of recrimination.

This disastrous situation has resulted in a great many shipping companies using any other port but Liverpool, with the result that cargo offered for lighterage has been spasmodic. However, bearing in mind the reduction of the barge fleet it is good to report that the barges have been well occupied over the twelve months ending 31st July 1969.

Cargo tonnages carried during the year included:-

	Tons
General Cargo from Liverpool to Manchester	27,250
Bulk Grain from Liverpool to Manchester	25,000
Woodpulp from Ellesmere Port to Thames Board Mills, Warrington	17,000
Storage of bulk grain in barge at Liverpool	26,000
Storage of bulk grain in barges at Manchester	14,000
Maize ex vessels to Messrs. White, Tomkins & Courage Limited, Stanley Dock	39,000
Bulk Fishmeal for storage and discharge	14,000

During the year there were 176 barge loads of General Cargo for accommodation and relief of quay congestion.

The earnings for the year totalled £243,000 approximately – an impressive figure which contributed a profit to the company after the deduction of wages, costs and depreciation.

Four years later on 11th January 1973, he wrote: 'There has been a marked decline in the demand for barges in the Mersey lighterage trade over the past few years and as our hopes for an improvement have not materialised we have reluctantly decided to withdraw from the trade.' This left Bulk Cargo Handling Ltd, who bravely invested in five new eight-hundred-ton twin screw vessels to move grain from the new Royal Seaforth Dock grain terminal to Manchester, and Lever Brothers with a single vegetable oil tanker. But these have both finished and only Frodsham Lighterage with the motor barge *Panary* and the ex-Lever tanker *Safehand* continue trading at present.

Leeds & Liverpool long boats crossing the Barton aqueduct on the Bridgewater canal in the 1950s.
E. W. Paget-Tomlinson

131

The Flatowners   8

In the eighteenth and early nineteenth century flats were owned by small partnerships rather than companies. Some of the owners were directly involved in running them, others used them to further their main business – possibly coalmining or saltmaking; and a few used them as an investment or even as a speculation. There was no profession of 'flatowner', although it is noticeable that the merchant or carrier with a fleet of flats tended to specialize and not become involved in the wider shipping business. The biggest owners were the canal proprietors and the major entrepreneurs in salt and coal, but there were many small flatowners – especially on the Weaver. Flats were always expensive to build because they were constructed of heavy, good quality materials. This meant that an owner could expect a flat, given regular maintenance, to last twenty to thirty years. On the evidence of the few surviving accounts the running costs were not particularly high and wage costs were linked to the number of freights carried. It is virtually impossible to estimate the rate of depreciation. Ralph Davis in *The Rise of the English Shipping Industry,* (1962) which focuses on the eighteenth century, estimates that four or five per cent per annum was the average. The only figure I can add to that for flats is for John Brockbank's sale of the *Minerva* of sixty-seven tons in 1790. She cost £460 new and he sold her for £430 when she was a year old, which just about fits Davis's estimate.

The aim of every flatowner was to keep his vessel filled with cargo and on the move at minimal cost. A flat did not pay when it was tied up loading or unloading or when sailing light. Voyage time and turn-round time were of crucial importance and often affected by factors outside the flatowners' control. The neap tides on the upper Mersey and congestion in Liverpool docks were two examples. The cost of dues on the waterways and in the docks were also largely beyond the owner's control. The rates for carrying could be affected by excess competition or by dictation from the major shippers. In the mid-nineteenth century the Weaver 'Number Ones' (masters who owned their flats) attempted to raise freights by collective negotiation through their society. The end result proved disastrous.

Flats were at risk from accidents; the Mersey was no inland lake and the coastal routes could be hazardous – especially in the eighteenth century, when many dangers were not marked. Collision, especially with steamers, became a major risk in the later nineteenth century. Yet from the evidence that exists, flatowners did not take out

Opposite page: *The proprietors of the Herculaneum Pottery, Liverpool, had one of their artists paint a lively portrait of their own flat* Phebe *(1813) on this flagon. The manager's wife was called Phoebe and the name suggests a pride in owning the flat. The mainsail is split in two and the upper section appears to be laced on to the lower, perhaps as a summer addition. This feature is not recorded anywhere else.*

133

insurance – at least, not for river work. The risks were greater for those that sailed coastwise and flats owned on the Dee and in North Wales are in the records of the various mutual insurance associations which were such a feature of that coast. Flats were also subject to the vicissitudes of the national economy; in the nineteenth century the shipping business was reckoned to run in a ten-year cycle of boom and recession. Given all the costs and the risks, a flat could turn a good profit and enable her owner to accumulate capital either to buy further vessels or to invest in other areas.

In the second half of the nineteenth century the introduction of tugs and steam packets concentrated ownership. They were more expensive to build and operate than sailing flats. Events in the salt and chemical industry consolidated the bulk of the Weaver vessels into either the Salt Union or Brunner Mond. Likewise, the Bridgewater in its various guises was the dominant owner on its own waterway; and the same tended to apply to the three other major waterways: the Shropshire Union, the Leeds & Liverpool and the Rochdale. The Sankey, on the other hand, did not own flats. There were still opportunities for small family firms to set up as limited companies on the estuary and around the docks, especially if they had a specialized or staple traffic. Cooper's at Widnes, for example, supplied sand from the river for Pilkington's glassworks at St Helens. Others had regular contracts to supply coal or perhaps grain to particular mills or factories. Success meant careful management, canny investment in second hand tonnage and perhaps building new flats using their own shipwrights.

The records of Thomas Patten, who operated a saltworks, a wharf and warehouse at Winsford between 1733 and 1746, give the earliest details of a flatowner. Patten and his partners owned six flats over the whole period of thirteen years and they earned £10,110 17s 7d (£10,110.88). The total expenses, including the building of the flats and about a fifty per cent share of the freight money for the skipper, came to £9,035 12s 6¼d (£9035.62). The profit including the cost of the flats was £1541 1s 8¼d (£1,541.08) or roughly £120 per annum and £20 per flat. The capital investment amounted to £77 12s 10½d (£77.64) per flat, which meant a substantial return of nearly twenty-five per cent. To this would be added the profits from the salt. In 1746 Patten leased the works – including the flats – to Isaac Woods, who seems to have controlled the Northwich–Winsford trade and who generated even more profit.

High earnings seem to have been a feature of early flatowning; there were also high returns in the accounts of the Douglas flat partnership in the seventeen-fifties. But here the owners were quite different from Patten and Woods. These two were entrepreneurs with large amounts of capital and businesses that could be expanded by owning the means of transport. The Douglas partnership raised the capital for a flat and on her earnings expanded by buying more flats.

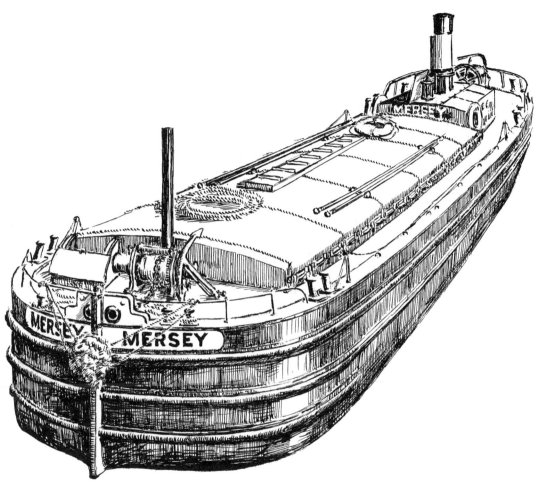

It seems to have been a loosely constituted partnership dedicated to running flats. However, one should not leave out the possibility that one or perhaps two partners had an interest in a coal mine at Wigan. In August 1752 James Winstanley and Richard Halton had a new open flat built for working the Douglas. They shared the cost of the *Expedition* – £104 9s 11d (£104.49) – between them. Two months later they met with Robert Howard and James Bradshaw, and 'twas agreed amongst them four to purchase a large Flatt to coast further to such places as they should think proper to send her'. A suitable vessel – the *Thomas* – was found, bought from a Mr Downall of Liverpool for £195 and renamed *Liverpool*. This suggests that she was intended for carrying Wigan coal to Liverpool. The four partners took a quarter share each and by May 1753 the trading prospects were looking good

Steamers – for example, the Mersey, *owned by* Rochdale Canal Company *– were invariably owned by companies rather than individuals because of the extra cost of building and maintenance.*

135

enough to consider buying a third flat. At this point Bradshaw seems to have had cold feet and agreed to sell his shares in the *Expedition* and the *Liverpool.* The matter was complicated because he had sold half his quarter-share in the *Liverpool* to her master, William Dandy. It was agreed to buy out both these men and three more partners – Topping, Crosfield and Fell – were recruited. The six partners then divided their shares in the two existing flats and a new flat, the *Sincerity*, which Fell – who was titled 'Captain' – had bought on their behalf. The *Sincerity* was bought for £237 18s 0d (£237.90), so a sixth share in all three came to £81 8s 9¾d (£81.44). This may not sound very much in modern terms but it was a substantial investment and was presumably financed from the receipts of the flat's coal cargoes and accumulated savings. There is no evidence that any of the partners borrowed any of the money. The risks were high, though not perhaps as high as with a deep sea vessel, and no insurance premiums seem to have been paid. The partnership also had unlimited liability. One of the partners was a flat master with practical experience who could advise the others on the acquisition and management of flats. James Bradshaw must have been a seafarer because in the subsequent accounts he is paid an additional five shillings (25p) for sailing to Dublin. Captain Fell is likely to have been a mariner rather than soldier because he bought the *Sincerity.* The arrangement whereby the master took a small stake in his vessel was common in the eighteenth century for bigger ships as well as flats. It ensured that he served the interests of the other owners because more often than not the master was the business manager as well as the navigator. This informal kind of partnership was common for flats and coasting vessels.

Although the accounts are difficult to interpret, it would seem that the *Liverpool* made a total of eleven voyages in 1753. Most of them included a return cargo and her total gross earnings amounted to £213 14s 1¼d (£213.71). Set against this were costs of £151 12s 6¼d (£151.62), leaving a profit of £62 1s 7d (£62.08) or twenty nine per cent. Each shareholder would have received £10 3s 7d (£10.18), which was a very handsome return on their investment. The *Liverpool* had cost the partnership £195 and a sixth share cost £32 10s (£32.50). Apart from the crew's wages the major costs were replacements of sails and spars. The most expensive single item was a new mainsail at £7 16s 9¾d (£7.84). The return per share was high compared with other coastal traders. The accounts for the Welsh sloop *Unity* launched in 1785, show that her annual dividend on an eighth share, £88 5s (£88.25), was only £5, and according to Dr Lewis Lloyd, who published the *Unity*'s accounts, this would have been considered quite a good return.

It was difficult on occasions to establish ownership of flats. There are some splendid letters in the Arley Manuscript Collection quoted in T. S. Willan's *The Navigation of the River Weaver in the 18th Century*

(1951) which demonstrate this. In 1761 the flat *Venus* sailed into Pickerings lock with her sails up in a gale and burst through the lower gates causing over seventy pound's worth of damage. The Weaver trustees had to conduct a long correspondence to discover who owned her. William Brock writing from Liverpool to Thomas Slaughter at Chester on 22nd January 1762, stated:

> The *Venus* is this day come down. I have seen the Master Brown. He says the flat did belong to Ard Docksey & Co. proprietors of the salt works at Middlewich, but that she is lately sold to Mr. Richard Heyes an attorney in Northwich and Mr. Thomas Leigh, an ironmonger there. It is a very difficult matter often to come to the true owners of a vessel and impossible to learn from any tradesmen in the town.

Flatowners were expected to have their names on the stern of their flats, but this was not always carried out. Most flats came within the jurisdiction of the Canal Boat Acts of 1877 and 1884 and thereafter had both their name and number painted on their sterns.

Towards the end of the century, the Liverpool Ship Registers from 1786 and the Quarter Sessions records for Cheshire provide a further view of flatowners. The Lancashire Quarter Sessions records for inland navigation also exist but were not accessible at the time of writing. The ship registers, which were documents of title, gave a list of all the shareholders and the name of the master, together with any subsequent changes in shareholdings. In the nineteenth century, the records become even more detailed with each shareholder's number of shares listed. The total number of shares in a flat or ship was limited to sixty-four.

Most flats in the Liverpool Ship Registers were owned by merchants and usually there were two shareholders to each flat. In 1786, out of thirty-four flats or galliot flats, ten had a mariner as a partner. A number of these appear to have been relatives of the other shareholders or in other cases the captain was clearly related to the shareholder or shareholders, without taking a share himself. There were no flats owned outright by mariners although the following year the *Friends' Goodwill* of 1740 was owned by Thomas Golding, mariner. The fact that it was a very old flat and therefore cheaper to purchase points to the fact that most flats were outside the pocket of the individual flat master. Shareholders could be 'sleeping partners', putting up the money and leaving the management to the skipper. The *John and William* of 1765, which was owned by Ralph Dickinson and a cooper from Haversage in Derbyshire, is a good example. The Derbyshire partner would clearly have not played much of a role because of distance. Some of the merchants had recognizable businesses such as colliery owning – including the Clares and Thomas Briggs. There was also Samuel Wylde, a Runcorn corn merchant and miller, who had an interest in the galliot flat *Dolphin* with six others –

including John Gilbert of Worsley who managed the Duke of Bridgewater's affairs and Michael Hughes who managed the copper smelting works at St Helens for Thomas Williams. Other occupations were marine related and included shipwright and sailmaker. The shipwrights may well have been responsible for the building of their vessels. In slack times flatbuilders probably followed the practice of bigger shipbuilders and laid down vessels as speculations. This helped to keep key members of the work-force employed and if no buyer could be found the flat could always be managed or hired out. The hiring out of boats to individuals or families was still practised on the Leeds & Liverpool into this century. Robert Alty's reminiscences include his father hiring a boat from Mayor's, the Tarleton builders, and on another occasion from the colliery owners Pearson & Knowles. Large owners would also charter additional flats if they had insufficient tonnage. The Bridgewater Navigation Company found themselves short in 1875 and hired twenty-seven flats. Alty would have considered himself a Number One because he worked for himself, even though he did not own his boat.

The *Happy*, forty-nine tons, built at Northwich in 1760 with a knee figurehead, had no fewer than twenty-nine shareholders in 1786.

11 merchants (3 Liverpool, 2 Burscough, 1 Burgh, 1 Chowbent, 1 Caton, 1 London)

8 yeomen (3 Lathom, 2 Ormskirk, 2 Shivington, 1 Sollom)
4 victuallers (1 Blackrod, 1 Burscough, 1 Lathom, 1 Newburgh)
2 grocers (Wigan)
2 clergymen (Upholland)
1 cooper (Liverpool)
1 widow (Parbold)

The master had no shares and came from Preston. What they each paid is not recorded, but she was a second hand flat, twenty-six years old. The *Fox* was built at Lancaster for £7 a ton in 1796, and if the *Happy* cost £5 per ton – which would be generous – then her value would be £245. Dividing by twenty-nine (assuming equal shares) shows that each shareholder would have invested about £8 10s (£8.50) – probably less. This was more like a lottery than a desire to operate a flat, and the question has to be asked as to why this disparate mixture of people decided to invest. I can only guess that John Atkinson and possibly Thomas Atkinson, two of the Liverpool merchants, knew or were related to the other shareholders. They must have been managing shareholders because they were at the top of the list in the register. Most of the shareholders lived in settlements close to the Leeds & Liverpool Canal and its Rufford branch to Tarleton, which had opened in 1781 to replace the inadequate Douglas. Perhaps they saw this as an opportunity to make some money and to improve the delivery of supplies to their various businesses. The facts that the skipper came from Preston and the *Happy* was re-registered at Preston in 1791 strongly suggest she was sailing out of Tarleton and into the Ribble. Some of this must remain guesswork, but the *Happy* illustrates a type of flat ownership which could be described as 'community ownership'. It was not all that common for flats, unlike the wide diffusion of shareholders in schooners and deep-sea ships owned in North Wales. The sloop *Bold*, seventy-seven tons, launched and registered in 1812, was another example. She was owned by an innkeeper from Penketh and five local farmers in the surrounding district.

The Liverpool Registers do not include the flats that were used on inland navigations. Fortunately, the Quarter Sessions records from Cheshire include a list of inland vessels for the period 1795 to 1812. Out of the 191 registrations forty eight were narrow boats and the rest flats – with two doubtfuls because of two missing pages. Only three flats had masters as owners: J. Hazelhurst's *Frodsham Trader*, Thomas Hazelhurst's *Compleat* and J. Jenkinson's *Mary*. All the other flats had masters who were employed by the owners. Out of fifty-two owners, twenty-four owned one flat each, twenty owned between two and five, and the other eight had over five flats each. Three of the owners were women: Elizabeth Tomlinson and Catherine Horabin with three flats each and Emma Jeffreys in partnership with Peter Banroft with four. There were also notable names such as Deakin's, who became salt producers in 1846.

It was the Weaver flatman's ambition first to own his flat and then to go on to have his own saltworks to supply cargoes. The salt business was so risky that there was continual movement among flatmen, flatowners and salt proprietors either on their way up or down. It is also clear that the single-owner flats were family based with relatives helping with capital and labour, and the same applied in the small saltworks. These single-owned flats were known as Number One flats, whether the owner skippered them or employed someone to do so on his or her behalf. The Weaver community was a close knit one and its influence on trade was reinforced by the Flatmen's Association, which was set up in 1792 and by the eighteen-fifties negotiated for both small owners and flatmen with the larger salt producers and merchants. In 1852 Poole recognized its existence:

> The custom of salt proprietors hitherto has been to load their own flats first and hire Number One flats afterwards, when required; and for the owners of saltworks, who are non-proprietors of flats, to hire them from one part or the other, indiscriminately. Now, however, the owners of Number One flats, having entered into a club, insist upon the salt proprietors also entering and classifying their flats in this club, to be valued at a rent according to a certain scale of hiring, which was formerly 6d a ton and is now advanced to 9d, for odd trips, or if for a year, fifty pounds or seventy pounds per flat, according to size and character, the owner keeping it in repair.

This dictation of terms was strongly resented by the larger salt proprietors, especially H. E. Falk, and his building of the first steam packet in 1863 was intended to cheapen salt transport and deal with the 'blackmail' of the Flatmen's Association. Steam packets took far more capital than a sailing flat. The prevailing price was about eight hundred pounds for a new sailing flat and a packet would be nearer fifteen hundred pounds, but the large salt proprietors could afford this without unduly straining their resources. After 1863 there was also the possibility of setting up a limited company which could issue shares and borrow money for investments.

Flats do not seem to have been mortgaged to any great extent. Larger ships were frequently used to secure loans from banks or merchants in the middle of the nineteenth century, at a low rate of about five or six per cent interest. Massive loans to shipowners caused local Liverpool banks to wobble and in two cases to crash. One might have expected flatowners to have borrowed as well. There are just a few instances; on 30th March 1831 Arthur Barron of Woolden Hall mortgaged the *Comet*, *Amy* and *Mary Jane* as security for a loan of £1,400 at five per cent interest per annum to George Wood, merchant of Manchester. The flat *Harry*, built by Clare & Ridgeway in 1880, was a later example. She was bought by William Clarke of Hough Green, Widnes, in December 1891 and a year later she was mortgaged to F. McGovern of Oakfield, Hough Green, for six hundred pounds at six per cent; this was paid off in three years. Another example showed that borrowing could be short term. In 1896 flatowner Thomas Robinson went bankrupt after he had built up a fleet of about ten new flats. They were sold off and the *India* (1892) and the *Albert* (1891) were bought by Henry Seddon, the salt proprietor of Middlewich. They were clearly too good a bargain to miss because Seddon bought the pair by borrowing from Robinson's liquidators. He sold them, probably at a profit, nine months later to the Northwich Carrying Company, discharging the loan at about the same time.

Some flatowners did turn themselves into limited companies and one, T. J. May, who owned some fine jigger flats, resorted to the device of the single ship limited company. This was commonly used by larger Liverpool shipping companies. It was partly a fund-raising device but more importantly it gave the managing owners first call on the revenue and limited their liability to an absolute minimum. T. J. May's fleet included the Gladys Flat Company, the Pilot Flat Company, the Progress Flat Company and so on – all single flat limited companies.

Falk's packets and the introduction of tugs led to a gradual concentration of ownership. The numbers of flats also tended to drive down freight rates. There was not the same earning power in 1852 as the early eighteenth-century flats had. There were four hundred flats on the Weaver and according to Poole this was double the requirement. As a result flats could take anything between fifteen and fifty salt

Bridgewater flats and tugs ('little packets') in the basin at the top of the Runcorn flight of locks, about 1900.
Trustees of NMGM

cargoes a year. The average was about thirty four at £10 10s (£10.50) freight money per trip. This had to be split between the flat's owners, who were responsible for repairs, and the master, who had to pay the crew, the dues and the loading and discharging costs. In 1856 the flat *Sprightly* earned her shareholders twenty-two pounds, coasting between the Mersey or the Dee and Barrow with coal at 2s 6d (12p) a ton and iron ore at 3s 9d (19p) a ton. The thirteen shareholders received £1 13s 11d (£1.70) and another £5 10s 9½ (£5.54) was carried over to help cover future repairs. This was fairly typical of the coasting trade generally. The accounts for the Ashburners' schooner *James Postlethwaite* in 1881–86 showed similar freight rates: as low as 1s 10½d (9p) for coal and 2s 6d (12p) for iron ore on the same routes. It should be pointed out that though expenses and earnings were different for vessels with a more complex rig and hull, more crew and more cargo capacity the returns were not dissimilar.

The most detailed surviving set of nineteenth-century flats' accounts is for six flats owned by Worsley Battersby and Company, coal merchants of Liverpool, and covers 1881, 1889 and 1895. Unfortunately 1881 and 1895 are for six months' working and it cannot be assumed that accounts for one six month period were the same as for the next. Moreover, the earnings varied from flat to flat according to the amount of repair costs. The *Avon*, for example, earned her shareholders £71 0s 7d (£71.03) up to June 1889 and only £28 10s 8d (£28.53) to December after paying the repair bills. These could be heavy. The *Elwy*'s account included – apart from routine replacements – an item of fifteen pounds for the 'collision with Shropshire Union flat'. This suggests the flats were not covered by insurance for damage to other owners' flats. The *Clyde*'s bills amounted to £32 10s 11d (£32.55) in December and included over twenty pounds' worth of repairs to the hull. The *Humber* needed a new boat at £8 17s 6d (£8.87), and then there was five per cent commission on earnings which went to the managers. The six flats earned £462 11s 4d (£462.57) for their shareholders for 1889, or £77 1s 10½d (£77.09) per flat and £1 18s 6¼d (£1.93) per share. When the fleet was valued for sale in 1896 the average value of a share was £3 8s 6d (£3.42). Earnings were steadily decreasing. Taking the *Clyde* as the average, in January–June 1881 she earned £135 1s 5d (£135.07), over the same period in 1889 £72 18s 8d (£72.93) and from July to December 1895 £41 6s 8d (£41.33). Worsley Battersby's decision to sell was not an isolated one. I have already mentioned Thomas Robinson's bankruptcy in 1896 and there was also the formation of the Liverpool Lighterage Co. Ltd in the same year. This company consolidated many of the small flatowners. By 1914 it controlled about 150 flats and packets. The instigators were the Mack family who also had interests in floating grain elevators, the Alexandra Towing Company and the Belfast & Mersey Steamship Company.

Pride of ownership: the wife of the owner launches the Ruth Bate *at Abels' yard, Runcorn, in 1953. Jack Abel, the owner of the yard is on the left. Note the carved diamonds on the bow. The tug in the background is the former Bridgewater 'little packet'* Dovedale. *Abels' had converted her into a smart motor tug.*
J. Abel

There was still scope for small firms in spite of this giant and the big canal company fleets. There were about thirty businesses operating flats in 1910 – mostly family firms such as Cooper's at Widnes, Abels' and Bate's of Runcorn and Burton's at Bromborough. There were even a few Number One family-owned boats still working up to the nineteen-twenties. Richard Hart, for example, remembered the Birch family of West Bank as Number One owners. There were also Number Ones among the coastal flats. John Sutton and Ralph Ashton, owners of the *Protection* and the *Sarah Lathom* could be considered Number One owners. It seems each one of them had a staple. With Abels' it was the grain contract for North Shore Mills at Bootle and for Burton's it was raw sugar for the Sankey Sugar Company The Liverpool Lighter & Barge Owners' Association was probably formed about the beginning of this century. Like its Weaver predecessor it presented a united front to shippers and agreed rates and conditions for carrying specific cargoes between its members. In the nineteen-twenties there was a minimum rate of eighteen pounds per flat from Liverpool to Manchester, for example. It would seem that there was at least an informal agreement about sharing available traffic too. Jack Abel, the last general manager of Abels', considered the rivalry was friendly and firms would try to help each other out in emergencies. George Wharton, marine superintendent of Cooper's, their competitors in the sand business felt the same. The association was run by T. H. Burton, who was also head of Burton's, the flatowners. He was both secretary and treasurer and claimed thirty-three member firms in 1929, with five-hundred barges – including a hundred powered craft – and two thousand men. By the nineteen-fifties this had declined to about eight firms, according to Jack Abel.

By the nineteen-twenties there were no more than about twenty flats under sail and they worked coastwise or out of Widnes. Their rigging was regarded as an encumbrance in dock, fouling steamers' mooring ropes. But there were still a large number of dumb flats, many of them ex-sailing flats, afloat. A. V. Hallwood the manager of Liverpool Lighterage – who contributed information for the article on flats in the Liverpool Museum's guide of 1935 – estimated there were 189 including forty-one built before 1860. There were not many replacements; Abels' and Burton's built a few new dumb flats and the flatowners gradually became barge or lighter owners. Business was much affected by the world trade depression in the nineteen-thirties and even the Salt Union put its packets into general lighterage to keep them in work. George Wharton blamed road haulage competition for Cooper's loss of lighterage business: 'and by the time the war started we weren't doing any lighterage at all. Just sand.' But the Second World War revived demand, which included a huge requirement for sand bags and ballast. Flats, however, were being scrapped at an increasing rate, to the point by 1960 that very few wooden flats were left working.

The prospects for the future were not good. Old traffics began to be cut off: the Sankey Sugar Company's decision to use road haulage put Burton's into liquidation in 1959. The closure of mills at Liverpool, Ellesmere Port and elsewhere as part of a reorganization of the milling industry meant further loss. Cooper's and Abels' continued to prosper because they both had thriving sand and gravel businesses. Cooper's suffered a major blow when Pilkington's changed from traditional plate glassmaking, which needed sand for polishing, to their new technique of float glass. But they diversified into producing ready mixed concrete and were taken over by Ready-Mix Ltd in the mid-nineteen-sixties. Abels' went the same way, being taken over by the large aggregates group Hoveringham Gravels. The Bishop's Wharf Carrying Company, established in 1870, specialized in traffic for Warrington. By the nineteen-sixties its two main cargoes were wood pulp in bales for Thames Board Mills and grain for the North-West Farmers Company, and they were taken over by Rea's, who shared the Thames Board Mills traffic. The once great Liverpool Lighterage Company had declined. By 1969 their fleet amounted to thirty barges, five packets and a steam tug of 1913. Many of them were reaching the end of their useful life. In 1971 the company was wound up. The repair yard at Northwich was closed and some of the fleet scrapped.

What was left was taken over by a new company, Bulk Cargo Handling Services, a subsidiary of the Alexandra Towing Company.

The canal proprietors and the manufacturers and mine owners were the biggest flatowners in the nineteenth century. The Salt Union and the Brunner Mond fleets of packets have already been mentioned. Coalowners such as the Clares and Bromilow at St Helens owned an above average number of flats, a dozen or more, and there seems to have been larger colliery-owned fleets on the Leeds & Liverpool. The biggest was the Wigan Coal & Iron Company, which ran to over a hundred. Some companies only needed a single vessel or so to maintain the business. Seddon's, the salt producers, had a packet, a dumb flat, narrow boats and coasters; Crosfield's and Gossage's, both soapmakers, and Griffith's, the millers, all owned small numbers. The canal companies varied. The Weaver trustees did not involve themselves with carrying, except for two of the first proprietors. The Leeds & Liverpool operated boats for general cargo, sold them in 1850 and then bought them back in 1874. The Rochdale also bought its way into carrying in 1888. The Canals Acts of 1845 and 1847 encouraged canal proprietors to enter carrying and gave them powers to borrow money to buy boats and run carrying services. The Duke of Bridgewater as a private individual needed no such sanction and he retained a tight monopoly on the Liverpool–Manchester traffic. Although bye-traders were allowed more scope after his death in 1803, the Bridgewater fleet expanded and dominated the valuable general cargo traffic.

This seems to be common to the other canal company fleets. This was the most valuable traffic and all companies invested not only in vessels but in depots to accept cargoes. Such investment was on a scale that could not be matched by an individual private owner although there were a number of 'Union' companies – consortia – in the early nineteenth century to compete with the canal proprietors on both the Bridgewater and the Leeds & Liverpool. In 1803 the Bridgewater owned sixty flats, rising to ninety-three in 1837 and 243 in 1888. It also owned lighters, narrow boats, 'coal boats', floats and tugs. The level of traffic peaked in the eighteen-eighties and the flats were split between different businesses and managed separately. So, in 1881, there were 115 Manchester flats, forty-nine Runcorn, forty Liverpool and Birkenhead and eleven Anderton. In 1885 the supporters of the Manchester Ship Canal finally succeeded in getting their Act through parliament. Under its terms, the Bridgewater Navigation Company, including the Mersey & Irwell, was vested in the Ship Canal Company from August 1887. The navigation company was reconstituted as the Bridgewater Department to manage the carrying. The volume of work was sustained for the rest of the eighteen-eighties. The ship canal was opened to Manchester in 1894 and this meant that much of the valuable Liverpool transshipment traffic was lost. Deep-sea ships could sail direct to Manchester, but this in turn meant there was an increase in

local lighterage around Manchester docks. This did not pay as well and the long term result was a gradual rundown of the fleet. There was very little new tonnage added: a new flat in 1889, three second-hand ones in 1895 and six large lighters between 1894 and 1897 – including two steel ones of six hundred tons capacity each.

The actual amount carried rose from 696,000 tons in 1892 to 857,000 tons in 1896, but the rise was due to the increased Manchester docks short haul work. By 1913 it was almost half the total of 831,000 tons. Only three more wooden flats were added and by 1918 the fleet had dropped to 181 flats. Old worn-out flats were discarded or converted for use as derrick barges to transship cargo over the sides of deep sea ships. The Big Pool at the Sprinch Yard became a graveyard of old flats. By 1928 no fewer than seventy-four were abandoned there. The working fleet was halved to 109 with only eighty-two permanently manned. The remainder were manned as needed, which did not help their condition. In 1928 there was a proposal to build replacements but the state of trade did not allow the investment and the wooden flats were the mainstay until supplemented by concrete barges from the Ministry of War in the Second World War. Only twenty-eight wooden 'Dukers' were left by 1947, only two of them less than fifty years old. They were replaced by a modern fleet of six motor and nineteen dumb barges and three tugs. These were devoted chiefly to the Kellogg's traffic and from the early nineteen-fifties used the ship canal except for the last three miles to Stretford. The last barge sailed on 29th March 1974; a few units were transferred to the maintenance department and the remainder were sold or broken up.

The Shropshire Union fleet, which was probably the second largest, stood at seventy-six in 1870 and had increased to a peak of 116 in 1889. This was followed by a decline which eventually led to a loss of £150,000 in 1921. This loss, plus rising costs, the effects of the war and the eight-hour-day legislation led to the decision to cease all carrying immediately with a loss of a thousand jobs. The Leeds & Liverpool and the Rochdale also sold off their fleets in the same year. The Leeds & Liverpool was still used for general merchandise carrying by three main private firms: John Hunt & Sons, Benjamin C. Wallis and Lancashire Canal Transport. In 1929 LCT were in financial difficulty and the canal company put up the majority stake in a new company, Canal Transport Ltd, which incorporated these three firms. The Liverpool Warehousing Company also took a share because they were the agents for the new company at Liverpool. New steel and wooden boats were bought by the canal company and sold to the new firm on a hire purchase basis. But this modernization did not stem the continuing drift to road transport. In spite of the efforts of Canal Transport Ltd to publicize their services by advertising, issuing handbooks and articles, the last through workings for merchandise as against coal were in 1960 under British Waterways. Coal carriers such

Opposite page: *Some canal companies, such as the Bridgewater, owned a large fleet of flats. Theirs was taken over by the Manchester Ship Canal Company. The* MSC Trafford, *which is clearly of similar design to the* Daresbury, *survived into the nineteen-fifties as a derrick barge.*
E. W. Paget-Tomlinson

147

as John Parke & Sons and Ainscough's the millers of Parbold and Burscough kept some traffic going to and from Liverpool until about 1962. Parke's fleet was subsequently bought by British Waterways and scrapped.

The consolidation of flats into larger fleets from the mid-nineteenth century meant that there had to be a degree of organization and shoreside back-up. The *Sprightly*'s owner-master-manager of the eighteen-fifties only needed a cheap notebook. A limited company needed printed, audited annual accounts. Each had a repair yard and most companies maintained an office in the centre of Liverpool because it was essential to be in close touch with the major customers such as the deep-sea liner companies and the grain millers. There might be smaller offices in the docks, with office runners who would tour the loading berths checking where flats were needed. The office staffs were small compared to those of the great shipowners. Abels' had twelve office staff in their heyday plus a hundred flatmen and twenty at their Runcorn yard. Cooper's, who owned a similar-sized fleet, had a total of nine office staff, three in the shipping department, two in the secretary's and four in accounts. The fleets of the larger companies such as Rea's, Spiller's and Rank's were managed by small semi-independent shipping or lighterage departments. Hours could be long according to need, and the management fairly dictatorial. When he left school George Wharton was told by Mr. Cooper that he was going to work in Cooper's office whether he liked it or not. George had wanted to follow his father and go on the boats:

> 'Why don't you want to work in the office?'
> 'I don't want to, it's like going back to school.'
> 'Well', he said. 'One reason is as good as another. It's Friday isn't it?'
> 'Yes, Sir.'
> 'Monday morning you start at the office at 9 o'clock. Get your clothes on, collar and tie, part your hair and you report at 9 o'clock. There's no argument.' He swung on his heel and walked away and I duly reported at 9 o'clock.

George got on well in the office and his love of the boats was partly satisfied by being put in charge of the *Duke of Northumberland* for the trip to Ditton Brook. He recalled:

> I was running the craft just going on eighteen. Yes, I arranged the loadings at the Bank. I kept liaison with Pilkington Brothers as to their requirements. I also arranged craft for lighterage and saw they were towed down by some means or other either by our own craft or somebody else's to Liverpool where they were loaded.

On the whole, the shoreside staff showed great loyalty over many years to their managers. There was also a pride in owning vessels, however humble. Most flats were named and not numbered, except on the Leeds & Liverpool. Most had a launching ceremony. Distinctive colour schemes and insignia contributed to a 'corporate identity' and some firms also went in for naming schemes. The Bridgewater department had 'meres', John Parke the 'O' suffix. Bishop's Wharf had the prefix 'Bishop's' and Ainscough's flats were named after their Shire horses. All the Abels' flats' names ended in 'Dale', but the dale had to be a genuine one. Cooper's, Abbott's, Burton's and Bate's added a Christian name to their surname. This was an echo of the old eighteenth-century flat names which had a high proportion of female christian names – *Olive, Mary, Nancy* and so on. There is a little evidence of commissioning ship portraits or models and of 'marketing campaigns'. I know of only two ship portraits of flats. One, which is in a private collection, shows three flats, the *George B*, the *Rose C* and the *Duchess*, owned by Thomas Thompson of 16 South Castle Street, Liverpool, the second is of the jigger flat *Petrel* built at Northwich in 1873 and owned by Liverpool Lighterage. Both pictures are by the local marine watercolourist Gilbert Stevens. There is also the Herculaneum Pottery's commemorative pitcher with the *Phebe* on it. Liverpool Lighterage had two models in its office at Liverpool, but these had been made by the manager, Mr Hallwood, who took a great interest in the boats and their past. Advertising was used sparingly, usually in trade directories.

The flatowner's social status varied from the aristocratic Duke of Bridgewater to the single owner. Even the latter had a standing in his own community because he owned his flat. Latter-day principals of the family firms were clearly 'comfortable', as can be seen from their home addresses and they had sufficient time to take an interest in community affairs. Henry Bloor, managing director of Liverpool Lighterage and chairman of the owner's association was a JP and a Liverpool alderman; T. H. Burton was a county councillor. Others, like the remarkable Joe Monks of Bank Quay – flatman, flatowner and then steamship owner – helped in the running of their local church or chapel.

The Flatmen 9

Flats normally carried a two-man crew of master and mate and sometimes a boy who was learning the job. Steam packets had the 'shovel-engineer' to tend the boiler and engine. There had to be an extra hand for coastal work and a 'Barrow flat' with her additional size and number of sails might carry five or six. In 1800, when there were at least three hundred flats, there must have been more than six hundred flatmen and this figure grew to thousands by the middle of the nineteenth century. There were four hundred flats on the Weaver, which meant at least eight hundred flatmen and indeed as early as 1817 it was claimed that the flats supported about five thousand people. In 1889 the *Liverpool Courier* estimated there were 1,500 flats with between three thousand and four thousand flatmen. By 1916 the *Liverpool Handbook of Employment* gave precise figures: twenty-one boys, fourteen women and 755 men; by the mid-nineteen-fifties this had declined to about 350, according to the Liverpool Health Inspector's reports. Sailing flats tended to be a traditional family calling. The 1916 handbook emphasized that recruitment depended very much on having a relative or knowing somebody who worked on flats. At that time at the beginning of this century a high proportion of the flatmen were drawn from Widnes West Bank, Sankey Bridges, Runcorn, Northwich and Winsford. Some families had three generations afloat. The Houghs, Athertons, Bowdens and Hulses of Winsford and the Crosses, Rogersons and Muskers of Northwich, among others, had ancestors whose names were recorded among the flat skippers in the Quarter Sessions of Cheshire reports on inland vessels between 1795 and 1812. Burscough Bridge was a similar centre for boating families on the Leeds & Liverpool Canal. Runcorn had more of a mix with the Manchester Ship Canal tugs and the coasting schooners. Flatmen were not exclusive but part of the wider community. At West Bank this included chemical workers and the shoreside staff of the docks and the local shipwrights. One family, the Kirbys, for example, were flatmen and river pilots and also owners of a cake shop in Mersey Road. The Browns and the Harts were organizers of the local gala with its races on the shore and its band and dance in the evening. At Bank Quay, the Lees, the Houghs and the Monks were the leading figures in the Working Men's Mission.

In Sankey Bridges the Warburtons remembered the flatmen as respected members of the community, 'never ragged, well dressed in blue melton cloth, with large blue guernseys knitted by their wives'.

Opposite page: *A man and a boy and a lot of sail. The bowler-hatted skipper strains to hold the flat's huge tiller in check. Flats were hard work for their crews.*
Colin Wilkinson Collection

151

Tom Lightfoot characterized the Winsford 'watermen' as a 'non-militant, decent living body of men, many of them fairly religious Church and Chapel goers'. He also emphasized how much pride they took in their boats: 'They were men who were proud of their job. The way those men looked after the boats they were in charge of and worked on would have made anyone think they owned them themselves.' This pride in the flats did not extend everywhere. In Connah's Quay, for example, it was the schooner masters who were at the top. Captain Robert Shaw's father was considered something of a failure because he skippered a flat. This may have applied in Runcorn too. Nevertheless, the flat skippers on the whole took pride in their craft and derived status and kudos from having an independent command. This assertive attitude – of parity with any other captain – is a feature that caught the sharp eye of the American novelist Herman Melville. In *Redburn* in which he tells the story of an up-state farm boy's adventures in an American packet ship he gives a graphic description of Prince's Dock, Liverpool in the early eighteen-forties. He was intrigued by the 'salt-droghers', as he terms them, and their skippers. He was rather patronizing but does make the point that the flatmen – whether Number Ones or employed – were their own men:

> It was diverting to observe the self-importance of the skipper of those diminutive vessels. He would give himself all the airs of an admiral on a three decker's poop and no doubt thought quite as much himself. And why not? What could Caesar want more? Though his craft was none of the largest, it was subject to him.

This pride in being in command and being a flatman was probably a long tradition. Unfortunately, eighteenth-century flatmen have left little or no record. The accounts for the *Liverpool* and the *Expedition* in the seventeen-fifties indicate that the skippers stayed with the same flat but there was a rapid turnover of crews. James Stonehouse's recollections, as recalled in Gomer Williams's *History of the of Liverpool Privateers* (1897) include the mention of one ex-Northwich flatman who was involved in salt smuggling in the estuary before he went to seek his fortune deep sea. It certainly argues for an independence of spirit. Similarly, the Flatmen's Association on the Weaver, founded in 1792 as a friendly society, was prepared to stand up for the rights of its members. The strike of the Mersey & Irwell crews in 1796, when strikes of any kind were uncommon showed the same spirit. The buccaneering attitude of the eighteenth-century salt smuggler can be seen in some of the later escapades of the Widnes flatmen. The wrecks left for breaking up on Tranmere beach were regarded as fair game and salvaging parties would drop down the river in a small boat with muffled rowlocks and with a lantern concealed in a sack to look for portable equipment – cabin lamps, linoleum, rope and the like. Much of the loot was sold to Cooper's at Widnes who often had the salvage

contract from the Dock Board. On one occasion, aboard the *Simbunga*, they found a body lying in the hold which turned out to be a half-inflated diver's suit; but it gave everyone a fright when it was first spotted. Although they were a peaceable crowd and did not fight amongst themselves, flatmen would defend their rights if required. There was always great rivalry between narrow boatmen and flatmen at Chester and fights sometimes broke out on the quayside after closing time. Pogney, the skipper of the *John and William* of Widnes, was a noted wrestler. Richard Hart remembered he was, 'only a little man, but he could cross-buttock a big feller. I remember him being in some do at Canada Dock with some Irishman. He'd been ashore to see the stevedore and some argument had cropped up. The Irishman went for little Pogney . . . and Pogney threw him right over his shoulder flat on to the stones.'

Most flatmen's sons were brought up with the river and boats:

> Course I'd been on it since I was a baby nearly, swam in it, fished in it done everything in it . . . We were brought up near the Cob at West Bank. There was always a buoy in the Cob . . . when we were kids, we used to go across there, stripped off and shouted to the Runcorn kids. . . Going to sea with me dad and in the river was a pleasure. Widnes was alive. All the lads when you was leaving the school they'd all go in the flats and some would drift to the sea.

This was how John Brown recalled his childhood at West Bank. Merseyside Maritime Museum has a child's toy sailing flat – the *Rob* – which must have been fashioned by a flatman for his son to sail and on

The inland flatman took much pride in their horses as well as their boats. These are some of Albert Wood's employees and horses at Castlefields Basin, Manchester.
Trustees of NMGM

153

the North Wales coast there was a well-known children's song. 'Hugh Pugh's flat'. These are just two examples of how a boy's interest in 'going flatting' would be engaged from an early age. Many lads had access to small boats. Richard Hart recalled how he learned to sail in a fishing boat:

> Course I'd been in these little things, these nobbies, with another lad. So, I had the hang of it. I was always playing about with them. I used to go down with a lad whose parents owned one and we used to land at Hale light-house, put ashore with a basket of shrimps, each of us, and we used to sell them, walking on the way home.

They would also go with their fathers at weekends and in the school holidays. George Wharton went with his father in Cooper's packet, the *Pirate*, every Saturday.

Playing on board for the occasional day at weekends and summer holidays was all very well and a good grounding, but the reality of working all the year round and especially in the winter was far less pleasant. Lou Atkin, who left school in 1929, hated the driving rain. He had no oilskins and got soaked even though he had an extra coat on. Captain Shaw's father's flat was once grounded in the Dee in a winter's storm and they spent a freezing night aboard with the flat's

The Atkin family, crew of the Keskadale. *Lou Atkin is on the left, his father in the centre and his brother Frank on the right.*
L. G. Atkin Collection, Trustees of NMGM

154

hull creaking and crashing in the surf. At daylight his father put him ashore for safety. He got into the cock boat and his father paid it out on the barrel line until it reached the shallows. He had to wade ashore and walk several miles in a biting east wind before reaching the shelter and warmth of a relative's house. Lou Atkin recalled:

> The hardest time was with flats, when you towed down loaded from Widnes, the rope, thirty fathoms would be dipping in the water as you was towing down. When it was freezing hard, it would get icicles on it. As soon as you got to the lock it was a case of let go . . . [the tug released the tow rope from her hook] . . . then you had to get it in quick. That was hard times.

Richard Hart also recalled having to beat the frozen canvas of the sails with a boat hook to stow them.

A lad would be expected to work for about five years before he was considered competent to be considered for a mate's job. In the early nineteenth century this stage could be seven years, starting from the age of ten. It would seem that in some cases this was a formal apprenticeship. The Salt Union lads would spend half their time on a dumb flat and half on a packet so that they could handle both kinds. Engineer apprentices served just on the packets. Dick Hart, who had been brought up in a Welsh sailing ketch, the *Ceres*, noted that when United Alkali reduced their fleet in 1929 they gave preference to the men who had been apprenticed with them. There was a great deal to learn, not just in handling the boat but in learning the sights and sounds of the river and the coast. While there was no formal instruction in navigation, the knowledge was passed down by word or mouth, by demonstration and by experience. 'You'd hear the captain shouting, "Can you hear the Dungeon buoy yet?" . . . The next minute you'd hear it and they knew where they were going . . . with time, tide and compass', recalled John Smith.

There were 101 practical wrinkles to navigating the Mersey. 'I asked him about entering Brunswick and he said, "You're all right, you can't hit the bull nose because of the tide. If you meet the tide coming in and if you miss the entrance, the tide will sweep you right out"', remembered John Brown. Fog was the worst hazard but experienced flatmen knew how to manage, as John Brown recalled: 'I studied that much I'd go out in the thick fog out of Eastham channel; I knew all my courses buoy to buoy and tide to tide. I've sat with the anchor, while he's [the skipper] shouting, listening. You get used to the sounds . . . you got to know the river that well.' The acquisition of detailed knowledge of all the landmarks, hazards and a whole gamut of techniques to handle a boat applied to inland boats – for example, shooting a bridge, entering a lock and handling a horse.

The flatmen worked long hours, partly because they were subject to the tides and partly because their wages depended on the number of cargoes delivered. 'It was night and day, night and day and you didn't get overtime, you got paid by the cargo or you didn't get no money', said Richard Hart. The hours tended to mount up because much time was spent while the flat was loaded and discharged and waiting to move. Saturday mornings were worked until after the Second World War. Although the men on the Winsford boats were supposed to be paid on a forty- seven hour week it was easy for those hours to be exceeded, and this was all the more likely with the sailing flats. The longest hours were probably worked on the Leeds & Liverpool when boats worked 'fly' across the Pennines and were kept running continuously except when stopping to pick or deliver goods. The long hours and the harsh conditions were recalled by many flatmen. Lou Atkin felt trapped by family tradition into going on to flats: 'It was the hardest and most soul-destroying job a man could do, but like a great many more I was from a family that had been river men for as long as we could trace our history.' It is easy for the maritime historian to be too nostalgic about this way of life.

Flatmen's wages always seem to have been more than the equivalent ashore. Between 1753 and 1755 the master of the flat *Liverpool* earned 10s 6d (52p) a week, his mate 5s (25p) and the boy 5s. It is difficult to make comparisons because labourers often received payment in kind and were paid by the day. In Lancashire in the mid-eighteenth century this was about 1s 6d (7p) a day. The skipper of the *Expedition* earned a grand total of £2 12s 6d (£2.62) for a month's work, and it is not surprising that flatmen were found with savings which they invested in shares in flats. The settlement of the wages of the flatmen handling the general cargo flats on the Mersey & Irwell in 1796 seems to have been very generous. The Old Quay Company agreed to pay captains 16s (80p) a week, 13s (65p) for mates and 6s (30p) for boys; plus bonuses for prompt delivery and cost of living allowances for wives and families living in Liverpool and Manchester; and on top of that a yearly bounty of £5 for good behaviour and eight annual bounties for the skippers who had done the most trips in the year.

By the eighteen-fifties the Weaver captains were averaging about twenty-two shillings (£1.10) a week after paying the flat's dues and the wages of the crew, and many economized by having members of the family, including their wives, working the boat. They could make even more money in times when there was a strong demand for salt by buying their own salt cargoes and selling them to the Liverpool salt merchants. Theirs was the most prestigious occupation on the Weaver and many owned their own houses and sometimes their own flats. While the independent flatmen were at liberty to employ wives and families to assist them, the larger owners – such as the Bridgewater – discouraged the practice and in 1837 their agent claimed 'besides affording many excuses for depredation, it leads to a system of morals extremely detrimental and therefore not to be considered'. Nevertheless, it flourished as long as there were Number One flats, as Melville recorded in *Redburn*:

> Often I used to watch the tidy good-wife seated at the open little scuttle, like a woman at a cottage door, engaged in knitting socks for her husband or perhaps cutting his hair as he kneeled before her. And once, while marvelling how a couple like this found room to turn in below; I was amazed by a noisy irruption of cherry-cheeked young tars from the scuttle, whence they came rolling forth, like so many curly spaniels from a kennel.

In living memory wives were always left ashore except for the occasional summer trip – other than on the Leeds & Liverpool. Even there most families had a house as well.

By 1890 a skipper's wage had advanced to an average of 30s (£1.50) a week. In August 1890 the skipper of the *Earl* earned 38s 6d (£1.92p) for a ninety-hour week. Griffith Brothers, the Chester millers, paid their crews a basic wage – £1 for the captain, 15s (75p) and 5s (25p) for the mate and the lad plus trip money of 12s, (60p), 7s 6d (37p) and 5s (25p) respectively for a three-day round voyage and tonnage money of 1s 3d (6p) light and 2s 6d (12p) loaded. This system of a basic wage whether the vessel was working, waiting to load

A female helmsman (perhaps a daughter rather than a wife) at the tiller of a Rochdale flat in Liverpool docks about 1890-1900. The flat is tied up rather than under way, but many women did share the hard work on board. Note the flower decoration on the water barrel and on the head of the rudder.
Trustees of NMGM

157

or in dry dock seems to have been universal by then because there were few Number One flats and the flatmen's unions could bargain with the owners for an agreed rate for the job. The flatman was not always as well protected. In February 1853 Griffith Williams had to take out a summons at Caernarfon magistrate's court against Gaskill Johnson, owner and master of the flat *No. I* because the latter 'neglected and refused' to pay the £8 due to Williams for his work as a seaman. Williams won his case and was awarded costs of £1 14s 6d (£1.72). In the nineteen-twenties the Salt Union masters received £2 12s 6d (£2.62) for a forty-seven hour week in a packet and 5s (25p) less in a flat. The mate and the engineer were paid £2 2s 6d and lads would start at 15s (75p,) going up in yearly steps to 26s (£1.30) at the end of their apprenticeship. Overtime was payable at 1s 6d an hour – except for lads – and there was tonnage money. On the other hand, there was no payment for keeping watch on board over a weekend, nor were there any travelling expenses. Some Salt Union men carried bicycles on board so that they could get home to Winsford without paying the rail fare – quite a saving when cargoes were scarce.

The rate of tonnage money seems to have depended on the type of cargo. In the United Alkali flats bulk saltcake paid better than bags. United Alkali also paid sailing money for moving a sailing or dumb flat around the docks without the aid of a tug. That was an extra 7s 6d (37p) a week; overtime was payable at 2s 6d after 5 pm and if the crew helped to discharge the cargo at night docker's rates of pay were applicable. Two trips a week from Widnes to Liverpool secured good pay, as Richard Hart recalled:

> When I went to sea in 1916, deep sea, it was only eight pounds a month, five bob [25p] extra if you were on look-out or in the wheelhouse, quartermaster. When I was mate with Frank Eastham I said this is blinking good . . . five pounds wages . . . When I got to be skipper regular in the *Comet,* I thought I was in the Lord's pocket.

The Second World War advanced wages still more because the flats were kept working round the clock. In the nineteen-fifties, they paid better than many shore jobs. One flatman left school and worked in a butcher's shop for just under three pounds a week but could earn over nine pounds aboard with his tonnage money. Between 1967 and 1970 the wages advanced by some eighty per cent on a reduced week of forty hours. In 1970 this put the weekly basic at eighteen pounds, including a four-pound productivity bonus instead of the traditional tonnage money.

Flatmen took great pride in the appearance of their flats and owners were usually prepared to supply generous amounts of paint, varnish and tar for their upkeep. They strove in particular to keep the cabin neat and tidy. The cabin was entered through a scuttle with a

sliding top and two vertical boards or two doors. Dumb flats and the long boats of the Leeds & Liverpool might have a simple hatch cover. There was an arrangement of three iron bars that could be slid across and locked so that air and light could be admitted to the cabin without allowing unauthorized access. Theft from boats in Liverpool docks was a perennial problem, especially in the mid-nineteenth century. The *Liverpool Mercury* for 2nd January 1855 reported that James Russell, a man of colour, was sent to gaol for two months for attempting to steal a quantity of bedding from the cabin of a flat in George's Dock. This sliding scuttle may have been a fitting of some antiquity. The accounts of the *Success* for 30th November 1765 have an item for piecing (welding) the scuttle bar, which seems to refer to this locking device.

The size of the cabin was small and the exact measurements were recorded in the Canal Boat Acts' registers. In the Runcorn registers, for example, the sailing flat *Comet*'s cabin measured 6 ft high (1.83 m), 6 ft 3 in. (1.9 m) long by 7 ft 5 in. (2.3 m) wide; and Burton's dumb flat the *Amelia*'s cabin was among the smallest – 4 ft 11 in. (1.5 m) high, 6 ft 2 in. (1.88 m) long by 6 ft 1 in. (1.85 m) wide. The cabin lay out was almost standard in flats or canal boats. Whereas sailing and dumb flats had their cabin aft, the packets had their cabin forward and the space might be subdivided to provide a separate sleeping cabin for

Weaver steam packet, cabin looking aft. The engines and boiler occupied all the space in the stern. The crew lived forward. The skipper had a small sleeping cabin off to the right. Like the sailing flat, it had a coal range or stove for heating and cooking, lockers that doubled as seats and a fold-down table.

the captain. The cabin was lit by glass deck lights overhead and a brass oil lamp might be in gimbals so that it stayed upright as the flat rolled or might be kept on the mantelpiece above the stove and put on the table when needed. A cast-iron stove was fitted for heating and cooking. The packets might have a complete range with an oven; but many vessels had a simple cast-iron box with an ashpan below and a bracket on which to lodge the inevitable kettle. Most had some brass as decoration and a brass towel rail above the fire. Flatmen were supplied with coal and oil for heating and lighting but unlike coastal and deep-sea mariners had to supply their own food. A frying pan was also supplied. This was a piece of equipment of long standing. A grate and frying pan were supplied for the *Lancaster* at a cost of 5s 6d (27p) in October 1754. The same account also recorded the supply of a

dozen bottles of ale for the open flatmen. Payments for beer were mentioned several times and this was a tradition that probably died with the growth of ideas on temperance afloat in the mid-nineteenth century. Cooking was inevitably of the bacon, eggs and sausage variety – hot and sustaining on a cold day – backed up by large quantities of tea and tobacco.

Whether it was a flat cabin aft or a packet cabin forward, there was normally a large cupboard for food and crockery flanked by two smaller ones at the opposite end to the stove – its door was hinged along its bottom edge. This dropped down to form the table. Its outer end was supported by an iron rod from the deckhead. There were bunk spaces on either side. The starboard side was traditionally the captain's. On the port there might be two bed spaces. If it was a family boat on the Leeds & Liverpool, the mate would have a bunk in the forward cabin. The bunk spaces had sliding doors and inside them the flats' frames were sheathed in a light boarding, clinker fashion, painted white or a light colour. There might be shelves and space for a suitcase with shore-going clothes. The slats at the bottom of the bunks could all be removed for cleaning. The crew supplied their own mattresses, which were usually the traditional 'donkey's breakfast' type – a large piece of sacking filled with chaff or straw. There were fixed bench seats around the cabin and these had flap tops so that lockers below could be used to store coal and utensils. There was a small door into the hold in the forward bulkhead of an aft cabin. Water was carried in a water cask on deck – except on the packets and the later dumb flats, which had a tank with a tap in the cabin.

The cabin walls were either panelled or made from tongue-and-groove boards. Many were painted in wood grain and varnished. In the Salt Union boats the painting was carried out by the painters of the dockyard, but elsewhere flatmen painted their own cabins. Richard Hart painted pictures of sailing ships on the cabin panelling of his flats – 'I painted them on the panels of the doors of the cabins. I did the *Cutty Sark*, the *Thermopylae* and the *Fiery Cross*' – and special pictures for a skipper he worked with: 'He couldn't eat. He used to booze pretty well. This particular time when he was away, I drew a mutton chop on the panel and a pint of beer on the other with a good top on it. When he came down to the cabin . . . it used to torment him.'

Hart's sailing ship pictures were well known in Widnes, as John Brown recalled 'They'd say, that's Dick Hart's flat. When I was a little kid, I knew which he'd been on with the sailing ships.'

The cabin was cleaned twice a week when the crew were on board and this meant scrubbing the deck and panelling, washing out the food locker and less often scrubbing out the bunk spaces. This helped prevent vermin and kept the health authorities happy. The 1877 and 1884 Canal Boats Acts included flats and under their terms inspectors were appointed by the local authorities to check and license all boats under their registration. In some cases the inspector's report could ensure that the owners carried out repairs. For example, if the crew complained about a leaking deck and the owners ignored it, the inspector could force them to carry out the work. The memories of flatmen of the recent past suggest that on the whole flats' cabins were well looked after. The Liverpool inspector's reports for the nineteen-fifties still contained instances of defects. In 1954 there were sixteen reports which were mainly of leaking decks and skylights or no certificates. One flat, the *William Sutcliffe*, was condemned as unfit for habitation. Two years later the *Gladys* and the *George Burton*'s cabins were also considered poor, but their crews were given a subsistence allowance and did not have to sleep on board.

Going back before the recent past and the canal boat inspectors, it is difficult to discover how good or how bad the flatmen's accommodation was. Melville waxed very lyrical:

> These craft have each a little cabin, the prettiest, charmingest, most delightful little dog-hole in the world; not much bigger than an old fashioned alcove for a bed. It is lighted by little round glasses placed in the dock; so that to the insider, the ceiling is like a small firmament twinkling with astral radiations. Upon one occasion, I had the curiosity to go on board a salt-drogher and fall into conversation with its skipper, a bachelor who kept house alone. I found him a very sociable, comfortable old fellow who had an eye to having things cozy around him. It was in the evening; and he invited me down into his sanctum to supper and there we sat together like a couple in a box at an oyster cellar.

But not everybody considered that flats' cabins were so inviting. The seamen's missionary described the canal boats in 1860 as 'not only dirty but filthy' and as for the 'Wigan boats', he was amazed at the mixture of 'ignorance, kindness, dirt, attention and sin'. The flatmen, along with other canal boat people, were characterized as being in poor spiritual and physical condition. Outside observers expressed great fear about 'immorality' because of heavy drinking and women living on board. No doubt there were those who lived a less than respectable way of life. The Warburtons remembered one occasion when a Bishop's Wharf flat sank in the Mersey in the centre of Warrington and a young woman who should not have been on board had to be rescued along with the crew. At Christmas 1840 Captain Thomas Wignett of the Liverpool flat *Jenny* drowned in the River Seiont at Caernarfon. After drinking in the Stone Lion in the company of a local prostitute known as Shany Caemawr, he repaired with her to the *Jenny*. Unfortunately Shany missed her footing on the plank and fell into the river. Wignett also fell into the water in trying to save her and was drowned. Shany was rescued by a passing seaman. Wignett's body was eventually recovered and buried in the local churchyard.

Harry Hanson showed in his *The Canal Boatmen 1760–1914* (1975) that the death rate for canal boatmen and bargemen nationally was above the average, but that the gap between the waterway workers and the rest of the population narrowed in the second half of the nineteenth century. This was in line with a national improvement which could be attributed to improvements in standards of living and hygiene and a decline in heavy drinking. Flatmen may have been better off at that time because many did not live on board their vessels all the time.

The other criticism that was levelled aginst the flatmen in the mid-nineteenth century was their ignorance of the Christian religion, and there was particular anxiety about the religious education of their children. Working on Sundays was normal until the eighteen-thirties and eighteen-forties. According to a report in *Gore's Advertiser* for 3rd September 1834, the Mersey & Irwell, which always seemed to have had a more conscientious attitude to its employees, agreed to suspend Sunday work. Mr Lingard, their manager, was presented with an inscribed silver tea and coffee service by the flatmen in thanks for supporting their case. In 1841 the Weaver trustees paid for the building and upkeep of three large churches for flatmen at Weston Point, Northwich and Winsford. They stopped all Sunday working on their waterway and imposed a five-pound penalty for breaking this ban. They also established three schools for the flatmen's children and charged a penny a week per child to help pay their teachers. There was a flatmen's bethel and reading room near Manchester Dock, Liverpool. The Mersey Mission to Seamen set up mission rooms at Ellesmere Port and Runcorn in 1879 and later at Burscough on the Leeds & Liverpool. The first one was a hayloft above a shop at Crabtree Lane. This became too small and a corrugated iron mission hall was built at New Lane (in competition with four beer houses) in 1905. At Chester there is a similar hall near the Shropshire Union's maintenance yard in Whipcord Lane which was intended to attract the local watermen.

As was the case for most of the nineteenth-century working population there was no provision for a flatman's old age or for his being put out of work by an accident on board. He had to continue working as long as he could, depend on his sons or daughters or go to the workhouse. The flatmen witnesses in a 1827 court case about the waters of the upper Mersey included two men who were both in their seventies and still at work. Some flatmen were in benefit or provident societies which provided some support when they were sick and unable to work. The Weaver Flatmen's Association probably undertook this task, and at Ellesmere Port Thomas Harper had been paid by the 'Provident Society' from 1898 to 1900 when he was suffering from chronic asthma. In 1900 his employers, the Shropshire Union, agreed to pay him a retirement gratuity of twenty-five pounds and he also

received 2s 6d (12p) a week pension from 'The Flatmen's Club'. This club seems to have been a friendly society based on Ellesmere Port, and there may have been similar clubs at Liverpool and on the Weaver. By the end of the nineteenth century the large fleet owners seem to have been more ready to help their flatmen in times of sickness and old age. This may have been fostered by the Employers' Liability Act of 1880, the Workman's Compensation Act of 1897 and possibly by a more enlightened attitude to the welfare of their employees. The Shropshire Union decided to supply their flatmen with greatcoats at a cost of 22s 6d each (£1.12) and in 1891 it was decided that flatmen were eligible to join the Provident and Pension Fund of the London & North Western Railway. Contributors were paid a pension of five shillings (25p) a week on retirement. In August 1900, for example, John Thomas, aged seventy-three, who had fifty-four year's service and William Leverett, sixty-eight with forty-five years' service, were both unable to continue working and were granted pensions.

One of the worst aspects of the flatman's work was caused by the rules and regulations in force at Liverpool docks. The 1802 Act imposed a no fires rule on all ships in the docks. This was rigidly enforced. The docks were always congested with craft and a fire could spread very quickly among the tarred hulls and rigging. Fines of up to ten pounds could be imposed for the worse violations. Even smoking pipes was supposed to be forbidden. It meant that the flatmen were put to the extra expense of going ashore to buy boiling water for their tea and have their food cooked. But what could be worse than a cold cabin? 'No place is pleasanter to a flatman than his own cabin but when the fire is out his best friend is gone. It is all gloom and misery, and he has no longer any comfort in it.' (Mersey Docks & Harbour Board Manager's file on tide-watch on flats) This was not the end of the misery, the by-laws brought in by the Mersey Docks & Harbour Board in 1858 stipulated that any vessel lying in dock should have a shipkeeper on deck two hours before and one hour after high water to be available to alter the mooring ropes. The dockmasters had bells to indicate the beginning and end of tide time and the dock police had powers to summons anyone who failed to keep the tide-watch. This was all very well on large vessels, but there were considerable difficulties on a flat with a crew of two. The rule seems to have gone largely by default until April 1889 when the matter came to a head in Birkenhead. Four hundred flatmen were summonsed and twenty-five cases were heard at the magistrate's court for failing to keep tide-watch. Mr R. B. Moore, who defended the flatmen at the expense of the owners, contended that flats were exempt from the rule because they could not be considered 'vessels'. The case was adjourned on this technical point and it caused a great deal of comment in the local papers. The *Birkenhead Advertiser*'s editorial for 13th April 1889 said:

> Truly a nice point and the question might be asked if a flat floating in a dock, a canal or on a broad river like the Mersey is not a vessel what is it? Then the question might branch off into various directions. For instance, there are steam flats and sailing flats, and canal flats, or barges, that can neither sail nor steam on their account, but to have to be towed, or dragged by horsepower, or pushed ahead or astern by the help of long poles. Are these all 'legal' vessels, or not, and if they are, what sort of vessels – steam vessels, sailing vessels or handy vessels merely?

Mr Moore then argued that as the by-laws were not posted the summonses were not valid. The prosecutions were upheld and the Dock Board continued its campaign because it felt unwatched flats were a danger to other shipping. Individual prosecutions were recorded in subsequent years. On 25th March 1892, William McDougall of the flat *Lord Stanley* was fined half a crown (12p) and another half a crown costs at Liverpool magistrate's court for having no tide-watch in King's Dock. The matter came up again in 1897 when the dock police tried to enforce the tide-watch, even resorting to rowing round the docks to spot offenders. This kind of action led to a petition and deputation to the board's officers from the Liverpool Lightermen's Union, the Mersey Flatmen's Association based at Liverpool, the Weaver Watermen's Association, the Upper Mersey Watermen & Quay Porter's' Association from Runcorn and the

Shropshire Union flatmen. They were supported by the owners. Henry Bloor for Liverpool Lighterage wrote, 'As a rule when flats are moored for the night, they are not required to be disturbed and it seems a hardship because of the infinitesimally small number of cases when anything is required to be done, that all flatmen should be compelled to expose themselves to inclemency of weather for three hours a night.' Bloor also felt the fines were too high and this would result in higher wage demands which the owners could not meet because 'flattage rates are much too low to enable owners to stand any further charges'. Bloor and Anderson, the general secretary of the Mersey Flatmen's Association met the board's officers again and it was eventually agreed that flatmen would not have to keep a tide-watch unless the dockmasters deemed it necessary. The police summonses were withdrawn. The arrangement was for six months and was successful enough to be continued to the end of 1900. The Liverpool Steamship Owners' Association then claimed that they had received too many claims for damage to flats by the members' ships and asked for rule three to be reinstated, and so the matter rumbled on until the rules had to be suspended in 1915 because of the wartime emergency and the lack of men. The original petition contained 353 names; out of that total fifty-three signed with an 'x', showing they could not write.

The existence of many small unions based on separate communities is noteworthy. The Liverpool Lightermen's Union represented the coal flats; the Mersey Flatmen's represented the other Liverpool flats. They were rivals and often had different points of view on the tide-watch problem. J. H. Rea of Rea's called at the Dock Office on 29th November 1900 to plead the case for his men's union (the Lightermen's) being represented. The manager of the Mersey Docks & Harbour Board recorded: 'The Mersey Flatmen's Association was not the only Flatmen's Union inasmuch as their flatmen and those of Nicholson's who were, Mr. Rea stated, a more reasonable body of men than those connected with the Associations named.'

The eighteen-eighties saw a general move to unionization of port workers. The first port-wide strike lasted three weeks in 1879, and there was growing agitation throughout the following decade. The Mersey Flatmen's Association was formed in March 1889 and the Liverpool flatmen went out on strike for three weeks again; curiously enough this was just before the spate of tide-watch prosecutions. The year 1889 seemed to have seen general restiveness among flatmen. On 6th July the sand hookers of Widnes struck because the London & North Western Railway barred them from discharging their sand in Widnes Dock. Twenty-three flats belonging to Cooper's, Hill & Grundy and Clare & Ridgeway and a hundred men were involved. The payment for unloading the sand was a substantial part of their pay. The owners and men met in Cooper's sail room and the owners urged the men to go back to work so that they could persuade the railway company to back down. Eventually they agreed to resume work and appointed a committee of six to go and meet a representative of the railway. The following month there was a strike at Ellesmere Port. This was in support of the crew of the flat *Earl*, who were dismissed because they refused to deliver an urgent order of forty-seven tons of sheet iron to Liverpool on a Saturday afternoon. Three hundred came out as members of the Upper Mersey Watermen & Quay Porter's Association, and they were supported by the district committee of a national umbrella organization known as the National Federal Union of Lightermen, Watermen, Flatmen & Canal Boatmen which claimed a membership of seventeen thousand. There were donations of forty and fifty pounds from the Mersey and the Winsford associations respectively towards the strike fund. There were processions in Ellesmere Port and Chester. In the end the Shropshire Union conceded right of membership of the union but insisted that the men work as needed. All these unions are now fairly shadowy organizations because of lack of records. A memorandum of agreement for round about this period exists. It was drawn up between the Weaver Watermen's Association and the salt proprietors and laid down rates of pay and times of working so that flatmen did not work continuously. This is quoted in full in Brian Didsbury's article on the Cheshire salt-workers in R. Samuel's *Miners, Quarrymen and Saltworkers* (1977). Flatmen also played a part in the 1911 general transport strike on Merseyside which resulted in 'Bloody Sunday' clashes with police and troops on 13th August. What the flatmen's role was is unclear, but their banner was clearly visible amongst the strikers standing in front of St George's Hall, Liverpool.

The flatmen's attitude to their employers and among themselves, apart from the instances cited above seems to have been tolerant. As Tom Lightfoot remarked: 'Most of them were very mild even-tempered men. Taking into account that they almost lived and worked in each other's pockets week in week out, month in month out on those small boats, it was surprising that there were so few arguments.' On the other hand, there was plenty of rivalry between boats, including unofficial races on the river and along the coast. There were also cock-boat races as part of the Winsford gala. There were occasional rowing races at Warrington too; some of the participants, such as Samuel Lee, were definitely flatmen. At Widnes flatmen sailed in the races of the local yacht and boat club. John Brown's father was a frequent winner and was almost barred from races. Sometimes his winning was through cunning as well as skill. Richard Hart recalled:

> I was on a tack through the bridge [Runcorn railway bridge], got to the Slag [Bank] below the bridge, another short tack and a longer reach. When we got below Hale lighthouse, I told one of the lads to take the tiller and I went to have my dinner. His father was under the lee of me in a smart little vessel called the *Robert* and he said "I'll report you, you are not

supposed to change helmsman, you know." I said, "What about my dinner?" He said, "Give me a piece then", and so he had to close haul to come up to me and I passed him a piece of this and through messing about like that, I comes about, I was jiggered and I hit the bank and that's how your father won the race.

Flatmen were always playing tricks on each other. A favourite one was to use a catapult to hit the cabin chimney. This sent a shower of dust down into the cabin. There were many nicknames: my own favourites are 'Scriking Ned', so called because of his high-pitched voice and 'Dump Nixon, also known as 'God's hammer' because of the noise his wooden leg made on deck.

In dock at Liverpool when staying aboard overnight, they would get together in one of the cabins for a yarn and a smoke or a game of cards or to read. They liked to build up a good 'fug'. There was not much drinking although there were recognized flatmen's pubs, such as the Round House in Widnes and the Sloop at Sankey Bridges. Much of the talk revolved around the flats, both past and present. All flatmen took a pride in their calling and their vessels. One, John Leigh, even took it with him to the grave; his tombstone reads:

This grave is not to be disturbed after the interment of John Leigh.

The old Quay Flats was my delight;
I sailed in them both day and night.
God bless the Masters, and the Clerks,
The Packet people, and Flatmen too,
Horse drivers, and all their crew,
Our sails are set to Liverpool;
We must get under way
Discharge our cargo, safe and sound,
In Manchester Bay.
Now all hands, when you go home,
Neither fret any, nor mourn;
Serve the Lord where'er you go,
Let the wind blow high or low.

This stone and grave is free gift of John Yates, Mariner, Captain of the Old Quay Packet. God Bless all British sailors, Admiral Nelson and all the English Fleet.

Upper Mersey lightship
Arthur Sinclair *(1901),*
was purpose built along the
lines of a flat and was
moored off Ditton on the
north bank. The chimneys
of one of the Widnes
chemical works can be seen
in the background.
Trustees of NMGM

Accidents and Disasters   10

Though stormy blasts on Mersey waves
Have tossed me to and fro
In calm repose by God's decrees
I harbour here below
My body now at anchor lies
My soul no more opprest
Has steeled its course
By love divine
And gained the port of rest

This was flatman John Maddock's epitaph at Hale churchyard. His death by drowning on 27th February 1819 is a reminder of just how dangerous the Mersey could be for a sailing vessel, with its treacherous shifting sandbanks, sweeping currents and tides and exposure to gales from the north west. The high loss of life among seafarers in the eighteenth and nineteenth centuries was accepted as an unfortunate but inherent risk of going to sea. In 1764, for example, eighteen ships were stranded at the entrance of the Mersey and seventy-five people drowned. Such tragedies were hardly surprising, for there were no regulations about the condition and loading of shipping and there were few navigational aids or rescue services. Liverpool Bay, the Hoyle Lake anchorage and the Mersey to Liverpool docks were only gradually buoyed and lit. In 1762 the Dock Committee applied for an enabling Act to build four lighthouses to mark each end of the Hoyle Lake and four years later a pilotage service was set up. Charts were published and about 1776 a lifeboat station was established at Formby. Further lighthouses and lifeboat stations were added, charts were improved and in 1813, the first of the lightships was moored at the outer end of the Hoyle Bank. This was a second-hand Dutch galliot, purchased at a cost of £425 and renamed *Good Intent*. But there was nothing on the upper Mersey for the flats delivering cargoes to Runcorn and Ellesmere Port. The Mersey & Irwell had gone to great expense in making new cuts to avoid the worst bends in the river and this included diverting the channel away from the dangerous Hempstone rocks. But below Fiddler's Ferry the main channel was constantly on the move. One year it could be on the south side of the river and the next it might have swung over to the north bank. Besides the changing channel – on which even the Admiralty 'Sailing Directions' declined to offer advice – there was the treacherous north bank; it was very rocky and rocks projected out into the river just above Garston and at Runcorn Gap. A report which accompanied the Bill of 1762 for the lighthouses mentioned the man-made hazards, such as V-shaped stone chevrons projecting into the river to protect the banks and long walls of basketwork fishtraps. According to the collector of Customs, writing in 1785, seagoing ships occasionally tried to sail up to Runcorn or Warrington to deliver cargo but many found it easier to transship into flats at Liverpool:

> Vessels from foreign parts have some years ago delivered iron at Warrington, but the expense of officers and the delay it occasioned were greater than the convenience of landing it there and all goods are now landed here [ie Liverpool] except a few instances of lime stone from Ireland which by special sufferance are allowed to be landed there. Vessels of the burthen of 120 tons have recently discharged clay from Poole and Exeter and flint stones from London at Runcorn; but as it frequently occasioned much delay by missing the channel and grounding on the banks for a whole neap, the masters in general prefer delivering their cargoes here which are afterwards carried up by the flat bottomed vessels.

Silting affected the entrances to the Bridgewater and Mersey & Irwell at Runcorn and the Weaver at Weston Point. The Duke's managers dug a flushing channel to try to keep their entrance clear. Traffic increased in spite of the difficulties and there is evidence by the eighteen-twenties, in a contemporary sketch, of stone markers set up to identify the Bridgewater entrance. In fact, the Bridgewater trustees took on the responsibility for marking the upper estuary. This was because steam towage of flats and coasting vessels and the steam ferries trebled the volume of Runcorn's traffic between 1835 and 1845. In 1838 they erected lighthouses at Hale Head and Ince and by 1859 another one had been installed at Garston. These, together with a light vessel off Speke and forty-three buoys, improved the flats' safety. The old ex-Mersey & Irwell paddle-steamer *Tower* was hired as a buoy tender and survey vessel. In 1867 she was replaced by a new steamer, the *Preston*, built at Brundit's yard at Runcorn. This was built along steam packet lines with a heavy derrick forward for lifting the wooden cooper-made buoys on deck. She also supplied the lighthouses and the lightships. The latter all seem to have been converted flats, such as the *Lyon* and the *Miner*. They were manned by a crew of four, a month at a time, and their lonely life was not without excitement or risk as there were frequent reports of flats colliding with them.

In 1842 the government appointed commissioners to oversee the conservancy of the upper estuary and to ensure that obstructions were not built which would impede the tidal flow. Its condition was vital to the safety of the port of Liverpool as a whole. The capriciousness of the river was frightening and the canal termini were all threatened with being cut off. In 1862 the Woodend channel leading to the entrance of the Sankey became badly silted. The Weston Point approach was also threatened and the following year the Old Quay entrance was causing anxiety. In the eighteen-seventies there was general alarm about the state of the Runcorn approaches. On 31st March 1875 forty-three flats and eleven coasters were reported aground off Runcorn with another thirty-five stranded on the Widnes side. The Bridgewater's superintendent hired fifteen flats to assist with scouring the channel, but by 10th September the situation was as bad if not worse with seventy-three flats, the buoy tender *Preston*, two canal tugs and five coasters off Runcorn Dock entrance and another twenty above the Runcorn railway bridge, aground.

In 1876 the Upper Mersey Navigation Commission was formed to take over responsibility for the lighting and buoyage from the Bridgewater trustees' successor, the Bridgewater Navigation Company, who had declined to continue the service. In addition it took over other navigational work carried on by the Hutchinson Estate at West Bank Dock, the Weaver Commissioners and the Shropshire Union Company – which had its own lighthouse at Ellesmere Port. In all they took over the two lightships, the *Rival* and the *Lyon*, with twenty-eight buoys, four lighthouses – Hale, Ellesmere Port, Ince and Weston Point – landmarks and tide gauges. The *Rival* marked the 'new channel', while the *Lyon* was stationed off Stanlow Point. The *Rival* was equipped with a mast, a lantern containing eight lamps, eight reflectors and two globe lamps, together with a small tender equipped with mast, oars and sails, valued at £432 12s 0d. (£432.60) The *Lyon* had a lantern with only three reflectors and lamps. Lightships and lighthouses were brought in and out of service as the channels changed. In 1877, for example, the Ince lighthouse was extinguished. The Commission chartered and eventually bought the *Preston* in 1885, and she served them well until broken up in 1929. They added more lightships, all of which were converted flats or built along flat lines. They were the *Shamrock*, built at Widnes in 1836 and acquired from the Bridgewater Navigation in 1887, broken up in 1922; the *Vencedora*, built at Northwich in 1875, acquired 1898 and sold to Abels' in 1923 to become the *Littondale*; the *Arthur Sinclair*, built new by Yarwood's in 1901 and sold to William Bate, flatowner, in 1920; and the *G. R. Jebb*, the last vessel built by Clare & Ridgeway – in 1913 – and sold to Abels' in 1922.

The Manchester Ship Canal granted free or reduced price passage to vessels which had hitherto used the upper Mersey channels. This meant a decline in the commission's income and probably accounted for the withdrawal of the lightships. The Commission continued to survey and buoy the channels for the many flats, coasters and schooners using Widnes and the Mersey locks into the Manchester Ship Canal. The access channel to the latter was narrow and often silted. The Ship Canal Company had an obligation to dredge and buoy this from where it left the main upper Mersey channel. This was the cause of some expensive litigation between Brunner Mond, one of

the main users, and the Ship Canal Company in the nineteen-thirties. The Commission continued its work right through to 1971, by which time there was virtually no commercial traffic. Only twenty-nine ships used the channel in 1970. Widnes docks were closed, although there was an occasional vessel brought up to be broken up on the shore outside West Bank Dock, and the Weston Mersey lock closed the same year.

Flats still got into trouble in spite of all the improvements. In 1862, for example, the flat *Peggy* sank and was swallowed by the sand, only to be scoured out four years later to become a danger to navigation. On 3rd and 4th December 1863 no fewer than ten flats were sunk or had run aground in the Mersey in a gale. These included the *Eagle* of Conway, which went aground at the mouth, and the coal flat *Weigher*, which sank off Salisbury Dock entrance. In 1874 the iron schooner *Domitilla* was wrecked and broke her back and the flat *Jackal* collided with her hulk before she could be blown up. H. F. Starkey's *Schooner Port* (1983) notes that between September 1879 and October 1886 the flats *Joseph, Greenland, Elk, Lilac, Willie, Samuel, Eliza, Diamond,*

Supplement (a steam packet) and *Spider* had been sunk between Oglet and Hale. Richard Hart recalled:

> There was one instance we did lose a flat on the river . . . we'd loaded manganese ore at Garston. The tide used to run pretty hard there, on the port side of the lock there were some rocks not covered properly and we got a sheer and we caught them and she leaked. We got her as far as Oglet and hit the bank there'.

Hitting a sandbank could cause a capsize; the great gale of the winter of 1928 is still remembered in Widnes because the sand dredger *Crinkle* capsized and drowned her crew. Her hull was completely swallowed by the sand in two days. Hart recalled, 'I went up with the *Comet* that same day on the afternoon's tide. It was blowing so hard I could practically sail on bare poles.' Heavy laden flats were always at risk for many were loaded until the gunwale was awash. Flats were gauged or measured on the Weaver to stop overloading because if an overloaded flat sank it could block the navigation. In the eighteenth century skippers overloading their flats could be fined up to five pounds. In the sand hookers the water in the hold had to be pumped out quickly, otherwise the flat would not lift off with the tide. Sometimes the flat bottom would create a vacuum with the mud and the flat would fail to rise with the tide. When it became clear that the flat was not going to lift, the flatmen would climb the mast and try to rock the flat to and fro to break the suction. George Wharton's father employed a slightly different method in the steam packet *Pirate*:

> My father had the *Pirate* for many years. . . . He was in Ditton Brook one time with a cargo of tanning extract and when the tide went out she duly sat on the mud and the tide as it always has done came in and she wouldn't move. The suction had got her. Dad said to me 'Go and stand by the windlass forrard and hold on tight." He put a hammer down the front of his trousers and he went up the mast. He got to the top and he gave the truck two or three hefty swipes with the hammer and up came the barge. I didn't know where to go. It shook me but it broke the suction. He came down. He said, 'Now don't forget that. If ever you are in that position you know what to do.'

George also recalled his mother's premonition of an accident to his father's boat:

> I used to go with Dad every Saturday. Wherever his barge was I went with him. Now she was at Birkenhead. The Friday night came, 'What train are you going on in the morning, Dad?'
> 'Six o'clock.'
> 'Can I come?'
> 'Yes'. My mother said, 'You're not going.' Of course there was tears. Now, she'd never objected before. 'You'll get drowned.'
> I wasn't allowed to go and at five o'clock a chappie called at the house that knew the family quite well: 'Mrs Wharton, I've come with bad news . . . Mr Wharton's drowned. George and Edith [that's my sister] have got no father

now . . .' Now we didn't know any different until turned midnight when Dad walked in!

The outer lockgates at Birkenhead had been charged down by a coaster and the *Pirate*'s lines had been snapped; she was carried out into the river and sank. George's father had been able to scramble ashore just before she went. It is not difficult to imagine the agony of the Wharton household when receiving such news – the loss of a loved one and the breadwinner – and the joy of his return. The experience of being brought bad news was all too common for flatmen's and other coastal seafarers' families, even in the early twentieth century. Tow ropes, rigging, anchors, tillers, handling cargo and moving machinery all presented hazards. These would not necessarily cause death, but crippling accidents and lost limbs were not uncommon around the river and the docks and such 'bad luck' could condemn a whole family to poverty.

Flatmen who left their hatches off were also at risk and there must have been quite a few eighteenth century 'open flatts' that were caught out by sudden squalls. It was quite common to leave the hatches off on short trips from one part of the docks to another or from Garston and Birkenhead. Most of them got away with this, but not always. On 11th July 1857 the *Warrington Guardian* carried the following story:

On Tuesday morning between four and five o'clock, the Mersey was again the scene of a mournful and unhappy occurrence. The flat *Samson* with a heavy cargo of salt from Northwich and five people on board was passing from the Canning Basin to the Nelson dock when the weather being very boisterous it is supposed that she shipped water and her cargo became saturated. The Captain, Henry Hill, began to feel alarmed as to the safety of the craft and in a short time afterwards the realisation of his fears became somewhat apparent as the vessel displayed every symptom of going down, not being able to make way against the gale of wind which was then blowing, with her increased weight of burthen. Seeing that all efforts to keep her afloat would doubtless prove ineffective and the imminent peril to all on board, the Captain at once began to avail of what means he had on hand for their safety. No sooner had he jumped into the boat and before anyone else had succeeded in getting clear of the vessel she sank and all with the one exception went down with her. The persons who have perished in this melancholy occurrence are Elizabeth Hill, wife of the captain of the flat; Albert Goss, a young man of 18 years, the captain's assistant; Henry Woodcock aged eight years, nephew of the Captain; and Ann Elizabeth Woodcock, niece of Captain Hill, aged eight years. They were all natives of Northwich. It is stated that on the captain getting into the boat, his wife and the young man Goss were on deck, the other two being in the cabin. The wife of the Captain immediately ran down to the cabin to bring the children up on deck and get them into the boat whilst Goss himself busied himself in procuring an oar and it was just at this moment amidst the terror and confusion that the vessel sank and the poor creatures were launched into eternity.'

As with most flats, the *Samson* was later salvaged and returned to use.

A similar incident was reported to the *Daily Courier* of 26th December 1898, in this Charles Houghton of 21 Ebenezer Street, Rock Ferry; his son Henry, aged ten; and Abraham Houghton, an unspecified relative, were all drowned when their flat *Ann* capsized. William Davies who had helped them move the *Ann* out of dock at Garston, told the coroner:

> It was high water when she went out and they had to hurry to get her into the river. She went out under full sail-mainsail and foresail. The weather looked dirty, but it was not blowing hard when the vessel entered the river. When she got clear, however, a squall came on so suddenly that the men had no time to take in sail and in their hurry to get out of the dock they had no time to batten down the hatches, seventeen in number. The result was that the water washed into the hold and the vessel became waterlogged and tilted over to one side. If the tarpaulin had been battened down over the hatches the water would have run off instead of going into the hold. As to the sails, they had no time to take a reef in when going out of the dock, as they did not want to miss the tide. The vessel tried to reach across the river and when about half way she was caught broadside by the squall and capsized.

A 'Barrow flat' aground, probably in the Dee estuary. This was an accident rather than an intentional grounding on the beach to deliver a cargo.
Trustees of NMGM

The catalogue of tragedies could go on and on, and the same applied to flats in the coastal trade. In *Schooner Port* (1983), H. F. Starkey lists nearly fifty Runcorn flats and schooners that were lost between 1860 and the beginning of this century. The Hoylake lifeboats assisted nine flats between 1895 and 1911 and saved fourteen lives. Some flatmen were not so lucky. The flat *Hecla*, loaded with a heavy cargo of iron ore, went ashore at Llandulas in February 1882. Two of the crew were drowned with only the captain managing to swim the fifty yards to the shore. The worst part of the story was that there was a lifeboat station near the wreck and the lifeboat stayed in its shed.

Some flats were converted into schooners in the eighteen-sixties and the wide hatches and additional sails made these flat schooners more of a risk. Many were lost. The *Kate* was built at Winsford in 1857; in October 1861 she was converted to a schooner for her owners – the three Evans brothers, coal merchants of Haydock; and she was wrecked off Land's End about 1871. The 'Barrow flat' schooners could end up in the casualty lists. The *John Stonard*, built at Ulverston in 1856 and owned in Aberdovey, left her home port on 30th October 1893 with cargo of 131 tons of slate bound for Limerick. She had a crew of four and a master, James Morgan, who held no certificate but had twenty years' experience in coasting vessels. On 6th November at 4 am she was off the Irish coast and had passed Crow Head. The master intended to pass between Dursey Head and the Calf Rock, but he had never made this voyage before and so was ignorant of the Lea Rock lying off Dursey Head. He had only got a small-scale chart on board which did not show the rocks which were just below the surface. By 5.30 am, the ship was in the channel midway between Dursey Head and the Calf when breakers were spotted straight ahead. The vessel was turned hard-a-starboard but struck her port bilge on the rocks and slid off. The pumps were tried but they could not cope with the inrush of water and one stopped working. The master then tried to find somewhere to beach her but the wind was slight and off the land and so the vessel was anchored. The boat was lowered and the ship finally sank at 11 the same morning. Human error as well as pressure of weather could be a major factor in these accidents. Unseen wrecks as well as unseen rocks could be a hazard as well. In October 1875 Clare & Ridgeway's schooner *Mary* hit an unmarked wreck west of Hoylake when bound from Llandulas with limestone for Sankey Bridges. A Widnes-owned schooner was fortunately at hand to rescue the crew and the sails.

Casualties could occur without pressure of weather. The misjudgement of the jigger *Joan* piled her into Canada Dock entrance wall. She smashed her bow and sank immediately. The steam packet *Lord Delamere* regularly carried wheat from Liverpool to Flint for Cobden Mills of Wrexham. She left Liverpool at 10.30 am on 12th October 1913 bound for Connah's Quay and arrived about 2.00 pm off Lannerch-y-mor, anchoring there until the following morning when they picked up the pilot to take them up to Connah's Quay. The tide was on the flood, the weather was fine and there was a light breeze from the south. Records of the subsequent court action reveal that she arrived off the paper mill at Pentre at 9.30 am and was just entering the New Channel leading to Connah's Quay:

> The *Lord Delamere* got a little to the east of the channel and caught the edge of the middle bank, the engines were reversed full speed astern but the flood tide was so strong it would not allow her to come out into the channel but drove her further on. We then tried full speed ahead to try and force her out into the channel but were not successful.

The steamer *Scotsman* tried to tow her off but the five-inch (127 mm) hawser broke and she proceeded on her voyage. 'We decided to do nothing further until the next tide. About 4 hours ebb she commenced to strain and take in water and when the tide made again she filled and remained and the cargo commenced to wash out of her. We were able to salve about thirty tons of the cargo.' The *Lord Delamere* became a total loss, apart from a few fittings, and her hull rapidly sank below the sands of the Dee, leaving only her mast exposed to mark her last resting place.

Collisions were another risk especially in the Mersey with so many large steamers moving at high tide. The famous flat *Daresbury* was run down by a Dock Board steam hopper barge in October 1885. Samuel Mason, the mate, was lost overboard. She left Langton entrance in tow with another flat. Their tug was preparing to pick up some flats from the wall at Sandon when the hopper barge came out of Sandon Basin and hit the *Daresbury* a blow on the starboard side. On 18th March 1943 the tug *Bridgeness* had four flats – the *Albatross, Dog Star, Edith Mary* and *Glittering Star* – loaded with groundnuts from Coburg to Waterloo Dock. It was foggy when they left the Brunswick lock and they proceeded down river cautiously, keeping close to the river wall, the tug sounding her whistle – one long and two short blasts. The fog worsened and immediately there was an answering signal. The tug's skipper spotted a salvage vessel lying at an angle to the river wall and steered out to avoid it. The whistle signals of another vessel were heard and the steam packet *Perso* was seen emerging out of the fog. The tug took avoiding action and the *Perso*, which had not slowed down, struck the bow of the *Albatross*, parting the tow rope and forcing her into the *Dog Star* and the *Edith Mary*. The poor *Albatross* was so badly damaged that she sank shortly afterwards.

More collisions happened at sea. In February 1867 the jigger flat *Ant* was loaded with slates bound from Port Dinorwic, Clare & Ridgeway's builder's yard at Sankey Bridges, when she was hit and sunk by the coaster *Jane* in the 'Wild Roads' at the mouth of the Dee.

A flat stranded on the weir of the River Dee at Chester about 1860–70. The men on board appear to be salvaging her cargo.
Chester City Council, the Grosvenor Museum Collection

Some accidents took place in the docks and on the canals. In September 1753 the collector of Customs reported

a very high tide which forced and broke down a barricade of timber which was fixed to keep the water out of the south dock [Salthouse Dock] while some men were employed to work there and, by the sudden rushing in of the tide, forced and drew in several ships, flatts and boats one upon the other and beat to pieces, oversett and damaged several of them

and there was an incident with the flat *Venus* charging down the lock in 1761 which has been mentioned in chapter eight. On the Sankey the Double lock walls at Blackbrook collapsed on two flats going up to St Helens chemical works in September 1852. The *Warrington Guardian* reported, 'the boats were not swamped but they lie fast embedded and almost loaded with the mass of earth and debris and there they will have to remain until that portion of the canal is again discharged and the necessary work contracted'. In 1866 there was a strange accident on the Sankey: the flat *Arthur* was hit by a railway locomotive. On the evening of 20th November Evans's (the coal-owners of Haydock) flat *Arthur* had to wait for the 6.15 pm passenger train to pass before the railway bridge at Sankey Bridges could be swung. Immediately the train had departed the stationmaster set the signals at danger and proceeded to swing the bridge. The *Arthur* was just passing through when a Great Northern Railway cattle train came up. The driver was unable to stop and his engine ended up on the fore part of the flat. It took some days to lift the engine back on to the rails and to repair the bridge. The damage to the *Arthur* was not recorded.

But for every extraordinary accident there were hundreds of daily hazards which a flatman recognized and avoided. The perils of the Mersey were obvious; what were not so obvious were the hazards of the inland waterways. Take the example of a Salt Union packet plying between Winsford and Liverpool. A packet skipper needed knowledge and prudence even though the trip was less hazardous and laborious than in a sailing flat. There were six locks to the Mersey and also six swing bridges and the fixed bridge at Hartford. Passages could take place at night to suit the tides on the Mersey and locks were manned until 10 pm. In the narrow Winsford reaches there were flats loading the different consignments. It was the custom to whistle two long blasts for going down, one for up river. If the packets met, the skipper would blow one short one to show he was going to go to starboard and two for port. Three meant going astern and four indicated a change of course and were followed by the port or starboard signal. The whistles could also be used to warn swing bridge and lock keepers of an approaching packet. At Vale Royal the abutments of the railway viaduct narrowed the width of the river, which caused an awkward eddy – especially if the river was in flood. The mast had to be lowered to pass under the old stone bridge at Hartford and in the centre of Northwich the rush of water from the tributary River Dane could push the packet sideways. Below the town the river widened out and was shallower. Going into locks called for a fine touch. Too much way and the packet would ram the gates, too little and she would lose steerage. The crew of the towed flats had to be pretty sharp about getting their ropes on to the bollards on the lock wall because this was the only way they could stop. The last lock gave access to the Mersey.

This changed in 1891 when Weston Marsh lock was opened and diverted the flats and packets into the Manchester Ship Canal. Weaver traffic had the option of going down the canal to Eastham locks at reduced dues. Bagged salt up to four hundred tons went free. The packet could also use any one of the three locks giving access to the upper Mersey from the canal free of charge. The ship canal had its hazards. For a start there were ten-thousand-ton cargo liners under tow for Manchester docks. But once out of Eastham the worst of the trip was the Mersey proper, for the river was unforgiving to steam and sail alike. It was no mean task steering a low-powered packet under a dripping canvas dodger into the teeth of a north-west gale. Everything on deck and in the cabin had to be lashed down. If the cock boat was being towed, the line would be paid out so that there was no risk of it bumping into the rudder. Skippers would try to avoid the worst of the tide. On big springs they might wait to lock out at three hours to high water instead of four so that they could make the passage in slacker water. If the packet had a load for the Liverpool South Docks – perhaps for the Elder Dempster Line's West African berth – she had to cross the river, avoiding other vessels, and inch her way up on the incoming tide. If the packet came out on the ebb, the outflowing tide would give her a fair speed. Rounding up to enter one of the dock gates could be tricky, especially the Brunswick entrance where the groynes built to stop silting created an awkward current. Rough weather made life difficult for the helmsmen of the dumb barges too, as Tom Lightfoot recorded in his book *The Weaver Watermen* (1982):

> It can be understood how difficult it must have been to steer a barge in a fairly straight line when it was rolling and pitching about. A tiller, when a barge was in rough water would jerk one way and then the other when the waves hit the rudder, but having a tiller rope on with a couple of turns wound round the end of the tiller would stop it. The man who was steering had to watch his hands and fingers, for he had to make sure he did not get them between the rope and the tiller or it was very painful. A tiller was certainly very dangerous if it was not kept under control, it might sweep across the quarter deck and knock a man flat on the deck, or it could have knocked a man over the side of the boat.

I have no record of flats being damaged or captured by enemy action. None of the jigger flats on the coastal trade was caught by enemy submarines in the First World War, although this befell some of the 'Barrow flats'. Sailing ships were normally stopped and the crew allowed to row clear in the lifeboat while the ship was destroyed by a demolition charge or gunfire. In the Second World War a number of flats were destroyed by enemy bombing in the Liverpool docks. The worst destruction happened when the ammunition ship *Malakand* blew up in Huskisson No 2 Dock, taking several flats with her, on the night of 3rd/4th May 1941. Lighterage was so important in the war campaign that a fleet of concrete barges was drafted in to supplement the existing flats. The flat *Hannah Beckett* was the victim of a peacetime accident. She was blown up by a mine in August 1887. The mine was part of the port defences, which were deployed for training the volunteers of the Submarine Engineers from the New Brighton fort at the mouth of the river.

Flats were sometimes used to assist with the salvage of larger vessels. They could come alongside a stranded ship to help lighten her by taking off cargo, and they were also used as salvage 'camels' or 'lumps' strapped to the hull of damaged ship to provide buoyancy. The Merseyside Maritime Museum has an undated painting of the dismasted ship *Dicky Sam* being towed into port by two tugs and supported by three flats on either side. T. & J. Brocklebank's barque *Valparaiso* ran ashore at Formby Point while leaving Liverpool in February 1845 and was refloated with the aid of flats. Again, a picture was painted to record her salvage. She was supported by five flats with their bows lashed to her sides and towed by three paddle tugs of the Liverpool Steam Tug Company. From another incident ten years later it would seem that the tug company retained 'lump' flats specially for salvage. The brig *Henry and Margaret* of Portmadog was sunk by the mail steamer *Imperadore* off the Formby light on 16th January 1855. The brig was lifted by the lumps and moved to Bootle Bay where she was beached. Her cargo was discharged into the 'lumps'. Once patched and lightened she was towed to Prince's Dock, and she and her cargo were put up for auction.

The salvage of the barque Valparaiso *in 1845 was effected by lashing flats along her hull to give her buoyancy. It took three paddle tugs of the Liverpool Steam Towage Company to bring her in for repairs.*
Sothebys

The Survivors   11

The last sailing flats to work on the river were the *Edward*, the *Comet*, the *George and Ann*, the *Ellen*, the *Olivet* and the *Keskadale* – all 'sand hookers' from Widnes. There were jiggers such as the *Eustace Carey*, *Winifred*, *Santa Rosa*, *Protection*, *Pilot*, *E. K. Muspratt* and *Sarah Lathom*. At Runcorn in the nineteen-twenties George H. Grounds owned the 'Barrow flat' schooners *Fanny Crossfield*, *J. H. Barrow* and *Gauntlet*, together with five other schooners from other builders. Fisher's and Ashburner's of Barrow had sold their fleets before 1914, and there were a few left at Connah's Quay. The *Happy Harry*, *Harvest King*, *J. & M. Garrett*, *Maude*, *Millom Castle*, *Nellie Bywater*, *Emily Barratt* and others survived in the hands of West Country and Irish owners. One by one all succumbed to old age, stress of weather or lack of work. The *Edward*, the *Comet*, the *George and Ann* and the United Alkali jiggers were laid up by their owners at the start of the 'great slump' of the early nineteen-thirties.

I have picked several examples among these last survivors to examine in detail. By good fortune, I was able to meet three men who worked on them, the *Keskadale*, the *Sarah Lathom* and the *Mossdale*. These three between them exemplify the last years of the flats, working on the edges of commerce, scratching a living and not being replaced. Of these only the *Mossdale* survives, preserved at the Boat Museum, Ellesmere Port. She also stands for another feature of the later history of flats. As they disappeared, so interest in them among maritime historians and ship enthusiasts increased; today there is a significant corpus of information about them and some key objects and a few full-size vessels have been saved for posterity.

Lou Atkin started work on the *Keskadale* with his father in 1929, straight from school. He left after only three years because he saw the end was in sight. He started as an apprentice with his father as skipper and one of his brothers, Frank, as mate. The *Keskadale* was employed at that time in carrying sand for the building of Otterspool promenade. The *Keskadale* anchored in Eastham deep on about fifteen fathoms of chain and was loaded by an ex-schooner, cut down to a dumb barge and fitted with a steam grab. Sometimes they were towed across to Otterspool, but nine times out of ten they had to sail. When they arrived they moored to two buoys close to the foundations of the wall and dried out at low water. The sand was discharged by a crane with a ninety-foot (27 m) jib on a platform built out into the river. His father retired about 1937; his eldest brother took the *Keskadale* and later went

Opposite page: *The* Keskadale *loaded with sand and under tow in light winds.*
L. G. Atkin Collection, Trustees of NMGM

185

on to the Salt Union boats. Brother Frank then took over the *Keskadale.*

The *Keskadale* was owned by Abels' and based at Widnes West Dock along with the sailing flats *Ellen* and *George and Ann.* The United Alkali Company still had a few 'mast' flats such as the *Florence,* the *E. K. Muspratt* and the *Eustace Carey.* They never sailed; they were always towed by the company's steamers, such as the *Osmium.* The flatman got extra for sailing the flat from Widnes West Bank to Eastham instead of being towed. They were paid 6½d (3p) a ton for sand and they could carry 150 tons out in one trip. The *Keskadale* was 76 ft (23 m) long, 19 ft (5.8 m) beam, 9ft 6 in. (2.9 m) depth of hold. She could carry 200 tons dead weight. When loaded with sand she was 'deck in'; the scupper holes from the deck were just level with the water, leaving 2½ in. (64 mm) free board in the waist. If there was a big tide, with enough water to cross the bank in time, they would put extra in and would be paddling in water on the deck. They wore no sea boots, but clogs with rubbers round the iron so as not to mark the deck. Lou Atkin used to go barefoot in summer. He was never allowed to run on board in case he marked the deck or made it leak. The *Keskadale*'s original name was *Herbert* and she was built as a jigger flat, Abels' bought her from United Alkali at Flint and rebuilt her about 1920. A thousand feet of oak were put into her. Her mizzen was removed and she continued sailing with a short main boom. The mast was fixed and went through the deck. There were two winches at the foot of the mast. One winch had a greater reduction than the other, and had a bigger square on its shaft which required a bigger handle. *Keskadale* was a good enough sailer, both light and loaded. Light she drew 4 ft (1.2 m), so there was no problem of leeway. She had the finest shape on the river, with a nice counter. The *Ellen* drew 6 ft 6 in. (2 m) loaded and 2 ft 9 in. (884 mm) light, but came straight down at the stern and this caused a lot of resistance and slowed her down. The *Keskadale* could beat the steam packets. If the tide was stronger than the wind, the anchor had to be used to keep her in the channel. This was known as 'springing her in', Lou Atkin recalled:

> There would be between twenty and fifty fathom of chain fleeted on deck ready to let go. The skipper would round her up to the tide; the anchor would be let go. The skipper would then steer her in across the tide, coming across the chain. The chain would be leading back to it practically, and she would spring head to it. You would heave the chain off the bottom. As soon as it got off the bottom. She would spring then, and could do this for anything up to half a mile, going right across the river to the hopper barge off Bromborough.

Widnes West Dock was difficult to enter because of the tidal eddies setting off the bull-nose. They would round her up off the Slag Bank at Ditton; with her head to the bank there was a good chance of being swept down on to Runcorn railway bridge. They dropped the anchor and dropped down stern first to the lock. Lou Atkin went on: 'The gateman took your stern rope for sixpence a time. Then you swum her round to go through the lock. The sails had to be made and the lad's job was to scull the small boat across the dock in case it got smashed by her stern. Then we laid out the barrel line and started heaving her in.' The barrel line could be worked through snatch blocks on the stem. If there was not too much tide it was possible to move a flat on the kedge anchor and the barrel line. The barrel held about 120 fathom of line. All flatmen were on piecework and they had to go out whatever the weather. Flats could be awkward to steer, especially under sail. When some of them got a bit of way on them it was impossible to push the tiller. The rudder was huge, about eight feet (2.4 m) long at its base with twelve-inch (305 mm) by twelve-inch reinforcing pieces. *Keskadale* was fitted with a double tiller rope. One end was made fast to the tiller, then stretched across the deck to a sheave in the rail, then back across the deck to another sheave in the rail on the other side, then back to the tiller. Some flats' tillers would scarcely move six inches (152 mm) in either direction. Sand was loaded by a two and a half ton grab and was usually half sand and half water. As Lou Atkin continued:

The dredger men were on piecework and only anxious to load you as quickly as possible. They started by loading sixty tons aft and the biggest load was put around the mast because it carried better and for the sake of stability. The forehold was not loaded. As soon as she was loaded the crew had to pump for up to an hour at a time. There were two old fashioned hand pumps, one at the foot of the mast and one on the after-coaming. They were made of iron; the first five feet from the bilge was narrow, then widened out. Where it widened out, there was a bottom box or clack. The end of the pump went to within an inch of the outer planking. An iron rod – the pump spear with a second valve – also of wood with a hook at the top which connected it with a short lever known as a brake. The brake pivoted on a bracket on the side of the pump.

While sailing the mainsheet was fixed to the headledge. Strips of rubber found in the sand or leather found in the same way were attached to the bottom of the block to stop it chafing the hatch covers. The crew did many jobs like this to save themselves work and on the whole took great care of their craft. A damaged or torn hatch cover would have to be humped across the footbridge on the Runcorn railway bridge to Abels' yard by the side of the Manchester Ship Canal. They never dry-docked flats except for accident damage. Caulking was done by flatmen. A rubber tyre was often fitted on the end of the rudder to prevent chafe or damage to the stem of the cock boat.

Abels' steamboats had yellow and blue bands on their funnels. Abels' flats had blue cabin funnels and blue waterways. They always bought second-hand usually from the Salt Union or United Alkali.

Coopers, their rivals at Widnes, bought Gossage's boats. Flats had a white streak from the stern to the mast. It was not extended beyond the mast because the sails flapping over the side and the sand would have soon worn it away. The cabin was oak grained by Charlie Roe, Abels' sailmaker – a relative of the Atkin family. The cabin had to be maintained in a good condition and free of vermin because there was a cabin inspector based at Runcorn who could stop them sailing if the accommodation were not up to scratch. The Atkin family slept on board for up to a week at a time. The main leisure pastime was playing cards. The week after Lou Atkin left school he started on board on Monday, docked on the Saturday night at Duke's Dock, Liverpool, then caught the last train home to Widnes – the 10.50 pm. He was back again for Sunday morning. Usually if they finished on a Saturday night they started on Monday morning. The forward 'cabin' was used as a store. It contained a lot of fish oil and red ochre for the sails, and plenty of tar. It was very good tar; it dried dull and always remained tacky. The tar worked into your hands. The shiny black varnish that replaced it was never as good.

No compass was carried on the *Keskadale*. On dark or foggy nights the skipper would instruct Lou Atkin to go forward to listen for a particular bell of buoy in the river. It was dead quiet in the river, but the skipper would often spot it first. When it was foggy there was usually no wind; they might lay up for the night off Ditton, on the 'fret' side of the bank. The kedge was put out for getting off the following morning. It was very frustrating to be in sight of West Bank. Being windbound in West Bank Dock was also frustrating. Sometimes they sailed to the company depot at Liverpool through Brunswick entrance if the tug was delayed. The *Keskadale* continued sailing, though she did less and less work under sail and more under tow. Abels' retained her sails until after the Second World War. By then she was worn out. She was broken up in 1948.

Ralph Ashton bought the *Sarah Lathom* in 1947. He had been an engineer in coasters and he wanted his own ship. He could not afford a coaster, so he settled for the *Sarah Lathom*, which cost him £1,500. She had been built by Ferguson & Baird at Connah's Quay in 1903 for Samuel Vickers, a noted local shipowner. She was rigged as a jigger flat and her dimensions were length 80 ft 8 in. (24.6 m), beam 21 ft 5 in. (6.6 m) and depth of hold 8 ft (2.4 m) with a gross tonnage of 77 tons. Before the war she was owned by Thomas Jones of Flint. He fitted her with a new Kromhout engine in 1943. She was sold to a Captain Barnes, who renewed her rigging in 1947 and kept her for about a year. She did not do much sailing so the mizzen sail was taken down and the mizzen boom was used to hoist the cock boat aboard. She also had her bowsprit taken out so that she was more of a motor vessel than a sailing vessel. Unlike other flats, she had a fine teak wheelhouse and wheel steering. Ralph Ashton refitted her and used the sails for about

fifty per cent of her voyaging. The mainsail needed three men to hoist it, and an old Morris Cowley engine was fitted at the foot of the mast to power a winch to hoist it. This could be used for discharging cargo. She was difficult to sail in light conditions, going easily to leeward. She drew 5 ft (1.5 m) light and 9 ft 6 in. (2.9 m) loaded. She was in fact a heavy boat to push along and at best could make 6½ knots under sail. Ralph refitted the mizzen and once the wind became strong he could be reduce her to foresail and mizzen. There was also a square foresail for light weather. The engine was a 2-cylinder hot bulb diesel, 40 horse power, 325 revs a minute. There were two blow lamps to heat the bulbs. These could be very temperamental and it was difficult to restart the engine under way. There was also an air bottle to help with starting, but it took an hour's hard pumping to fill it sufficiently to give two starts. On one occasion while she was on passage to Port Dinorwic to dry dock for a four-year survey, the propeller lost two blades when she caught the mooring chain of a buoy. It seemed to make no difference and the *Sarah Lathom* reached the dock with only one blade left. Ralph bought a replacement cast-iron propeller from Liverpool for seventeen pounds.

It took two men to steer her in heavy weather, especially when she was light. The windlass which went right across the ship was labour intensive as well. It was worked by a pump action and was very slow. There was a dog clutch so that each side could be operated indepen-

The Sarah Lathom *in the Mersey on 2nd March 1948, with a Liverpool–Dublin cross-Channel steamer in the background.* K. Lewis

189

dently. The anchors were heaved on deck by means of a tackle from the main mast and were lashed on deck. She had about forty-five fathoms of chain on each and only dragged her anchors once, in Holyhead harbour, when she collided with a lightship without causing any damage. The master's quarters were below the wheelhouse, and there was a bogie stove with a copper flue that went right through to the wheelhouse and helped to warm it. There was a beautiful mahogany sideboard with brass rails and a half-moon table with a sofa shaped to fit against the aft bulkhead. At the forward end there was a double bunk athwartships raised about six feet (1.8 m) high with lockers below and a ladder to climb up to it. The crew of three lived in the foc's'le forward. This was simply fitted with three bunks and a coal stove for heating and cooking. The crew were expected to provide their own food, but the skipper or his wife usually supplemented their supplies.

Crews were very difficult to recruit. At best he had a mate, two boys and his wife Mary and no engineer. The oddest crew member was 'Sparks'. He had been a radio officer and was from a wealthy Birmingham family. But he chose to live rough, sleeping under an upturned boat at Connah's Quay and catching his fish from a borrowed boat. He had long hair and a beard down to his waist and wore a shirt and trousers and no shoes, summer and winter. He was very tough and strong and would think nothing of swimming with a line to a mooring buoy in the middle of winter. He was adept at repairing machinery and devised an ingenious bilge pump which worked off the propeller shaft. Unfortunately, Sparks was totally unpredictable and on occasions would run up the mast for no good reason. His lack of washing and squalid eating habits made the fo'c'sle uninhabitable for the rest of the crew and so Ralph had to sack him.

The *Sarah Lathom* traded mainly between Connah's Quay, Anglesey, the Isle of Man and the Mersey. Ganister rock, which was loaded at Holyhead, was an important cargo. It was shot into her hold in ten-ton loads, with the ship being moved along the quay to trim the cargo. It was heavy cargo and the shock of those ten-ton loads was not good for her timbers. She also carried a lot of scrap iron, bricks, tiles, clay and firebricks. On 18th July 1948 she left Connah's Quay with 148 tons of bricks for Belfast. A few hours out, she met a heavy summer gale and started to make water. The bricks absorbed a great deal of water, the two 'Deluge' pumps could not cope and the engine was put out of action. She struggled as far as Langness Point on the Isle of Man in the early hours of 19th July and anchored, and the skipper, his wife and crew were taken off by the Port St Mary lifeboat. The poor old *Sarah Lathom* – the last sailing jigger flat – sank later that morning in twenty-four fathoms of water. This still left the *Protection* at work carrying stone on the River Severn, but she was no more than a motor barge without masts or sails.

The *Keskadale* and the *Sarah Lathom* did not survive long enough to be considered for preservation, and it was only ten years after their demise that one senses there was a growing awareness of the urgent need to record the last of the flats and flatmen. Very little had been written about them. There were three pages in Liverpool Museum's guide to the shipping collection of 1935 about the museum's three model flats, the *Avon*, *Elizabeth* and *Pilot*; a brief mention in Frank Carr's *Sailing Barges*, the Science Museum's *British Fishing Boat and Coastal Craft* catalogue (1952) and two articles in *Sea Breezes* in 1948 and 1949. By 1956 Kenneth Rathbone, a journalist, had discovered the eighteenth-century flat *Daresbury* laid up as a derrick barge at Northwich. He made strenuous but unsuccessful efforts to persuade British Waterways to preserve her and carried out a measured survey and detailed research into her history. This marked the beginning of a growing interest in flats: more articles and a small book by Edward Paget-Tomlinson in 1973 were written. Unfortunately there were no sailing flats in good enough condition to act as a focus for a preservation group. The Thames barges survived long enough to be considered, as did the Norfolk wherry *Albion*. Dr Frank Howard spent many muddy hours in the late nineteen-sixties and the nineteen-seventies crawling around the *Bedale* at Runcorn and the hulks in Widnes West Bank Dock, photographing and measuring in great detail. The results were two detailed sets of plans of flats and two superb models: one of the *Bedale*, which filled a major gap in the Science Museum's collection, and a second one of a sailing flat based on the lines of the *Sir R. Peel* at Widnes for the Boat Museum. William Salisbury, a fellow-researcher who was an expert on the construction and design of eighteenth- and nineteenth-century wooden sailing ships, drew up plans of the model of the *Wesley*. Don Sattin, who had started work as a builder of Thames barges built two models of flats based on the photographs of the two Liverpool Museum models *Avon* and *Elizabeth* – which had unfortunately been destroyed in the bombing of the Liverpool museum building in the Second World War.

In 1970 a small group of people, each with an interest in one or more historical canal craft ranging from flats to narrow boats, decided that something should be done about preserving at least one boat of each key type for the future. Eighty people attended an inaugural meeting in 1971, and under the chairmanship of Dr David Owen, director of the Manchester Museum and a historian and supporter of canals, interest and enthusiasm grew. Plans were prepared to acquire vessels and a site at which to restore and display historic canal craft. Various places were investigated, including Preston Brook, Runcorn and Anderton; in the end, the derelict docks at Ellesmere Port offered the best opportunity. The Boat Museum grew from a one-room exhibition in 1976 to a complete renovation of the docks complex including the dock basins, warehousing, workshops, company cottages and a dry dock. The collection of boats has been built up to over seventy, and these include the Mersey flat *Mossdale*, the Leeds & Liverpool short boat *George*, the long boat *Scorpio*, the steel motor boat *Bacup*, the float *Cedar*, the Bridgewater steel barge *Bigmere* and the diesel Weaver packet *Cuddington*. The museum also owns the hulk of the *Daresbury* at Sutton Level locks on the Weaver. The Manchester Ship Canal Company's directors' steam yacht *Daniel Adamson* is tied up in the 'bottom basin'; she started work as the Shropshire Union tug *Ralph Brocklebank* of 1903.

The *Mossdale* is probably the most historic survivor of all these. Her building date is not known. Her first name was *Ruby* and she was chartered then bought by the Shropshire Union in 1867 for £350. It is not clear who her original owners might have been because she was not entered on the Liverpool or Runcorn registers until 1920. It could have been John Smith of Liverpool who sold them the *Onward*, *Onyx* and *Pearl* in 1869. Given the low price compared with rigged flats built by Deakin's at Winsford in the same decade – they cost eight hundred pounds apiece – it is likely that she always worked as a dumb flat. This would fit in with the Shropshire Union's main line of work but they did employ the sailing flats *Despatch* and *Onward* for working only on the river. The Shropshire Union gave up its fleet in 1921 and the *Ruby* was sold to Abels' of Runcorn. According to Jack Abel, the last managing director of the firm, his grandfather Richard had started

Being preserved for posterity, the Mossdale *under repair at the Boat Museum, Ellesmere Port, 1990.*
Trustees of NMGM

the business in 1865 with sailing flats and in Jack's time the fleet consisted on average of about thirty dumb flats and barges, three sailing flats and three steam tugs. The firm started at Runcorn and developed depots at Liverpool, Widnes and Manchester. When the *Mossdale* was bought the main business was grain deliveries to local mills. The sand and gravel business was built up in the nineteen-twenties to counteract the decline of the lighterage business. By the Second World War, when demand for sand rose rapidly, it was the main source of income. Many of the sand barges and the dredgers were conversions from old schooners such as the *Mary Sinclair*. Abels' had to be very frugal to stay in business, and expected plenty of work from their crews. Jack's father would make a point of checking the progress of the sand fleet when he crossed the Runcorn bridge in the train on his way to work at his Liverpool office. He expected them to load 150 tons of sand in two tides.

The *Mossdale* was not employed in the sand fleet. She was used for grain, and was Abels' best carrier on the Bridgewater; sixty-four tons on a draught of four feet three inches (1.3 m) to Manchester and seventy on another three inches (76 mm) to Preston Brook. She was completely rebuilt at Abels' own yard in 1933 and never took on much water. She might leak a little bit if she was loaded down by the head. Albert Caldwell was her skipper between 1943 and 1948. He had started work as mate of the *Olga Bate* and moved to Abels' in 1940 to become skipper of the *Liddiesdale*. He then moved on to the *Matterdale* before the *Mossdale*. Abels' made him skipper relatively young because they did not want him to be conscripted. His main work was to Manchester. The Bridgewater tugs towed four flats and the trip took about ten or eleven hours. Abels' later bought one of the tugs, put a diesel engine in her and called her *Dovedale*. The *Mossdale* went as far inland as Springfield Hall, Worsley, across the Barton aqueduct – this once took two days because of ice and snow. Grain and flour were also delivered to Preston Brook, and crates of pottery were loaded as return cargo for Liverpool. The *Mossdale* carried many cargoes to and from Ellesmere Port for the Wolverhampton Corrugated Iron Company and the flour mills.

In 1964 Abels' were taken over by Hoveringham Gravel who had no interest in the lighterage business or ageing flats. Peter Froud, who ran a fleet of hotel boats on the narrow canals, bought her with the idea of converting her into a floating restaurant. She was laid up at Northwich for several years. In 1971 Peter generously donated her to the infant Boat Museum. She was dry-docked and caulked and was generally tidied up and looked after by volunteers at Northwich until towed to Ellesmere Port in June 1976. This was not entirely uneventful; she sustained a slight knock while being towed out of Hunt's locks by the tug *Dolphin*. The portable motor pump gave up after an hour and a half and had to be rebuilt. The narrow boat *Ibis* then took her as far as Anderton where the ICI packet *James Jackson Grundy* took her down to Ellesmere Port two days later. Fortunately she did not leak again when she was tossed around by speeding ship canal tugs which refused to slow down. She was then squeezed through the locks to bring her to the museum in the top basin. Since 1976 she has undergone much rebuilding, including the replacement of the tops of frames, replanking and renewing deck beams. The work is not yet finished nor is the research. Her preservation in particular has stimulated others to attempt to save flats.

The *Ruth Bate*, the last flat ever built, was the headquarters of the Maghull branch of the St John's Ambulance Brigade for many years. When she became leaky they sold her to an enthusiastic owner who unfortunately did not have the resources to rebuild her. She lay sunk at Burscough for a time and was then raised and towed to the Bootle Barge Company's depot at Stanley locks, Liverpool. In 1988 she was patched up and towed up to the recently restored canal basin at Widnes. It is planned to restore her as part of the history trail around the canal. Funds are short and she lies sunk in the basin awaiting better times. Her near sister, the *Oakdale* (1950), survives in better condition. She was a floating youth club at Lydiate on the Leeds & Liverpool. The club folded and she was left to sink. David Keenan rescued her and has worked on her single handed. He fitted her with an engine and miniature flat rig and turned her hold into comfortable living quarters. Her owner has very correctly retained her original cabin aft which in spite of her late date was the traditional layout and design. Most of the time she lies alongside the Canning half-tide dock quay of the Merseyside Maritime Museum, going out into the river for summer excursions and to clean off, weed and repaint her bottom at low tide.

The *Scorpio*, the Leeds & Liverpool long boat, could only work on the main line as far as the bottom locks at Wigan because she was seventy two feet (21.9 m) long. She was built as the *Helena* for the Wigan Coal & Iron Company and was capable of carrying seventy tons of coal. It is believed she was towed by a horse at first but her owners used steam tugs as well. In 1920 the *Helena* was sold to Thomas & William Wells, coal carriers of Wigan. In 1948 she was sold to John Parke & Sons of Litherland and renamed *Scorpio* to fit the firm's naming scheme. She was given an extensive refit by Parke's and continued working in the coal trade until 1971. Keith Williams bought her for a nominal two pounds and gave her to the Boat Museum. Between 1971 and 1976 she was tied up at Crabtree Lane at Burscough, where she sank regularly in spite of much hard work and several dry dockings. A retired boatman, of whom there were many at Burscough remarked that she had always been 'a sinker'. In 1973 she was joined at Burscough by the square-sterned short boat *George*. At the time the *George* was something of a mystery. No one seemed to know her origins but she was clearly important because she really was the last surviving wooden short boat. In June 1976 *George* and *Scorpio* were taken down the Leeds & Liverpool for the very last time by a British Waterways Bantam tug to Stanley locks. Volunteers then worked them down to Nelson Dock where they were lifted on to two low loaders and carried under the Mersey to Ellesmere Port. Like the *Mossdale* they have both undergone major restoration. Reg Clarke, the shipwright in charge, estimated that there was only about five per cent of the *George*'s original timbers left by the time his team had finished. Both *George* and *Scorpio* were repainted in their highly decorative Leeds & Liverpool livery. In 1991 Phil Speight, the Boat Museum's painter, was determined to establish the *George*'s identity so that he could paint her in her true colours. After intensive enquiries among surviving boatmen and boatbuilders and some research in the Wigan archives, he established that the *George* was built in 1910, most probably at Springs Bridge, by the Wigan Coal & Iron Company. Although she was initially registered as a horse-drawn fly-boat, she appears to have been employed as a coal carrier between Haigh and Liverpool. In addition she carried moulding sand and coke for the company's steel works. Her first owners merged with the Wigan Coal Corporation and she finished her working life carrying coal on the Bridgewater Canal for the National Coal Board. One old boatman was able to recall precisely how she was painted, right down to all the small changes her crew made to make her individual and different from her sisters.

The steel motor and dumb boats that succeeded the wooden flats survived in good numbers into the nineteen-seventies. British Waterways used the Leeds & Liverpool motor boats for maintenance. One brave owner revived through working to Yorkshire on the *Wye* with cargoes of cereals from Liverpool to Selby; but the enterprise was defeated by the shallowness of the Liverpool end of the canal and by harassment from the local youth. Two of Ainscough's boats were turned into floating restaurants. The Bootle Barge Company used two of the Bridgewater barges for collecting rubbish around Liverpool docks. One, the *Barmere*, has been sold to SCARS – the Sankey Canal Restoration Society. In 1989 the society was able to arrange her lifting out and transport to the landlocked section of the Sankey at St Helens. She will be restored and used to display the history of the canal. The *Bigmere* has already become a museum exhibition and concert hall for the Boat Museum. The museum's *Bacup* is of the second generation of Leeds & Liverpool motor boats built by Yarwood's in 1950. Her original engine was a Widdop single-cylinder twenty-four horse power diesel. She was invariably crewed by the Robinson family, father and son, and used on general cargo carrying: sugar from Tate & Lyle, Liverpool to Wigan, Blackburn, Burnley and Leeds; aluminium from Manchester to Warrington; grain from Liverpool to Burnley;

A working survivor, the ex-Bridgewater Arleymere *steel flat, is still used for rubbish collection around Liverpool docks. Three others of the same class have been preserved, two at Ellesmere Port and one at St Helens.*
Trustees of NMGM

cotton in bales from Liverpool to Wigan, Blackburn and Burnley; wool to Leeds and Bradford and coal from Wigan and Leigh. John Freeman, the area maintenance engineer, recalled one incident when she was pressed into service to save the canal bank collapsing at Giant's Halt near Burscough. What had started as a small leak was turning into the imminent collapse of a high embankment:

> The situation was becoming desperate, a breach of the canal was imminent when along came the *Bacup* with the Robinsons crewing. We stopped them and begged the tarpaulin hatch covers off them, placing them on the bed of the canal and up the sides and weighting them down with stones to staunch the flow. Then we got the Robinsons to tie up the boat over the affected area, with a view that if the bank gave way, the *Bacup* would act as a partial dam. This saved the situation. We stood by all night and next day set to work, piled the bank and put in a new clay core. The *Bacup* saved the day for at the time the Leeds & Liverpool Canal was under threat of closure; a breach would have given those in high places the perfect excuse.

There are no wooden Weaver packets or wooden 'Duker' or Rochdale flats left, but the last steel steam packet, the *Davenham* (now with a diesel engine), is being privately preserved. Three other ICI diesel packets are also afloat. The *John Jackson Grundy* is the Sea Scouts' base at Northwich. The *Cuddington* belongs to the Boat Museum, is painted in her original ICI colours, and operates in the Mersey for Mersey river festival parades. The *Wincham* is her great rival and is painted in the Bulk Cargo Handling Company's colours. She is owned

196

by the Wincham Preservation Society and is based at Merseyside Maritime Museum. Both boats have only a light foremast but the Wincham's crew have acquired a mast from a scrapped coaster as an eventual replacement for the original.

The *Emily Barratt* is the only true 'Barrow flat' to survive afloat. The *Kathleen and May* which is preserved at Southwark on the south bank of the Thames, was built by Baird & Ferguson at Connah's Quay in 1900 as the *Lizzie May*. She has a dainty counter stern instead of the 'Barrow flat' type. The *Emily Barratt* was built at Millom in 1913 by Hugh Jones. She was named after the daughter of one of the Hodbarrow iron mine directors. The launching ceremony on Easter Monday had a special significance because not only was she the last vessel built at the little yard at Millom, but the last of two wooden schooners built in the United Kingdom. She was not much bigger than a jigger flat, and was employed carrying iron ore away from Millom and returning with coal. In 1920 she was sold for a mere £925, less seventy-five pounds commission and sixty pounds for repairs undertaken while the sale was being negotiated. The Welch family of Braunton in north Devon bought her, converted her into an auxiliary ketch and kept her trading until 1960 except for a spell as a barrage balloon barge in the Second World War. Captain Bruce, the master of the restored clipper *Cutty Sark* at Greenwich, bought her then and turned her into a smart yacht, sailing in and around the Thames estuary. In 1977 she was sold to John Goddard and was allowed to deteriorate. By 1982 she was almost derelict. George Patterson, a builder of St Bees, Cumbria, bought her and had her pumped out and towed to Maldon, where she was patched up. With a new engine and a set of sails she set sail in July 1984 bound for Workington via the Caledonian Canal. Her new owner based her on the newly restored harbour of Maryport. Unfortunately the cost of restoration proved too much for his pocket and he had to put her up for sale. Her future was precarious again. The Furness Maritime Museum bought her for their new development at the Ashburners' dry dock at Barrow. At the time of writing, the museum has made some progress towards her final salvation.

There is not one single flat sailing now. The *Oakdale*'s cut-down rig cannot really count although her owner says she sails quite well and in any case she was not designed to sail. There was a long debate as to whether it was both feasible and ethical to raise the remains of the *Daresbury* to rebuild her back to sailing condition. A recent underwater survey revealed that her sunken hull was in quite sound condition. The exposed timbers and decks were pretty rotten, however, and it is questionable whether she could be removed from Sutton Level lock where she lies hemmed in by other sunken hulks. It is also doubtful whether there are the resources to restore her and whether it is in fact right to rebuild a precious piece of archaeological evidence. There are

The fate of most flats, abandonment or breaking up. These Bridgewater flats were dumped in the bottom basin of the flight of locks from the Mersey to the canal at Runcorn. Today the whole area has been covered and none of them is visible. The eighteenth-century building in the background is the Duke of Bridgewater's House, which is still in use as offices for the Manchester Ship Canal Company.
J. Parkinson

a number of other sunken or buried flat hulks at Runcorn and Widnes, but it is unlikely that any one of them would be intact enough to be considered for rebuilding. Those at the Big Pool, Runcorn, have been buried for over sixty years. The *Eustace Carey* and the *John* – the most intact hulks at Widnes – were set on fire and burned to the water-line. An alternative might be to rig one of the Bridgewater steel barges. This would be a replica but it would give a good idea of what a sailing flat was like. Indeed if the sailing flat had not been displaced by steam towage, steel flats of their dimensions would have been built. The steel hull would be stronger and easier to maintain as the Humber Keel & Sloop Preservation Society have found with their keel *Comrade* and sloop *Amy Howson*. It also makes it easier to obtain insurance and to fit the obligatory engine. The other possibility would be to build a new wooden flat from scratch. The information certainly exists and modern lamination techniques make it feasible to build up heavy frames from smaller section timbers. The massive pitch pine mast might be a difficulty but this kind of obstacle has not stood in the way of other replicas and restorations. Rigging, blocks and duradon sailcloth, which is a fair representation of tanned flax canvas but more durable, are all available. The chief stumbling block must be finance both to build and then to maintain. The replica Liverpool pilot boat *Spirit of Merseyside* cost eight hundred thousand pounds in 1986. A replica flat could cost almost as much. Perhaps, a more realistic approach might be to build a smaller eighteenth-century flat along the lines of those in the Brockbank's specification book. This is a dream for the future. For the present it is important to ensure the long-term future of the 'survivors' and to continue the task of gathering archives and memories of the flats. Flats played an important role in the economy of the North West and by implication the rest of the kingdom. They deserve to be remembered.

Models such as that of the Wesley *are important sources of evidence for the construction and rigging of flats.*
M. Clarke

199

Dimensions of Locks on the Major North-west Waterways

		Length	Width	Draught
WEAVER	1732	68 ft	15 ft 6 in.	4 ft 6 in.
	1848–50	100 ft	22 ft	10 ft
	1871–91	220–9 ft	42–100 ft	12 ft
MERSEY & IRWELL	1736	68 ft	17 ft 6 in.	4 ft
DOUGLAS	1742	50–60 ft	15 ft	4 ft
SANKEY	1757	68 ft	16 ft 9 in.	5 ft
St Helens	1833	79 ft	20 ft	5 ft
BRIDGEWATER	1773	72 ft	14 ft 2 in.	4 ft 6 in.
ROCHDALE	1804	74 ft	14 ft 2 in.	4 ft
LEEDS & LIVERPOOL	1820			
Liverpool–Wigan		72 ft	14 ft	4 ft
Wigan–Leeds		62 ft	14 ft	4 ft

(These dimensions have been taken from Paget-Tomlinson, E. W. *The Complete Book of Canal and River Navigations.* Waine, 1978, except the Douglas which is from Clarke, M. *The Leeds & Liverpool Canal, a History and Guide.* Carnegie, 1990.)

Typical Dimensions (in feet)

FLATS

Date	Name	Length	Breadth	Depth of hold	Tons	Place of build
					(register)	
1766	*Friendship*	57	15	5.1	55	Liverpool
1786	*Amity*	61.6	16.3	6	70	Northwich
1803	*Merry Harrier*	63.1	16.8	6.8	76	Frodsham
1832	*Miner*	66	15.2	6.4	67	St Helens
1849	*Stanley*	67	14.9	5	38	St Helens
					(gross)	
1858	*Jane*	67.3	16.7	6.6	53	Sankey Brook
1880	*Harry*	66.1	17.1	7.7	67.5	Sankey Brook

SLOOPS

Date	Name	Length	Breadth	Depth of hold	Tons	Place of build
					(register)	
1783	*Pattys*	60	16.6	5.9	70	Manchester
1814	*Frances Mary*	68	17.4	7.8	87	Frodsham

GALLIOTS

Date	Name	Length	Breadth	Depth of hold	Tons	Place of build
					(register)	
1797	*Happy Return*	64	16.1	7	83	St Helens
1807	*Lane*	68	18.3	7.9	97	St Helens

JIGGERS

Date	Name	Length	Breadth	Depth of hold	Tons	Place of build
					(gross)	
1890	*Polar Star*	77.1	20.3	9	101	Northwich
1906	*Eustace Carey*	74.3	19.5	8.7	93	Sankey

WEAVER STEAM PACKETS

Date	Name	Length	Breadth	Depth of hold	Tons	Place of build
					(gross)	
1864	*Champion*	81.7	19.2	8.1	103	Winsford
1908	*Gwalia*	95.8	21.6	10.2	162	Northwich

BRIDGEWATER CANAL FLATS

Date	Name	Length	Breadth	Depth of hold	Tons	Place of build
1900	Manchester type	71	14.25	4 (draught)	80 (capacity)	Worsley or Stretford

20thC	Preston (Brook) type	71	14.25	5 (draught)	90 (capacity)	Runcorn

LEEDS & LIVERPOOL CANAL BOATS

19th–20thC	Long boat	72	14.25	5 (draught)	70 (capacity)	Various
	Short boat	62	14.25	3.5 (draught)	40 (capacity)	Various

ROCHDALE CANAL FLATS

19th–20thC	Flat	72	13.5	4–5	60–90 (capacity)	Various

'BARROW FLAT' SCHOONERS

1870	*Millom Castle*	81.2	20.6	9.5	91 (gross)	Ulverston
1913	*Emily Barratt*	76.8	20.0	8.3	71.4	Millom

OTHER COASTAL CRAFT

19thC	Humber keel	62.5	15.5	8	100 (tons capacity)	Various
19thC	Severn trow *Wave*	71.5	18.75	5.5	72	?
19thC	Thames barge	84	20	6	135 (tons capacity)	Various

APPENDIX THREE

Models of Flats and Packets in Museums

Name	Type of vessel	Date	Scale	Type of model	Maker	Collection
Bedale	Dumb flat	c1890	$\frac{1}{2}$ in. = 1 ft	Exhibition with full details of construction	Dr F. Howard	Science Museum
—	Sailing flat	c1860–80	$\frac{1}{2}$ in. = 1 ft	Exhibition with full details of construction	Dr F. Howard	Boat Museum, Ellesmere Port
Charity	Sailing flat	1858	$\frac{1}{8}$ in. = 1 ft	Waterline model	—	Merseyside Maritime Museum
Crescent	Steam packet	1910	$\frac{1}{4}$ in. = 1 ft	Builder's model	—	Merseyside Maritime Museum (33–137)
Elizabeth	Sailing flat	1827	$\frac{1}{2}$ in. = 1 ft	Exhibition model	Don Sattin	Boat Museum (loan from Manchester Museum)
Elizabeth	Sailing flat	1827	$\frac{1}{2}$ in. = 1 ft	Exhibition model	Don Sattin	Salt Museum, Northwich
Eustace Carey	Jigger flat	1906	$\frac{1}{2}$ in. = 1 ft	Exhibition model	Tony Lewery	Merseyside Maritime Museum
—	Sailing flat	c1860–80	$\frac{1}{2}$ in. = 1 ft	Builder's half-model	—	Merseyside Maritime Museum
Herald of Peace	Steam packet	1877	$\frac{1}{2}$ in. = 1 ft	Exhibition model	Malcolm Wilson	Salt Museum, Northwich
—	Leeds & Liverpool short boat	c1900	$\frac{1}{2}$ in. = 1 ft	Builder's half-model	—	Merseyside Maritime Museum
—	Steam packet	c1870	$\frac{1}{2}$ in. = 1 ft	Builder's half- model	—	Merseyside Maritime Museum
Pilot	Jigger flat	1894	$\frac{1}{4}$ in. = 1 ft	Exhibition model	I. Balfour	Merseyside Maritime Museum (33–139)
Ribble	Leeds & Liverpool motor boat	1934	$\frac{1}{4}$ in. = 1 ft	Builder's model	—	Mersyside Maritime Museum (34–118)

The Boat Museum and the Merseyside Maritime Museum have models of Leeds & Liverpool boats made by Mr Bradley of Adlington which, though not to scale, give a very good impression of the different types. The Merseyside Maritime Museum also has the toy flat *Rob*.

203

Glossary

A

Apron   The inner timber of the stem post.

B

Bill of lading   A confirmation of the goods carried on the flat and a promise to deliver them in the same condition as they were received on board.

Bolt rope   The rope sewn round the edges of a sail to protect the canvas.

Brail   A rope passing round both sides of sail with blocks at its luff to lead it down to the deck and used to furl it; found on sprit and standing gaff-rigged boats.

C

Cable laid   Thick, strong rope with its three strands twisted from right to left as against left to right in ordinary ropes.

Camber   The curve of the deck across a ship.

Cant frames   Frames at the bow and stern which are angled or 'canted' to the keel.

Carlin   Timbers fitted between the deck beams.

Centre board   A sliding keel for shallow draught sailing vessels that can be raised and lowered.

Chain plate   Iron strips bolted into the side of hull to which the shrouds can be fixed.

Clew   In fore and aft sails like the flats the aftermost bottom corner.

Coaming   The raised sides of a hatch.

D

Deadeye   Circular sheaveless blocks with three eyes, used in pairs to secure a shroud to a chainplate. A lanyard (rope) is threaded through the eyes to tighten the shroud.

Deadwood   A timber in the bow or stern to reinforce the stem or stern post.

E

Ejector   As in a railway locomotive injector, high-pressure steam forced through a narrow pipe could be used to force water out of the bilges of a packet. Two were normally fitted at each end of the hold.

F

Feedwater   Water for the boiler which was pre-heated by exhaust steam before going into the boiler.

G
Garboard   The plank (strake) next to the keel.

H
Half-tide dock   An entrance dock in the port of Liverpool where the lock gates were opened for access at three hours before high water (ie half-tide).
Headledge   The raised ends of a hatch.
Hounds   The point at which the upper part of the mast is reduced in diameter to fix the shrouds and stays.

L
Leeboards   Sliding keels fitted on each side of shallow-draught sailing vessels such as Thames barges to prevent them going to leeward.
Leech   The after side of a sail.
Luff   The fore edge of a sail.
Lutchet   The mast case on a Rochdale flat, a term derived from Humber keels.

M
Manrope   A safety rope temporarily fitted along the sides of a packet when on the River Mersey.
Mast case   A three-sided heavily timbered box from keelson to above the deck into which the mast is fitted, also carrying the halliard winches. See also: tabernacle.

O
Ochre   A natural mixture of silica and alumina which turns a reddish brown when burnt; ground up as a colouring and preservative for sails when mixed with fish oil.

P
Parcelled and served A method of protecting the rigging from rot by winding tarred strips of canvas round the rope and then tightly winding on (serving) thin twine (spunyard).
Poop   The aft deck usually higher than the main deck.

S
Scull   Propelling a cock boat using a single oar over the stern in a figure-of-eight action.
Sheer   The upward curve of the deck towards the bow and the stern.
Shroud   Rigging to support the mast (standing rigging) from the hounds to the chainplates on each side of the hull. Stays perform a similar function fore and aft.
Sloats   Two horizontal timbers to hold the vertical rudder boards in position.
Sprit   A diagonal spar to support a sail – for example, on a Thames barge – pivoted at its bottom (heel) next to the mast and running to after top corner of the sail.

Stephenson's link   A type of valve operating and reversing mechanism commonly used on railway and marine engines.

T

Tabernacle   A wooden mast case which is fixed on deck to support a mast.

Tack   The lower forward corner of a sail.

Tack to   To go about, the operation of bringing a sailing flat head to wind and across it to bring the wind onto its opposite side. Gybing (or wearing) is similar except the stern is taken across the wind. It is a more dangerous manoeuvre than tacking because the boom can crash across the vessel out of control – not recommended in heavily rigged flats.

Bibliography

Books

Anon. *Handbook and Guide to the Shipping Gallery in the Public Museums, Liverpool.* Liverpool City Council, 1932 and 1935.

Ayland, N. (ed.) *Schooner Captain.* D. Bradford Barton, 1972.

Baines, T. *History of the Commerce and Town of Liverpool.* Longman and author 1852.

Barker, T. C. & Harris, J. R. *A Merseyside Town in the Industrial Revolution; St. Helens 1750–1900.* Liverpool University Press 1954.

Burton, V. (ed.) *Liverpool Shipping, Trade & Industry.* Trustees of NMGM, 1989.

Burwash, D. *English Merchant Shipping 1460–1540.* Toronto University Press, 1947.

Butterworth, E. *A Statistical Sketch of the County Palatine of Lancaster.* Longman, 1841.

Clarke, M. *The Leeds & Liverpool Canal, a History and Guide.* Carnegie 1990.

Coppack, T. *A Lifetime with Ships.* Stephenson, 1973

Craig, R & Jarvis, R. *Liverpool Registry of Merchant Ships.* Chetham Society, 1967.

Davis, R. *The Rise of the English Shipping Industry.* David & Charles, 1972.

Diggle, G. E. *A History of Widnes.* Widnes Corporation, 1961.

Eames, A. *Ships and Seamen of Anglesey.* Anglesey Antiquarian Society ,1973.

Elis-Williams, M. *Bangor, Port of Beaumaris.* Gwynedd Archives & Museum Service, 1988.

Fenton, R. *Cambrian Coasters.* World Ship Society, 1989.

Fenton, R. *Monks' Navy.* World Ship Society, 1981.

Forman, C. *Industrial Town.* Cameron & Tayleur, in association with David & Charles, 1978.

Greenhill, B. *The Life and Death of the Merchant Sailing Ship 1815–1965.* HMSO, 1980.

Greenhill, B. *The Merchant Schooners.* Percival Marshall, 1957.

Greenwood M.T. The Rochdale. Author 1978

Hadfield, C. & Biddle, G. *The Canals of North West England.* David & Charles, 1970.

Hadfield, C. & Biddle, G. *The Canals of the West Midlands.* David & Charles, 1966.

Hanson, H. *The Canal Boatmen 7160–1914.* Manchester University Press, 1975.

Harris, J. R. (ed.) *Liverpool and Merseyside: Essays in the Economic and Social History of the Port and its Hinterland.* Frank Cass, 1969.

Hyde, F. E. *Liverpool and Merseyside; the Development of a Port 1700–1970.* David & Charles, 1971.

Jarvis, A. E. *Ellesmere Port, Canal Town.* North West Museum of Inland Navigation, 1977

Kennett, A. (ed.) *Chester & the River Dee.* Chester City Council, 1982.

Leather, J. *Gaff Rig.* Adlard Coles, 1970.

Leather, J. *Sailing Barges.* Adlard Coles, 1984.

Lightfoot, T. S. *The Weaver Watermen.* Cheshire Libraries ,1982.

Lloyd, L. *The Unity of Barmouth.* Gwynedd Archives Service, 1977.

Lloyd, L. *The Port of Caernarfon 1793–1900.* Author, 1989.

Lockett, A. *North Western Sail.* Countryside Publications, 1978.

McCaughan, M. & Appleby, S. (eds) *The Irish Sea.* Institute of Irish Studies, Queen's University, Belfast, Ulster Folk & Transport Museum, 1989.

McGowan, A. *Tiller & Whipstaff 1400–1700.* HMSO, 1981.

MacGregor, D. R. *Fast Sailing Ships 1715–1815.* Nautical Publishing, 1973.

MacGregor, D. R. *Merchant Sailing Ships 1715–1815.* Argus, 1980.

MacGregor, D. R. *Merchant Sailing Ships 1815–1850.* Conway, 1984.

MacGregor, D. R. *Merchant Sailing Ships 1850–1875.* Conway ,1984.

MacGregor, D. R. *Schooners in Four Centuries.* Argus, 1982.

McKee, E. *Working Boats of Britain.* Conway, 1983.

Marriner, S. *The Economic & Social Development of Merseyside.* Croom Helm, 1982.

Matthias, P. *The First Industrial Nation 1700–1914.* Methuen, 1969.

Melville, M. *Redburn.* Penguin, 1976.

Moss, W. *The Liverpool Guide.* Crane & Jones, 1796.

Musson, A. E. *Enterprise in Soup and Chemicals.* Manchester University Press, 1965.

Norton, P. *Waterways and Railways Around Warrington.* Cheshire Libraries & Museums, 1984.

Paget-Tomlinson, E. W. *The Complete Book of Canal & River Navigations.* Waine, 1978.

Paget-Tomlinson, E. W. *Mersey & Weaver Flats.* Robert Wilson, 1973.

Parkinson, J. R. *The Rise of the Port of Liverpool.* Liverpool University Press, 1951.

Poole, B. *The Commerce of Liverpool.* Author, 1854.

Ritchie-Noakes, N. *Liverpool's Historic Waterfront.* HMSO, 1984.

Rothwell, C. *Fleetwood as it Was.* Hendon, 1975.

Samuel, R. (ed.) *Miners, Quarrymen and Saltworkers.* Routledge & Kegan Paul, 1977.

Schofield, F. *Humber Keels and Keelmen.* Terence Dalton, 1988.

Smith, P. *A Pictorial History of Canal Craft.* Batsford, 1979.

Starkey, H. F. *Schooner Port.* G. W. & A. Hesketh, 1983.

Stewart-Brown, R. *Liverpool Ships in the 18th Century.* Liverpool University Press, 1932.

Strickland, R. *Report for the Pennsylvania Society for the Promotion of Internal Improvement*, 1826.

Taplin, E. *Liverpool Dockers and Seamen 1870–1970.* Hull University Press, 1974.

Thornton, R. H. *British Shipping.* Cambridge University Press, 1945.

Wheat, G. *On the Duke's Cut.* Author, 1977.

White, E. W. *British Fishing Boats & Coastal Craft, Part 1.* HMSO, 1950.

White, E. W. *British Fishing Boats & Coastal Craft, Part 2.* HMSO, 1952.

Willan, T. S. *The Navigation of the River Weaver in the 18th Century.* Chetham Society, 1951.

Manuscript sources

Only major sources have been included. Note oral history sources are acknowledged in the preface.

Boat Museum, Ellesmere Port

Alf Hayman's collection on the Bridgewater Canal.
T. Kavanagh's extracts from the Shropshire Union Canal & Railway
Company's manager's minutes.

Cheshire Record Office

Canal Boat registers.
Quarter Sessions records on inland navigation.
The Yarwood Collection.

Chester Record Office

Chester City Council River Dee committee minutes.
Daniel Peck's letterbook, 1703, and notes on lead shipments.

Lancashire Record Office

Accounts for River Douglas flats 1752–55 and 1764–68.
Bryan Blundell's journal.

Lancaster Library

J. Brockbank's day books.

Liverpool Record Office

Canal Boat registers.
Liverpool Lighterage Company annual reports.

National Museums and Galleries on Merseyside

Brocklebank Collection.
Bryson Collection (Worsley Battersby material).
Dr Frank Howard Collection.
Liverpool Nautical Research Society Collection.
Liverpool ship registers.
Mersey Docks & Harbour Board Collection.
Taylor Collection.
Upper Mersey Navigation Commission Collection.

Wigan Record Office

Leigh MSS (extracts transcribed by M. Clarke).

Newspapers and Periodicals

Birkenhead Times.
Bromborough Society Annual Report.
Cymru a'r Mor/Maritime Wales.
Journal of Commerce.
Liverpool Courier.
Liverpool Echo.
Liverpool Mercury.
Lloyds Register of Shipping.
Maghull Advertiser.

Manchester Guardian.
Mariner's Mirror (journal of the Society for Nautical Research).
Port of Manchester Review.
Port News (newsletter of the Mersey Docks & Harbour Company).
Report (newsletter of North West. Museum of Inland Navigation).
Sea Breezes (new series).
Transactions of the Lancashire & Cheshire Antiquarian Society.
Transactions of the Lancashire & Cheshire Historical Society.
Transactions of the Liverpool Nautical Research Society.
Warrington Guardian.
Waterways World.

Directories

Cheshire directories - various.
Leeds & Liverpool Canal Company Official Handbook, 1928.
Liverpool Directory 1766 and subsequent editions by various publishers.
Liverpool Shipping Who's Who? - various editions.
Port of Liverpool Annual Handbook - various editions.

General Index

Illustrations in bold type

Ship's Index

Illustrations in bold type

214

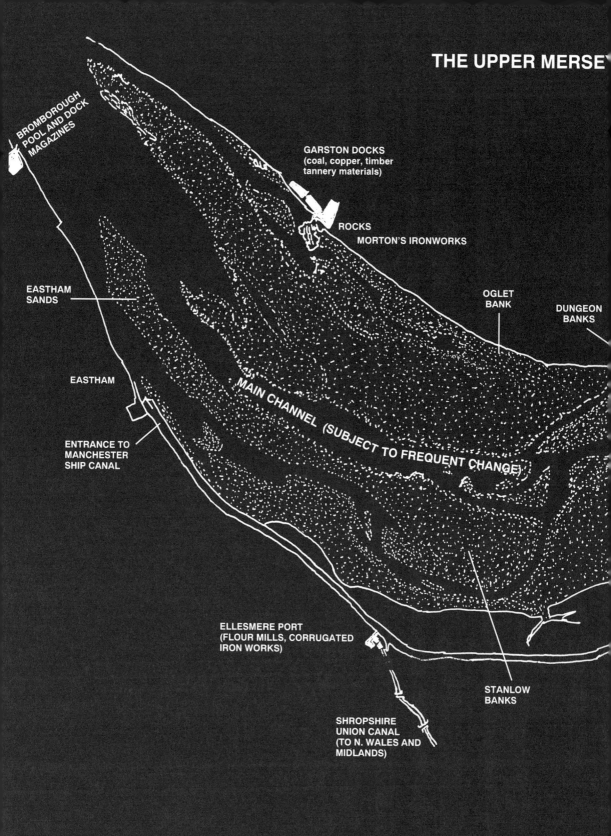

THE UPPER MERSE

BROMBOROUGH POOL AND DOCK MAGAZINES

GARSTON DOCKS (coal, copper, timber tannery materials)

ROCKS

MORTON'S IRONWORKS

OGLET BANK

DUNGEON BANKS

EASTHAM SANDS

EASTHAM

MAIN CHANNEL (SUBJECT TO FREQUENT CHANGE)

ENTRANCE TO MANCHESTER SHIP CANAL

ELLESMERE PORT (FLOUR MILLS, CORRUGATED IRON WORKS)

STANLOW BANKS

SHROPSHIRE UNION CANAL (TO N. WALES AND MIDLANDS)